The
MIDDLE *of*
EVERYWHERE

ALSO BY MARY PIPHER, PH.D.

Reviving Ophelia

Hunger Pains

The Shelter of Each Other

Another Country

MARY PIPHER, PH.D.

The
MIDDLE of
EVERYWHERE

THE WORLD'S REFUGEES
COME TO OUR TOWN

HARCOURT, INC.

New York   San Diego   London

www.HarcourtBooks.com

Translation of "Hoa Sen" ("The Lotus Flower")
taken from *The Lotus Seed* by Sherry Garland.

A portion of the proceeds from this book will be donated to
The Pipher Refugee Fund, Lincoln Action Program,
210 O Street, Lincoln, Nebraska 68508.

Library of Congress Cataloging-in-Publication Data
Pipher, Mary Bray.
The middle of everywhere: the world's refugees come to our town/
Mary Pipher.—1st ed.
p.   cm.
Includes bibliographical references and index.
ISBN 0-15-100600-8 (perm. paper)
1. Refugees—United States.   I. Title.
JV6601   .P56 2002
305.9'0691—dc21   2001005863

Text set in Bembo
Designed by Linda Lockowitz

Printed in the United States of America
First edition
A C E G I K J H F D B

To Sara, Zeke, Jamie, and Kate

There seemed to be nothing to see, no fences,
no creeks or trees, no hills or fields. If there was a road
I could not make it out in the faint starlight.
There was nothing but land. Not a country at all but
the material out of which countries are made.

—WILLA CATHER

CONTENTS

PART THREE: *The* ALCHEMY *of* HEALING— TURNING PAIN *into* MEANING

FOREWORD

As long as there is respect and acknowledgment of connections,
things continue working. When that stops, we all die.
—Joy Harjo

I finished this book on refugees in Nebraska on September 9
and on September 10 my husband and I flew to Canada. This
was our first vacation in a year, a well-earned vacation—a time
to catch up on laughter, sleep, hikes, and novels. We drove from
Calgary to a cabin nestled along Baker Creek in a valley between Castle Rock and Storm Mountain. On our way we
stopped to watch caribou and mule deer. The bushes and grasses
were turning mauve and rose, the aspens golden. In the late afternoon sunlight, we marveled at the luxury of living cradled in
these mountains for a week.

Tuesday morning we woke early and planned our first hike.
As we walked out into a blue and gold day, a man stopped us and
asked if we were Americans. When we nodded, he said, "Some
terrible things are happening in your country. You'd better go to
the basement gym and watch television."

We sat on folding chairs with other tourists for several hours. No one talked—we just watched and cried. At first I was in shock, then slowly I began to piece together the personal implications. I worked with three publishing companies in New York and I worried if my friends were safe. My daughter was scheduled to fly to D.C. from Cape Town, South Africa, Tuesday morning. Where was she? The Canadian/United States border and the airports were closed. How would we get home? Yet never had my own little life looked so petty. There were bigger issues: How many people were dead? What did this mean for America? What would happen to my refugee friends? Was the world as we knew it gone?

Later we walked outside into the crisp September afternoon. The world had changed and the world was the same, the same golden aspen and purple grasses, the same ripe rose hips and rushing water over smooth gray stones. We were safe in a beautiful place, but we weren't thinking and feeling what we had planned to be thinking and feeling.

As I looked through our binoculars for grizzlies and mountain sheep, I was thinking *is my editor dead? Are people trapped under the rubble right now, scared and in pain?* I imagined how frightened the passengers on the hijacked jets must have been, and I kept hearing imaginary airplanes. Watching the river, my husband said sadly, "No matter how crazy we humans act, the water keeps on flowing."

The beautiful time and place seemed to deliberately induce irony and contrast. The silver glaciers, emerald forests, and turquoise lakes humbled us. I kept thinking about all this sacred beauty in our sad, deformed world.

On 9/11, the book I had just finished seemed meaningless. *The Middle of Everywhere* felt like it had been written in and for a world that no longer existed. But later that afternoon, as I tried to read the books I'd brought with me—one on the Sand Hills of Nebraska and another on the life of Ben Franklin—I realized they were irrelevant, too. On September 11 everything—Shakespeare, Broadway, flower gardens, Bob Dylan—was irrelevant. Only Jihad and death seemed to matter.

Fortunately time didn't stop on September 11. As weeks passed we all began to put our terrible tragedy into perspective. My book began to seem applicable to the new world, maybe even more so than before. Refugees were still here, and they were even more beleaguered. A Kurdish family called to say, "We are confused and frightened and cannot eat. We have been harassed at work for being Muslim." Mohamed told me, "Bintu and I fear we have brought the war from Sierra Leone to America. We thought America was safe. Now we don't know where to run."

One of our greatest needs as a nation is to understand how other people see us, and this book is filled with stories about how people from different countries and religious traditions view Americans. In the aftermath of the disaster we all have images of Arab terrorists in our heads. In spite of our values and best intentions, we all are occasionally guilty of racial profiling. This book gives readers other images and replaces fearful stereotypes with stories of real and interesting people. I truly hope it will be an antidote to hatred and fear.

I have been struck by the kindness of many Americans toward our Muslim neighbors. One of my friends, a psychologist, lost his brother who worked at the World Trade Center. As he flew back to New York to pack up his brother's apartment, he made arrangements to start a Muslim-support group for local people. At Lincoln High students asked their teachers how they could organize to help Muslim kids. Twenty members of our South Street Temple volunteered to help refugees who were frightened by the recent events. Our politicians, our newspapers, and our churches have worked non-stop to make sure no hate crimes were committed in our town.

All over our country people have an impulse to help, to make our country safer and stronger. One of the best ways to help is to befriend newcomers. As we welcome refugees and teach them about us, we learn about them, and we develop wiser and more nuanced views of our world. This book encourages Americans to become involved with newcomers and offers many ideas about how to do that.

After September 11, we are all refugees from what was once our America. We have been exiled from a country that felt safe and calm and now we live in a new country filled with fear. We can learn from the refugees among us how to deal with our fears and sorrows. Our newcomers have experienced panic, loss, disruption, and vulnerability. They have learned to cope with catastrophes, and they can teach us how to survive these things. They can help us learn to live in the world with broken hearts.

Now that we have been terrorized, we have more empathy with others. When I returned from Canada I told Mohamed that, for the first time, I felt I could understand how he felt in Sierra Leone, not that our situation was as terrible, but that I had experienced similar feelings of shock, fear for my children, confusion, and depression. He was very quiet and then said, "I'm sorry you have to know how I feel."

On September 11 Americans felt what many of the world's people have felt for years. That day ended our illusions about our invulnerability and our isolation from the rest of the world. We joined the world's huddled masses yearning to breathe free. We need more than ever what I call "the attributes of resilience." We all want and need what refugees want and need.

We yearn for family and friends, meaning, calmness, routines, useful work, and spiritual solace.

One of the main points of this book is that identity is no longer based on territory. The world community is small and interconnected. We are all living in one big town. This tragedy has provided us with the most significant teachable moment in our history. We can learn from this to be kinder and more appreciative of life. And we can learn the importance of understanding the perspectives of all our neighbors in our global village. We can learn that the entire world needs stronger international courts and policing bodies and an agreed upon standard of acceptable conduct. All of us can work together to enforce the Universal Declaration of Human Rights in all countries and to provide our global community with economic and social justice.

The great lesson of September 11 is that we are all connected. Either we all are safe or none of us is safe. Either we are all free of fear or none of us is. Right now we have a window of opportunity to rethink our policies and to deal with the world differently, more fairly and compassionately. These events can lead to a national renewal of energy and compassion as well as to what Gay Talese called "an enlargement of our capacity to be human."

Buddha was asked about the effects of enlightenment on his life. He said, "Before enlightenment I chopped wood and carried water. After enlightenment I chopped wood and carried water." That is how I feel about life now. Everything is totally different. I see the world and feel the world in a new way and yet, I carry on as before. In the end, I decided that to let this book die was to let terrorists be the storytellers for our global village. *The Middle of Everywhere* is my way to chop wood and carry water.

The
MIDDLE *of*
EVERYWHERE

ELLIS ISLAND

Jane and I sailed to Ellis Island from Battery Park on a gorgeous summer morning. As Manhattan, once called New Amsterdam, sparkled in the distance, we found a place on deck among the other tourists.

Jane has been my editor for the last seven years. She's the first-generation daughter of Polish-Jewish immigrants. I'm the great-granddaughter of Irish peasants who came to America escaping the potato famine and of Scottish immigrants who came as bond slaves.

Our ferry retraced the immigrants' voyage into the harbor. We stopped briefly at the Statue of Liberty to unload sightseers. Jane told me that one immigrant saw the statue and asked, "Is that Mrs. Roosevelt?"

Jane recited from memory the famous words:

Give me your tired, your poor,
Your huddled masses yearning to breathe free,
The wretched refuse of your teeming shore,
Send these, the homeless tempest-tossed to me,
I lift my lamp beside the golden door.

Then she said proudly, "A Jewish woman, Emma Lazarus, wrote that poem."

We docked at Ellis Island and walked under sycamores into the same central hall immigrants once entered. A poet described this hall as a haunted ballroom where people danced their lives away. She was referring to the ghosts of those quarantined and IQ tested, then sent back home. Or perhaps to the twenty thousand people who died here in one month during an influenza epidemic.

Today the park employees were friendly. We had all the fresh water and food we needed. People were clean, polite, well-rested and well-clothed. Jugglers entertained us. Still, children cried as they grew tired and thirsty, and old people looked for places to sit. All of us, wandering around or standing in lines, created a resonance with the past.

As we explored Ellis Island I remembered a trip I'd made with my husband, Jim. It took thirty-six hours to fly home to Lincoln, Nebraska, from Chiang Mai, Thailand, and on the way we'd stopped in Bangkok, Tokyo, and Chicago. We took our picture in each of the airports. At Chiang Mai we were fresh, alert, and smiling. By Lincoln, we had rumpled stained clothes, bags under our eyes, and spaced-out expressions. If we looked like this after thirty-six hours of business-class travel, what must have become of people in steerage for three weeks crossing the North Atlantic?

Jane and I walked first to an exhibit of languages, a tree whose branches were countries and whose leaves were words. On the Spanish branch hung the words VAMOOSE and HOOSGOW; on the Yiddish, KLUTZ and NUDNIK; on the German, OUCH and CATALPA; on the West African, JUKEBOX and BANJO; on the Chinese GUNG HO; and on the French, PUMPKIN and one of our most beautiful words, PRAIRIE.

We joined a tour. The historian asked if we were from immigrant families. Most hands went up and he gently chided the others: "Unless you are full Native American, you are the child of immigrants." He added that the people on the *Mayflower* who landed at Plymouth Rock were our first "boat people." He said 40 percent of all Americans could trace their roots to Ellis Island. At its peak, the island was bigger than many towns in Europe, and some immigrants thought that Ellis Island was New York City.

The rich didn't come through Ellis Island; they were met on the boats by customs officials and doctors who allowed them to disembark in Manhattan. The poor immigrants were mostly Italian, Caribbean, or Russian. Many had never seen electricity and were afraid of people in uniforms. The food confused them. One woman thought spaghetti was worms. Some children, seeing bananas for the first time, ate them with the skins on.

The immigrants had just crossed three thousand miles of ocean and were sick and broke. They had come to escape racial or religious persecution or because they'd heard the streets of America were paved with gold. One immigrant later said, "There were few streets, no gold, and I did most of the paving."

As the immigrants walked in, those who looked ill were chalked by doctors for later exams. Officials asked each immigrant twenty-nine questions designed to see if they were prostitutes, bigamists, or criminals. People who were mentally ill, had communicable diseases, or were likely to need welfare were not allowed in. Names often were Americanized. Schmidt became Smith, Johannsen became Johnson. Only after passing the medical tests were those immigrants who had the proper papers and twenty-five dollars admitted. One man said, "I'm not going to be afraid of the gates of hell, I've been to Ellis Island."

With five thousand to seven thousand people admitted per

day, the processing was hurried and fraught with misunderstandings. One young man tried to say he was going to Houston (pronounced *Howston*) Street, where his family waited. The
officer thought he meant the city of Houston and put him on a
train to Texas. He went to Houston and never saw his family
again.

Most newcomers left the island for New York City, but
those riding the railroad went to New Jersey. Recently there has
been a dispute over whether New York or New Jersey owns
Ellis Island. Appearing in court on behalf of New York, Mayor
Giuliani argued, "No one ever set out from the old world for
Jersey City."

All morning Jane and I looked at names, faces, and objects.
Edward G. Robinson, Irving Berlin, Al Capone, and Felix
Frankfurter all came through Ellis Island. However, we were
most interested in the ordinary people, tired, frightened, and
yet hopeful. We walked past black-and-white photos of Finns,
Czechs, Jamaicans, Byelorussians, and shell-shocked Armenians,
the lucky ones who escaped being burned alive in their own
country. We smiled at the photos of a Japanese woman with
wooden slippers, a stylish Greek girl, and a Russian poet in a fur
cap. People had brought over leather-bound books, carved
wooden spoons, a mandolin, and a yellowing lace baby cap. We
examined wildly impractical shoes—Chinese jeweled moc-
casins and a pair of black Turkish sandals decorated with blue
feathers.

At lunch, we sat outside under the sycamores. Near us, an
Indian mother breast-fed her baby, a Latino family in starchy
new clothes shared tortillas and rice, and an old couple spoke
Italian as they fed the birds. Jane talked about her grandmother
who had carried her mother, an infant, in this place. Orphaned

in the flu epidemic, Jane's mother had raised her little sisters in poverty in a slum on the Lower East Side.

Our hearts and eyes were full. We headed back to our boat, back toward Manhattan for a sushi dinner. We sailed past the Statue of Liberty, aka Eleanor Roosevelt. When we arrived at Battery Park, we maneuvered through the sea of hawkers. Men from the Caribbean, West Africa, and Southeast Asia sold watches, Ellis Island T-shirts, snow cones, and hot dogs. An East Indian displayed his charmed cobra. One of the salesmen wore a shirt that quoted John Lennon, "You may say I'm a dreamer, but I'm not the only one."

Ellis Island had always welcomed dreamers. Jane's relatives and mine had dreamed the dream and so most likely did your relatives. America was freedom, the land of opportunity, and the promised land. And the dreams of our ancestors are the dreams of our Kurdish, Vietnamese, Sudanese, Afghani, and other new-comers today. Gold Mountain is Silicon Valley. The land of milk and honey is our land of Coke and french fries. America is where the streets are lined with compact discs and SUVs. We have free schools and free people. Everybody has a dream in America.

HIDDEN *in* PLAIN SIGHT

PART ONE

CHAPTER 1

CULTURAL COLLISIONS *on the* GREAT PLAINS

I AM FROM

I am from Avis and Frank, Agnes and Fred, Glessie May
    and Mark.
From the Ozark Mountains and the high plains of Eastern
    Colorado,
From mountain snowmelt and lazy southern creeks filled with
    water moccasins.
I am from oatmeal eaters, gizzard eaters, haggis and raccoon
    eaters.
I'm from craziness, darkness, sensuality, and humor.
From intense do-gooders struggling through ranch winters in
    the 1920s.
I'm from "If you can't say anything nice about someone don't
    say anything" and "Pretty is as pretty does" and "Shit-
    mucklety brown" and "Damn it all to hell."
I'm from no-dancing-or-drinking Methodists, but cards were
    okay except on Sunday, and from tent-meeting Holy
    Rollers,
From farmers, soldiers, bootleggers, and teachers.

I'm from Schwinn girl's bike, 1950 Mercury two-door, and
     West Side Story.
I'm from coyotes, baby field mice, chlorinous swimming pools,
Milky Way and harvest moon over Nebraska cornfields.
I'm from muddy Platte and Republican,
from cottonwood and mulberry, tumbleweed and switchgrass
from Willa Cather, Walt Whitman, and Janis Joplin,
My own sweet dance unfolding against a cast of women in
     aprons and barefoot men in overalls.

As a girl in Beaver City, I played the globe game. Sitting out-side in the thick yellow weeds, or at the kitchen table while my father made bean soup, I would shut my eyes, put my finger on the globe, and spin it. Then I would open my eyes and imagine what it was like in whatever spot my finger was touching. What were the streets like, the sounds, the colors, the smells? What were the people doing there right now?

I felt isolated in Beaver City, far away from any real action. We were a small town of white Protestants surrounded by cow pastures and wheat fields. I had no contact with people who were different from me. Native Americans had a rich legacy in Nebraska, but I knew nothing of them, not even the names of the tribes who lived in my area. I had never seen a black person or a Latino. Until I read *The Diary of Anne Frank,* I had never heard of Jewish people.

Adults talked mostly about crops, pie, and rainfall. I couldn't wait to grow up and move someplace exotic and faraway, and living where I did, every place appeared faraway and exotic. When I read Tolstoy's book on the little pilgrim who walked all over the world, I vowed to become that pilgrim and to spend my life seeing everything and talking to everyone.

As a young adult, I escaped for a while. I lived in San Francisco, Mexico, London, and Madrid. But much to my surprise, I missed the wheat fields, the thunderstorms, and the meadowlarks. I returned to Nebraska in my mid-twenties, married, raised a family, worked as a psychologist, and ate a lot of pie. I've been happy in Nebraska, but until recently I thought I had to choose between loving a particular rural place and experiencing all the beautiful diversity of the world.

Before the Europeans arrived, Nebraska was home to many Indian tribes. The Omaha, the Ponca, the Pawnee, and the Nemaha lived in the east, the Lakota Sioux in the west. In the late 1800s immigrants from Europe pushed out the Native Americans. Wave after wave of new pioneers broke over Nebraska and we became a state of Scots, Irish, British, Czechs, Swedes, and Danes. For a while, we had so many Germans that many schools held classes in German. But after World War I, when nativist sentiments swept our state, our unicameral made instruction in German illegal.

Mexican workers came to build the railroads and to work on farms and in meatpacking. African Americans came to farm and to work in our cities. Nebraska's first free black person, Sally Bayne, moved to Omaha in 1854, and an all-black colony was formed at Overton in Dawes County in 1885. Malcolm X was born in Omaha in 1925.

Even though people of color have a rich history in our state and, of course, the Native Americans were here first, our state's identity the last 150 years has been mainly European. Until recently, a mixed marriage meant a Catholic married to a Methodist. After World War II, so many Latvians came here that we became the official site of the Latvian government in exile. Our jokes were yawners about farmers or Lutherans—"What did the

farmer say after he won a million dollars in the lottery?" "Thank
God I have enough money to farm a few more years." Or,
"Wherever four Lutherans are gathered there is always a fifth."

However, in the last fifteen years something surprising
has happened. It began with the boat people, mostly Vietnamese and Cambodians, coming in after the Vietnam War. In
the 1980s Lincoln began having a few Asian markets, a Vietnamese Catholic church, a Buddhist temple, and English Language Learners (ELL) classes. Around the same time, Mexican
migrant workers, who had long done seasonal work in our area,
bought houses and settled down. Refugees from the wars in
Central America trickled in.

The real change occurred in the 1990s. Because Lincoln had
almost no unemployment and a relatively low cost of living, we
were selected by the U. S. Office of Refugee Resettlement as a
preferred community for newly arrived refugees. Now we are
one of the top-twenty cities in America for new arrivals from
abroad. Our nonwhite population has grown 128 percent since
1990. We are beginning to look like East Harlem.

Suddenly, our supermarkets and schools are bursting with
refugees from Russia, Serbia, Croatia, Bosnia, Hungary, and
Ethiopia. Our Kurdish, Sudanese, and Somali populations are
rapidly increasing. Even as I write this, refugees from Afghanistan, Liberia, and Sierra Leone are coming into our community.
Some are educated and from Westernized places. Increasingly,
we have poor and uneducated refugees. We have children from
fifty different nationalities who speak thirty-two different languages in our public schools.

Our obituary column shows who came here early in the
1900s. It is filled with Hrdvys, Andersens, Walenshenksys, and
Muellers. But the births column, which reflects recent immigration patterns, has many Ali, Nguyen, and Martinez babies.

By midcentury, less than half our population will be non-Latino white. We are becoming a brown state in a brown nation.

Lincoln has often been described by disgruntled locals and insensitive outsiders as the middle of nowhere, but now it can truthfully be called the middle of everywhere. We are a city of juxtapositions. Next to the old man in overalls selling sweet corn at the farmers' market, a Vietnamese couple sells long beans, bitter melons, and fresh lemongrass. A Yemeni girl wearing a veil stands next to a football fan in his Big Red jacket. Beside McDonald's is a Vietnamese karaoke bar. Wagey Drug has a sign in the window that says, TARJETAS EN ESPAÑOL SE VENDEN AQUI. On the Fourth of July, Asian lion dancers perform beside Nigerian drummers. Driving down Twenty-seventh Street, among the signs for the Good Neighbor Center, Long John Silver's, Fat Pat's Pizza, Snowflakes, and Jiffy Lube, I see signs for Mohammed's Barber Shop, Jai Jai's Hair Salon, Kim Ngo's jewelry, Pho's Vietnamese Café, and Nguyen's Tae-Kwon Do.

We celebrate many holidays—Tet, Cinco de Mayo, Rosh Hashanah, and Ramadan. At our jazz concerts, Vietnamese families share benches with Kurdish and Somali families. When my neighbor plays a pickup basketball game in the park, he plays with Bosnian, Iranian, Nigerian, and Latino players. I am reminded of the *New Yorker* cartoon which pictured a restaurant with a sign reading, RANCHO IL WOK DE PARIS, FEATURING TEX-MEX, ITALIAN, ASIAN, AND FRENCH CUISINES.

Women in veils exchange information with Mexican grandmothers in long black dresses. Laotian fathers smoke beside Romanian and Serbian dads. By now, every conceivable kind of grocery store exists in our city. And the ethnic shelves in our IGA grocery stores keep expanding. The produce sections carry jicama and cilantro. Shoppers can buy pitas, tortillas, egg rolls, wraps, and breads from all over the world. My most recent cab driver was a Nigerian school administrator who fled his country because he was in a pro-democracy group. S. J. Perelman's description of Bangkok—"It seemed to combine the Hannibal, Missouri, of Mark Twain's childhood with Beverly Hills, the Low Countries, and Chinatown"—could now apply to Lincoln.

Our city's experience is not unique. As writer Pico Iyer puts it, "More bodies are being thrown more widely across the planet than ever before." America keeps taking people in. By 2050, whites of European origin will no longer be the majority race in our country. We're becoming a richer curry of peoples. Before 1990 most of our refugees settled in six big states: California, Texas, New York, Florida, New Jersey, and Illinois. But during the 1990s refugees moved into the Midwest, including Nebraska. And what they found was a vast farm and ranch state defined by its most beautiful river.

Nebraska is from an Oto word, meaning "flat water," or the river we now call the Platte. That glorious brown river has been an east-west thoroughfare for thousands of years. It has provided a resting place for cranes and geese as they travel along the great American flyway.

Willa Cather wrote of our vast prairies where tall grasses undulated in a way that reminded her of a great red sea. However, especially in eastern Nebraska, there is almost no natural landscape left—only a few scraps of prairie, an occasional prairie dog town or burr oak forest. Instead, we have fields of wheat, corn, soybeans, and sorghum, little towns, and, increasingly, suburban sprawl.

Our state's best feature is our low population density. If they have to drive around the block for a spot to park, the locals complain about parking problems downtown. The difference between rush and nonrush hour commutes is, at worst, ten minutes. Three-fourths of Nebraska residents live in Omaha and Lincoln. Our third-largest city has around forty thousand people. In the rest of the state there is "a lot of dirt between the lightbulbs." The little towns are, to quote Greg Brown, "scattered like fireflies across the dark night." Some towns are so quiet that your own footsteps echo as you walk the empty streets. There are many places where you can hear the breeze in the cottonwoods or the sound of a killdeer. An international astronomical organization meets in western Nebraska because it has less light pollution than almost anywhere on earth.

We have ten-foot-tall sunflowers, accessible quiet places, and gentle people. Long-term Nebraskan residents tend to be large, rather plain white people whom my husband swears he can recognize in any airport in America. Nebraskans are the kind of people who compete to ride in the backseat, who put money in Salvation Army buckets, and who bake casseroles for grieving neighbors. We are humble people, proud of our football team, our Sandhills, our Native American heritage, and our few celebrities—Warren Buffett, Henry Fonda, Johnny Carson, and Tom Osborne. We don't expect to be invited any place glamorous and we don't make demands. We are happy just to be included.

Most of us come from farm families whose grandparents barely survived the Great Depression. We like our state, but worry that we won't be able to keep our children here. Wal-Marts and Pizza Huts are moving in. Family farms and city cafés are dying.

Lincoln is our capital city. Its skyline is dominated by our capitol building with its golden dome crowned by *The Sower* scattering seed across the land. The year I wrote this book, the capitol was being repaired and refurbished for the new century, a nice metaphor for the changes in our state. The men who worked on the capitol scaffolding spoke thirty different languages, which prompted my friend Sarah to call our capitol "the tower of Babel."

Loren Eiseley, Willa Cather, Mari Sandoz, and Kent Haruf all lived in Lincoln, and many fine writers live here now. Historically we've been a white-collar town with three universities and many insurance companies and banks. In our town of 210,000 people, we have 170 churches, a symphony, a performing arts center, and a university film theater. Two tall-grass prairies and a wilderness park border Lincoln and make it possible for anyone to be "in the country" in fifteen minutes. In the last decade, we have had years in which no one was murdered.

At the same time we are becoming a much more diverse community, we are also becoming more like everywhere else. Lincolnites eat at the same chain restaurants and shop at the same corporate stores as everyone else. We have the same glitzy malls, movies, and music that people do in London, Manila, and Moscow. By now, the world is connected by American Express cards, media, computers, and airline companies. People can buy Kentucky Fried Chicken in Chiang Mai and Dallas Cowboy memorabilia in Burmese markets. The Marlboro man rides in Warsaw and, no matter where people travel, they can sleep in a Sheraton or Hilton. People in Siberia eat pizza and play golf, and people in Lincoln play bridge over the Internet with people from Taiwan.

Our city library now has books in Hindi, Arabic, Spanish, and Urdu. Our colleges educate people from all over the world. Our citizens travel to the Galápagos or search for the wild ponies of Manchuria. But nowhere can they escape corporate logos. The local is no longer protected. The unique is vanishing.

In *The Lexus and the Olive Tree,* Thomas Friedman quoted a man as saying, "There are two ways to make a person homeless—destroy his home or make his home look like everyone else's."

These trends can be called many names but, for shorthand, I will call them globalization. Many writers have explored this phenomenon, but they have ignored the questions that most interest me. How do these processes change us humans? How do they affect our choices, our relations with one another, our allegiances, our mental and social health, our sense of place, and—at core—our identities?

Researching this book has been my grown-up version of the globe game. I wanted to understand what the deal is everywhere. Studying newcomers to Lincoln, I have learned more than a traveler. I have asked questions about family life, cultural collisions, dreams, and value systems. I have had long-term relationships with people who grew up in the mountains of Laos, in war-torn Bosnia, in a village in Jalisco, or on the steppes of Russia. I have talked to a Nuer tribesman about the refugee camps in Kenya and to a Muslim schoolteacher about the war in Sierra Leone. I have heard stories about small villages in Hungary and listened to Afghani women discuss the effects of the Taliban on their lives.

I have celebrated Eid al-Adha with northern Sudanese, the Holi festival with my friends from India, and attended a Latina girl's quinceañera. I have done family therapy with refugees from Macedonia or Romania, gone to a Southeast Asian Buddhist Parents Day festival, and still slept in my own bed at night.

Bill Holm, a writer from Minnesota, taught for a year in China. Afterward he wrote a book entitled *Coming Home Crazy.* In its preface he said that while he didn't necessarily know that much about China, his year there had taught him a tremendous amount about America. I feel that way about my experiences with refugees. They've helped me see my country with fresh clear eyes.

Tillie Olsen said there are five colleges: the college of motherhood, of human struggle, of everyday work, of literature, and of contrast. Refugees have taught me about contrasts. How do I see the world versus how do they see the world? What are my assumptions? What are theirs? What is particular in the human experience and what is universal?

The borderland where cultures collide is the best vantage point for observing human resilience. Where cultures intersect, all of a sudden everyone must do things differently. I love to be present when teenagers who don't know the earth is round or who have never seen a toothbrush collide with teens who play violins or scuba dive in the Bahamas. I like to watch people who have no written language in their home country learn to use the World Wide Web or to see what happens when third-generation Swedish farmers hire day laborers who have lived for generations on the island of Haiti or in the mountains of Peru.

Like all people, I see the world through my own cultural lenses. My view of reality is dependent on my Nebraska perspective. As I write this, I am a wife, mother, and a grandmother. I was raised Methodist although now I am a Unitarian. I am middle-class, middle-aged, and very ordinary in most ways. I have lived in the Midwest almost all my life.

Like most Americans I speak only English fluently. I value freedom and personal space. I am time conscious. I am comfortable with only certain forms of touch. A certain amount of eye contact and distance between bodies seems right to me. Some things seem much more edible than others. Certain clothes—jeans and T-shirts—feel best to me. I do not cover my head when I go out and I wear shoes inside my house. I like to talk.

In many ways I look, think, and act like a Nebraskan. But it is more complex than that. Nebraska culture is not coherent and homogenous. We have many Native American tribes with powwows all through the year and we have strong African American communities in Lincoln and Omaha. We have liberals and conservatives, sophisticates and provincials who have never left their county of birth. We have evangelicals and Sufis, hate groups and Nebraskans for Peace. Within Nebraska culture there are the cultures of academics, businesspeople, farmers, and artists. There are cultures of folk musicians, pheasant hunters, cyclists, and vegetarians. (Although in Nebraska, the beef state, vegetarians are pretty low-key.)

I have more in common with my editor in New York and with psychologists in Europe than I have with some Nebraskans. And I belong to other cultures—the culture of women, of gardeners, of my neighborhood, of writers, of Piphers, and of my family of origin. After I lost my parents, I was for a while in what Renato Rosaldo calls "the invisible culture of the bereaved," a culture all of us belong to if we live long enough.

Each of these cultures is different from the others. I move among them, switching roles and rules as I move. My everyday life is crisscrossed by borders. It is at those borders between cultures that much of my most interesting experience occurs.

Garrison Keillor wrote that, "If we knew the stories of refugees, they would break our hearts." As I've worked on this book, I've heard stories of mythic scope—of grandparents carrying children across raging rivers, of families barefoot in the snow, trudging across mountain passes, and of a poet surviving torture in an Iraqi prison by remembering the beauty of a flower garden. I've met Vietnamese men who, while they were in reeducation camps, were sent on their hands and knees into fields to find land mines. I've met members of the Polish Solidarity movement, former slaves, and women abducted and raped by soldiers. I've heard children tell of bombs that they thought were fireworks until they saw bodies explode. I have seen the full scope of what human beings do to each other and for each other.

I've interviewed high school students in ELL classes and worked with an elementary school classroom where the kids spoke twenty-two different languages. I've consulted at summer camps for refugee kids and attended English classes for parents of students in the public schools. I've trained members of different cultural groups to be liaisons between the mental health community and their ethnic community, consulted with our community action program's staff, and been a member of the New Americans Task Force.

As both a therapist and interviewer, I came to the conclusion that a formal question-and-answer format is not the best way to learn about newcomers. Partly, that format is too similar to an interrogation. People are fearful they will say the wrong thing. Mainly, I noticed that all the really interesting experiences came before and after those formal sessions. A grandmother would offer me some fresh naan and a bottle of Pepsi. Then she would ask me if Americans ate blackbirds and cardinals. A woman would whisper as I left, "Can you help me get my son out of jail in Saudi Arabia?" A man would ask, "Do you know where I can get a used car for sixty dollars?" A dignified widower would shyly ask if I could help him find a wife. A teenager would show her father the Walkman she bought with wages from her after-school job. The father would shout, "In the Ukraine, my brother has no food and you bought a toy?"

I have lived, as much as a white person born in the Midwest can, in the world of refugees. I've tried to be what Rosaldo calls

a "connected critic," not judgmental but involved and obser-
vant. I have tried to write about others with the respect that I
would want for myself. In the face of so much tragedy, humility
has been the only possible emotional stance. I didn't want
to turn anyone's life into an anecdote. The only justification
for writing these stories is to help others. As I've worked to
understand the world of refugees, I've been aware that they
were working to understand mine. We observed, analyzed, and
changed each other.

The first time I met a family of Sudanese from the Kakuma
Refugee Camp, I had to deal with my fear of the other. I was
alone in a room with Nuer and Dinka men, tall blue-black
Africans who spoke very little English. Some had *gaar,* facial
scarring done in manhood ceremonies. I was anxious, mostly
about making a fool of myself, but also that these men might
somehow hurt me. I had to admit I harbored the rudiments of
racism, an unconscious attitude that I fight daily, but that none
of us can totally escape. As I sat with them, I marveled that I was
even in a room with people from southern Sudan, tribal people
I had read about in college in the 1960s. One of the Nuer men
asked me, "Are you an anthropologist?"

I laughed and said, "No, not really." That broke the ice. I
realized, that strange as these men looked to me, I seemed
equally weird to them. They must have been looking at me, a
plain-faced, curly-haired, middle-aged woman in blue jeans,
and thinking, "What is she doing here?" Or even, "Is she animal, vegetable, or mineral?"

My immersion in the world of refugees has not been
anxiety- or mistake-free. At first, like many people who have
lived mostly in a world of their own kind, I was clumsy with
people who didn't look and talk like me. I worried I wouldn't

be able to understand people for whom English was a second, third, or fifth language. I wondered if I would be accepted and understood. I was embarrassed that I was fluent only in English.

I had trouble mastering names of people from foreign cultures. I knew too many men named Ali or Mohammed and especially on the phone I had trouble keeping them straight. I wasn't quite sure how to talk or touch, what behavior was appropriate in what settings, and when I might inadvertently offend. Encounters with people very different from me were hard work. Often I was anxious, awkward, and even suspicious. What were they saying about me?

Ridiculous misunderstandings occurred. One time a mother from Iraq told me her son had been hit by a car. I thought that she had said that he had a ride to school and I asked, "Are you happy?" Understandably, she was angry and insulted.

Another time, an African woman pointed at her daughter's bosom when the girl was wearing a tight shirt and said over and over, "Beautiful, beautiful." I was confused by this. Was she asking me if I thought her daughter's breasts were beautiful? I didn't know what to do. Fortunately, I just waited for the situation to become clear. At last, I understood that the mother was praising the cloth of the shirt, which came from Nigeria.

Gradually, I learned to relax and even to laugh at mix-ups. I learned to tolerate more ambiguity in conversations, to speak more slowly and clearly, and to smile and hug when other ways of communicating fell apart.

I was often overwhelmed. Families had so many problems with language, finances, health, housing, jobs, schools, and the Immigration and Naturalization Service (INS). They needed lawyers, doctors, and help with taxes. They wanted everything at once—to learn to drive, to read, and to find dental work and day care. They didn't have cars, shoes, or telephones. Most of their early problems were crises—the INS would deport them if they couldn't get fingerprinted, or it was January and the gas had been turned off, or grandmother had a stroke and there was no health insurance or Medicaid. And, even as they struggled to survive here, they had relatives in their old country who desperately needed money.

Sometimes I felt burned-out and discouraged. Eventually I figured out where to get good legal advice, who to call about INS problems, where decent health care could be found, and who had free bus passes, bicycles, clothes, and food. There were many people in our town eager to help, but it took a while to find them.

The other thing that saved me was the occasional remark that let me know that what I did mattered. A young woman from Romania thanked me for a scarf that I had wrapped and given her on her birthday. She said, "No one has ever given me a present before. I never had a birthday until I met you." I drove a Somali man to the doctor and paid for his appointment. He said afterward, "I didn't like Americans until today. People have not been friendly. Some steal from me. But now I know some Americans are good."

Writing about people from other cultures is fraught with social peril. Sentimentalism or romanticizing can be insidious forms of dehumanization. Generalizations about ethnic groups can easily become stereotypes. It's hard to master even the rudiments of knowledge about the fifty different cultures in our community.

I apologize in advance for the terminology with which I refer to people and places. Respectful language changes monthly. Different people prefer different words. Do I refer to people as from traditional cultures, developing nations, or the Global South? Do I use the word *Latino* or *Hispanic?* What is the best way to refer to whites and nonwhites? These are highly charged political and personal questions. I am reasonably sure I will inadvertently offend someone. I have been as careful as I could be in my use of language, and no offense is intended.

I use the word *American* rather loosely, to refer to native-born Americans and to some others who have become citizens or lived here long enough to become Americanized. Essentially, I use the term *American* as a contrast word for newcomers. Almost all the refugees I discuss are new arrivals, here only a few years at most, and not yet sure what the deal is. Of course, I acknowledge that Americans are not monolithic—we have many value systems among our native-born people—and not all Americans are Nebraskans, the Americans I write about most of the time. But for brevity and flow, it's better not to constantly reclarify the word.

This book is not an academic tome or an in-depth analysis of our policies toward refugees. It doesn't tackle many systemic issues, such as the root causes of the worldwide displacement of people or the political, economic, and social issues that come with this displacement. There are academics far more competent to discuss these issues. Rather, I attempt to show, by telling the stories of real people, the effects of our current policies. My goal is to increase the interest of ordinary Americans in refugee issues with the hopes that they will then dig deeper into more scholarly works.

The United Nations defines a refugee as a person who is unable or unwilling to return to his or her country because of a well-founded fear of persecution. These claims of persecution must be based on race, religion, nationality, or membership in a particular social group or political party. Refugees are resettled in a third country when they are unable to return home and cannot stay in the camp or country in which they were granted asylum.

Latinos are underrepresented in this book even though they are the largest ethnic group in our state. I met newcomers through refugee services and most Latinos are not legally refugees and therefore do not qualify for many of the services in our community.

Of all Latino populations, only Cubans are considered refugees by our government. Colombians are not considered refugees, even though their country has 2 million displaced people and is rapidly becoming unlivable. This classification system is a remnant of the cold war. The United States government destabilized governments in Chile, Argentina, Bolivia, Uruguay, and Brazil and helped build the death squads in Honduras and Nicaragua. People fleeing those places couldn't be called refugees without acknowledging our government's foreign-policy errors.

In many ways, newly arrived Latinos have the hardest time in Nebraska. They have experienced as much trauma as other groups and they tend to work under the harshest conditions in our state. However, because they are not labeled refugees, they don't get the social services other groups do. They are almost invisible except as workers. They are even called "illegal aliens" which sounds like they came from Mars.

I don't in any way attempt to discuss all refugee populations in America, just the major ones in Lincoln. There is not much in the book on the Hmong, for example, because Lincoln doesn't have many Hmong people. And I do not claim to be an expert on any of the cultures I discuss. I do try to understand and to present honestly the lives of the people I met. My hope is this presentation will give readers a glimpse of worlds they didn't even know existed in their hometowns and motivate them to discover more about these worlds for themselves.

This book is written for ordinary people, especially those who live in communities with refugees. It's for teachers, doctors, nurses, counselors, police officers, lawyers, employers, church workers, community volunteers, anyone who works with or knows someone from another country. My hope is that this book will open the eyes of ordinary Americans and allow them to see refugees with knowledge, empathy, and respect.

It is also written for refugees. I hope the book is a guide to America, but also a warning that here there are new dangers and perils. American streets are not paved with gold. Freedom is not absolute. Credit-card bills can create new kinds of servitude. Families can cross the tundra on horseback, fearful all the way of being shot, only to encounter what they consider a worse crisis here: children who won't come home at night and don't obey their parents.

Looking at America through the eyes of refugees, I have seen a very different America than the one I've inhabited for fifty years. I've seen Americans' kindness and eagerness to help newcomers. But I have also seen how some businesses use up their employees, how some landlords manage not to rent to people who have accents or brown skins, and how some doctors and police give very different kinds of service to the rich and the poor. I have seen the INS treat refugees like criminals and make their lives needlessly anxious and difficult.

Refugees reveal the strengths and flaws of America. To be fair, we are the country that takes people in. We educate refugees and allow them to become citizens. And yet, when they arrive, we often exploit them and make them suffer needlessly. And, for the most part, we Americans are abysmally ignorant

about the rest of the world. We have both an immense innocence and an enormous sense of entitlement. We are spoiled
children in a world of hurting people, and we take far too much
for granted. As my friend Pam put it, "We were born on third
base and we think we hit triples."

I do not want to idealize refugees. All cultures have lazy,
cruel, and even dangerous people. All cultures have malcontents
as well as people who are wiser and kinder than others. Some
people are more open to experience, more eager to learn, harder
workers, and more fun to be around. Some operate on a higher
moral plane. I wanted to study this variation between people
across cultures. Why do some people crumble and withdraw
while others with equally difficult situations move into mainstream America? I identified what I call the attributes of resilience, which are the personal qualities that help refugees make
it in their new situations. These attributes have relevance to all
of us as we move in an increasingly new world with all our familiar props left behind.

Refugees come from a fire into a fire. Like all who live in
crucibles, their experiences are defining ones for them and for
all who witness their lives. We all are interested in what happens
to people in extreme conditions. That's why *Tuesdays with Mor-
rie, The Perfect Storm,* and *Into Thin Air* were best sellers, and
that's why *Titanic* was a hit movie. After we see or read a story
of trauma we ask, "What would I do in that situation?"

Ernest Shackleton said, "Optimism is true moral courage."
The ways people are damaged are also the ways they are made
strong. Suffering can create bitter people but it often creates
people with depth of character and empathy with other people's
suffering. Easy lives can produce spoiled, soft people. Hard lives
can produce lovers and fighters. Refugees who make it in Amer-

ica manage to find meaning in their suffering. Many become kinder and more generous people. Anne Frank's father, Otto, a refugee himself, said, "Giving never makes anyone poorer."

Another great survival strategy is connecting with family and community. Many have lost some loved ones, but they have held on to others under extraordinarily difficult circumstances. Their attitudes toward family put ours into perspective. An American might be in therapy complaining of an intrusive mother. An immigrant will be working three jobs so that she can bring her aunt to this country.

Globalization will change everything forever. Soon we will all be as mixed together as a bowl of salt and pepper. Refugees in our town offer us a heightened version of the experiences we'll all share as our world becomes one vast fusion culture. They are the harbingers of our future. The coping skills that refugees need—flexibility, the ability to make good decisions in the face of a dazzling number of choices, the ability to stay calm in a tough situation, and the ability to deal with people different than themselves—are the skills we will all need. All of us will require a global positioning system to tell us who and where we are.

A track is not the shape of a foot; it is the shape of a foot in the ground. Identity can only occur in a context, that is, in a social environment. Refugees, displaced and disoriented by their rapidly changing world, have shaky identities. Increasingly, we will all have identity issues in our globalized world. Who are we when we don't have a hometown, when we don't know our neighbors or our kin? Who are we don't know the history of our land or the names of common plants and birds in our area? Or when our stories come from television sets instead of grandparents or village storytellers? Who are we in a world where the universal language is, to quote Pico Iyer, "french fries"?

"We think the world apart," said Parker Palmer. "What would it be like to think the world together?" Teilhard de Chardin had a word—*unfurling*—to describe that "infinitely slow spasmodic movement towards the unity of mankind." He saw education and love as the twin pillars of progress. At this amazing point in history, we have the opportunity to get things right.

CHAPTER 2

The BEAUTIFUL LAUGHING SISTERS— *An* ARRIVAL STORY

THE BEAUTIFUL LAUGHING SISTERS
"It was hard, but we got used to hard."

One of the best ways to understand the refugee experience is to befriend a family of new arrivals and observe their experiences in our country for the first year. That first year is the hardest. Everything is new and strange, and obstacles appear like the stars appear at dusk, in an uncountable array. This story is about a family I met during their first month in our country. I became their friend and cultural broker and in the process learned a great deal about the refugee experience, and about us Americans.

On a fall day I met Shireen and Meena, who had come to this country from Pakistan. The Kurdish sisters were slender young women with alert expressions. They wore blue jeans and clunky high-heeled shoes. Shireen was taller and bolder, Meena was smaller and more soft-spoken. Their English was limited and heavily accented. (I later learned it was their sixth language after Kurdish, Arabic, Farsi, Urdu, and Hindi.) They communicated with each other via small quick gestures and eye movements. Although they laughed easily, they watched to see that the other was okay at all times.

Shireen was the youngest and the only one of the six sisters who was eligible for high school. Meena, who was twenty-one, had walked the ten blocks from their apartment to meet Shireen at school on a bitterly cold day. Shireen told the family story. Meena occasionally interrupted her answers with a reminder, an amendment, or laughter.

Shireen was born in Baghdad in 1979, the last of ten children. Their mother, Zeenat, had been a village girl who entered an arranged marriage at fourteen. Although their father had been well educated, Zeenat couldn't read or write in any language. The family was prosperous and "Europeanized," as Shireen put it. She said, "Before our father was in trouble, we lived just like you. Baghdad was a big city. In our group of friends, men and women were treated as equals. Our older sisters went to movies and read foreign newspapers. Our father went to cocktail parties at the embassies."

However, their father had opposed Saddam Hussein, and from the time of Shireen's birth, his life was in danger. After Hussein came to power, terrible things happened to families like theirs. One family of eleven was taken to jail by his security forces and tortured to death. Prisoners were often fed rice mixed with glass so that they would quietly bleed to death in their cells. Girls were raped and impregnated by the security police. Afterward, they were murdered or killed themselves.

It was a hideous time. Schoolteachers tried to get children to betray their parents. One night the police broke into the family's house. They tore up the beds, bookcases, and the kitchen, and they took their Western clothes and tapes. After that night, all of the family except for one married sister made a daring escape into Iran.

Meena said, "It was a long time ago but I can see everything today." There was no legal way to go north, so they walked through Kurdistan at night and slept under bushes in the day. They found a guide who made his living escorting Kurds over the mountains. Twice they crossed rivers near flood stage. Entire families had been swept away by the waters and one of the sisters almost drowned when she fell off her horse. The trails were steep and narrow and another sister fell and broke her leg. Meena was in a bag slung over the guide's horse for three days. She remembered how stiff she felt in the bag, and Shireen remembered screaming, "I want my mama."

This was in the 1980s. While this was happening I was a psychologist building my private practice and a young mother taking my kids to *Sesame Street Live* and Vacation Village on Lake Okoboji. I was dancing to the music of my husband's band, Sour Mash, listening to Van Morrison and Jackson Browne and reading P. D. James and Anne Tyler. Could my life have been happening on the same planet?

The family made it to a refugee camp in Iran. It was a miserable place with smelly tents and almost no supplies. Shireen said this was rough on her older siblings who had led lives of luxury. She and Meena adjusted more quickly. The sisters studied in an Iranian school for refugees.

They endured this makeshift camp for one very bad year. The Iranians insisted that all the women in the camp wear heavy scarves and robes and conform to strict rules. The soldiers in the camp shouted at them if they wore even a little lipstick. Shireen once saw a young girl wearing makeup stopped by a guard who rubbed it off her face. He had put ground glass in the tissue so that her cheeks bled afterward.

They decided to get out of Iran and traveled the only direction they could, east into Pakistan. They walked all the way with nothing to drink except salty water that made them even thirstier. I asked how long the trip took and Shireen said three days. Meena quickly corrected her: "Ten years."

Once in Pakistan they were settled by a relief agency in a border town called Quetta, where strangers were not welcome. The family lived in a small house with electricity that worked only sporadically. The stress of all the moves broke the family apart. The men left the women and the family has never reunited.

Single women in Quetta couldn't leave home unescorted and the sisters had no men to escort them. Only their mother, Zeenat, dared go out to look for food. As Meena put it, "She took good care of us and now we will take care of her."

The sisters almost never left the hut, but when they did, they wore robes as thick and heavy as black carpets. Meena demonstrated how hard it was to walk in these clothes and how she often fell down. Even properly dressed, they were chased by local men. When they rode the bus to buy vegetables, they were harassed.

Without their heroic mother, they couldn't have survived. For weeks at a time, the family was trapped inside the hut. At night the locals would break their windows with stones and taunt the sisters with threats of rape. Meena interrupted to say that every house in the village but theirs had weapons. Shireen said incredulously, "There were no laws in that place. Guns were laws."

One night some men broke into their hut and took what little money and jewelry they had left. They had been sleeping and woke to see guns flashing around them. The next day they reported the break-in to the police. Shireen said, "The police told us to get our own guns." Meena said, "We were nothing to them. The police slapped and pushed us. We were afraid to provoke them."

During the time they were there, the Pakistanis tested a nuclear bomb nearby and they all got sick. An older sister had seizures from the stress of their lives. Shireen said defiantly, "It was hard, but we got used to hard."

Still, the young women laughed as they told me about the black robes and the men with guns. Their laughter was a complicated mixture of anxiety, embarrassment, and relief that it was over. It was perhaps also an attempt to distance themselves from that time and place.

They'd studied English in the hut and made plans for their future in America or Europe. Shireen said, "I always knew that we would escape that place."

In Quetta the family waited ten years for papers that would allow them to immigrate. Shireen looked at me and said, "I lost my teenage years there—all my teenage years."

Finally, in frustration, the family went on a hunger strike. They told the relief workers they would not eat until they were allowed to leave Quetta. After a few days, the agency paperwork was delivered and the family was permitted to board a train for Islamabad.

In Islamabad they lived in a small apartment with no air conditioning. Every morning they would soak their curtains in water to try to cool their rooms. It was dusty and polluted and they got typhoid fever and heat sickness. They had a year of interviews and waiting before papers arrived that allowed them to leave for America. Still, it was a year of hope. Zeenat picked up cans along the roads to make money. One sister ran a beauty parlor from their home. They all watched American television, studied English, and dreamed of a good future.

Finally they flew to America—Islamabad to Karachi to Amsterdam to New York to St. Louis to Lincoln. Shireen said, "We came in at night. There were lights spread out over the dark land. Lincoln looked beautiful."

We talked about their adjustment to Lincoln. Five of the sisters had found work. They didn't have enough money though, and they didn't like the cold. Meena needed three root canals and Zeenat had many missing teeth and needed bridge-work, false teeth, everything really. Still, they were enjoying the sense of possibilities unfolding. Shireen put it this way, "In America, we have rights." She pronounced "rights" as if it were a sacred word.

Meena mentioned that traffic here was more orderly and less dangerous than in Pakistan. The girls loved American clothes and makeup. Two of their sisters wanted to design clothes. Another was already learning to do American hairstyles so that she could work in a beauty shop. Meena wanted to be a nurse and Shireen a model or flight attendant. She said, "I have traveled so much against my will. Now I would like to see the world in a good way."

Shireen said that it was scary to go to the high school. Fortunately, her study of English in Pakistan made it easy for her to learn Nebraska English. She liked her teachers but said the American students mostly ignored her, especially when they heard her thick accent.

One boy had accosted her in the hall and asked her, "Do you suck dick?" She hadn't even known what he meant, but she'd asked her teacher to translate. The teacher had encouraged her to report the harassment and she had. "I am through suffering," Shireen said. "If it happens again, I will slap him."

I was struck by the resilience of these sisters. In all the awful places they had been, they'd found ways to survive and even joke about their troubles. These young women used their intelligence to survive. Had they lived different lives, they would probably have been doctors and astrophysicists. Since they'd been in Lincoln, they'd been happy. Shireen said, "Of course we have problems, but they are easy problems."

I gave the sisters a ride home in my old Honda. They invited me in for tea, but I didn't have time. Instead I wrote out my phone number and told them to call if I could help them in any way.

When I said good-bye, I had no idea how soon and how intensely I would become involved in the lives of this family. Two weeks later Shireen called to ask about an art course advertised on a book of matches. It promised a college degree for thirty-five dollars. I said, "Don't do it." A couple of weeks later she called again. This time she had seen an ad for models. She wondered if she should pay and enter the modeling contest. Again I advised, "Don't do it." I was embarrassed to tell her that we Americans lie to people to make money. Before I hung up, we chatted for a while. I liked her enthusiasm and openness to experience. I asked, "Do you need some help?" She said, "My sisters and I need to learn to drive."

DRIVING LESSONS

I went by the family's rental, a small house on a street of grocery stores, fast-food places, and pawnshops. The house was decorated Goodwill-style with Kurdish touches. The sisters came and went in various stages of dress, all with skin creams on their faces. A big can of cashews and a pot of strong black tea sat on the table. The rooms smelled of garlic, onions, and cooking oil. Later I learned that someone was always cooking something delicious.

I met all the sisters and their mother. Zeenat was short, with reddish hair and deep worry lines around her eyes. She couldn't speak English, but she smiled broadly. It was amazing how much we could communicate to each other with no language in common. Zeenat could convey a great deal with her dramatic body language. At first she mainly conveyed humor and joy at seeing me. Later, I would sense her deep sorrow.

At fifty-five, Zeenat was lost in America. She'd been left by her husband and she couldn't learn the language or find a job. She had many health problems and a deep persistent depression. Nevertheless, she remained earthy, affectionate, and expressive. She reminded me of strong women, like Thelma Ritter or Bea Arthur, with heart and spunk.

The sisters were all beautiful, smart, and assertive, with straight black hair and flashing black eyes. Their assertiveness and their sticking together was what had kept them alive. All of them loved to laugh, sing, and dance. But all of them were coping with nightmares, anxiety, intrusive thoughts, heart palpitations, and other physical symptoms of stress. Quickly, I learned how different they were from one another.

Nasreen, the oldest sister, was small and slender with a large beauty mark on her cheek. She had been educated in a private school before the family fled Baghdad. She had read feminist and political writers, poetry, and philosophy. There was an aura of sadness about Nasreen that never left, even when she smiled her slow smile. She was a poet in a factory.

Leila, the second oldest, was the tough workhorse, the leader of the family, and the moral authority. She was kindhearted and sensible. She had shopped for the family's first car and she made all the tough calls. Leila kept the family focused and calm.

Tanya had a shiny curtain of hair, a curvaceous body, and languid moves. Men were crazy about her. She often had a bouquet of roses on the table from some Back Door Johnny or other. But she seemed indifferent to these admirers, resigned to their attentions rather than pleased by them. Tanya was about as un-Nebraskan as a woman could be. She was intuitive and dramatic and spoke with her eyes and her body. Later I learned she was the family comedian and mimic. She was beautiful and sensual and could have been a great actress. But she was a lonely person, too, set apart by her strengths, too sensitive for the hard life she'd led, and isolated from American peers by her terrible history.

Shehla seemed healthy, both mentally and physically. She was pretty in a girl-next-door way, if the girl next door can be from Kurdistan. She had an eager smile and an easy laugh. She favored jeans and crisp cotton shirts. Shehla had an endearing habit of letting her sisters talk when they could, but jumping in when their English faltered. As time passed, it seemed as if Shehla allowed herself to have more problems. She had generously waited her turn and let her sisters have their problems first. When everyone else was doing better, she allowed herself the luxury of being sick.

Jabha was the second-to-youngest sister. She was fun-loving, sweet-natured, and lighthearted. She had been born during a famous battle and named Jabha, which means "battle," to commemorate that event. However, Jabha was a terrible name for her, so she was nicknamed Meena. Meena always wanted to go everywhere and to do everything. She asked lots of questions and made jokes whenever she could. Her favorite word was "tasty."

Shireen was the baby of the family. She could have been a model if we allowed our models to be size eight and of medium height. Partly because she was in school, she was the quickest to learn English and to understand American ways. She was very focused on getting a good education. Shireen had a close relationship to her mother and was used to getting star treatment in the family. Even as a new refugee in town, she was poised and confident.

That first day we talked about buying a car. The sisters had only been here for three months and didn't have much money. All had learner's permits. Leila said they had three thousand dollars and wanted to buy a Honda or Toyota.

Later I called a friend who sold used cars. He said he would look for a good deal. I said Jim and I would contribute some money, too. Leila came with us to the car dealer. She wore a scarf and carried a big plastic purse. It was a bitterly cold day and she shivered in the icy Nebraska wind. She test-drove the car and listened as my dealer friend explained the warranty and the car's flaws and virtues. I thought we had a deal, but after I took her home, I got a call. To my surprise, she said in her heavy accent, "I went to the library and the blue book value isn't so good for this car you showed me." I marveled that Leila, in a foreign country, somehow knew to use a blue book.

The sisters eventually bought a car and I began driving lessons with Shehla, Meena, and Shireen. These driving lessons allowed us many quiet hours to talk. After we got through the harrowing first stages of learning to drive with a stick shift, on the right side of the road, and in city traffic, I became their cultural broker for jobs, education, and physical and mental health.

We started out driving on Saturdays, in parking lots and on empty streets. Shireen or Shehla would drive first, then the others. We laughed a lot. I kidded them about my hair getting grayer every time we drove, and we teased Meena, saying she would be a race-car driver because she skidded on the corners. Shireen and Shehla had practiced driving in Pakistan, but Meena started from scratch. She was nervous when the car jerked, died, and screeched. When Meena finally executed a smooth start, Shireen shouted, "You go, girl."

I noticed that Meena became anxious whenever we passed a speed limit sign. Finally, I asked her what made her upset when she saw these signs. She explained that it was hard to drive the car at exactly the speed limit, not one mile faster or slower. This misconception made me remember a Hungarian woman who thought that at intersections she was supposed to drive right under the red light and stop. Before I figured out what she was thinking, she almost got us killed.

Later the sisters practiced driving at the Department of Motor Vehicles. There were always other immigrants in the parking lot learning to drive in old beat-up cars. I pretended to be the examiner and said officiously, "Young lady, you have done very well." Even such a small joke elicited a laugh.

The sisters wanted to know how I became a psychologist and writer. They didn't understand how the different colleges in our city connected with the GED program. They were desperate to catch up. Meena wanted her GED immediately, but her teacher had urged her to be patient. I said, "Don't worry, Meena, someday you will be president." But she told me, "Only people born in America can be president."

We talked about what psychologists would label posttraumatic stress disorder. The sisters had nightmares and trouble sleeping. They had memories that kept them from concentrating on their schoolwork. Shireen had visited a doctor who gave her sleeping pills. I encouraged them to talk to each other, to write in journals, and to consider seeing counselors. I worried about what we didn't talk about. Today they were stylish young women learning to drive, but I wondered what psychological damage had been done. What must they forgive in order to be healthy?

Shireen loved learning to swim at school. She passed her lifeguard training and joined the synchronized swim team. She taught her sisters how to swim, and they joined a club so that they could swim regularly. Otherwise, they worked long hours in a factory. In Iraq they had a sister with breast cancer to support and they had to repay their passage from Pakistan.

I wanted to make sure they learned about the good things in our city. Advertisers would direct them to the bars, the malls, and anything that cost money. I told them about what I loved: the parks and prairies, the lakes and sunsets, the sculpture garden, and the free concerts. I lent them books with Georgia O'Keeffe paintings and pictures of our national parks.

For a while I was so involved with the lives of the sisters that Zeenat told me that her daughters were now my daughters. I was touched that she was willing to give her daughters away so that they could advance. I tactfully suggested we could share her daughters, but that she would always be the real mother.

The sisters talked about the differences between the United States and Pakistan. They said even the light was brighter here. I taught them the names of trees and, when spring came, I taught them to identify jonquil, tulip, redbud, cardinal, and finch. One day we passed a goldenrain tree and I said its name. Meena said it could be called the tree of golden tears.

Sometimes I inadvertently frightened them. During the Bush/Gore presidential race, I explained the differences between the two candidates to the sisters. To my puzzlement, they looked increasingly alarmed as I talked. I finally asked, "Are you okay?" Shireen explained that they had been in Iraq and seen the rise of Hussein. Then they were in Pakistan after Benazir Bhutto lost her election. They'd seen women stoned in the streets. Meena asked, "If Bush is elected, will you be killed?"

They thought ordinary neighborhoods were for rich people. I never showed them the starter castles south of town because I was too embarrassed by our distribution of wealth. What would I say? "This is the home of the factory owner who pays you minimum wage?"

Very soon we all grew to depend on our weekly lessons. They needed my advice and support and I needed their joy at seeing me and their curiosity about the world. Often we talked of their nightmares about being chased or locked up. I was struck by how little they complained and by how eager they were to share everything they had, including stories.

When someone asked the sisters where they were from, they didn't know what to say. Meena laughed as she told me that one time in frustration Tanya said, "We are from Italy."

Whenever I showed up, I was offered food—fresh naan made by Tanya or spinach soup or curried fish. And always there was black tea or juice. Before we drove, the sisters would show me their schoolwork. The older sisters had enrolled in GED classes. Often, they worked overtime and were too tired to study. I felt sad that after losing so much of their lives to refugee camps they were now losing their lives to boring factory work.

I tried to act as a full-time encourager and helper. All the sisters tried out ideas on me—one week Meena asked me if she should join the army. Leila wondered if they could find factory work that didn't involve periodic layoffs.

One day Shireen said that in her human behavior class, they had just watched the movie, *Alive,* the grisly story of survivors of a plane crash. After the film the teacher showed interviews with the survivors. Shireen found it very upsetting and cried in class. The American students weren't so moved. Another day the sisters watched *Titanic*. They loved the movie but cried and cried. I found that this movie was a favorite of refugees. I suspect it is because it makes tragedy heroic and romantic, instead of merely sad.

IMPERIAL PALACE

One night I took the sisters to my favorite Asian restaurant in Lincoln. I also invited Anna, who is the pretty and sophisticated daughter of a friend of mine and someone I trusted to help the sisters with fashion and young adult activities.

While we waited at our table for Anna, I talked about the sandhill cranes. Every year between Valentine's Day and St. Patrick's Day, the cranes come to the Platte, hundreds of thousands of them. They sleep at night on the sandbars and feed in the fields along the river by day. Their cries sound like "something you heard before you were born," to quote writer Paul Gruchow, and they fill the air at sunset and sunrise. Some mornings they all lift off the river en masse like a great white cloud rising.

Anna arrived, energetic and friendly. The sisters were a little intimidated by her sophistication and were quieter than usual. They were also overwhelmed by the hundreds of menu items. They were picky eaters and wary of new foods.

We talked of many things, including how Kurdish women remove body hair by roping it with tiny threads and then yanking it out. The sisters asked Anna about her makeup, hair-styles, and clothes. Tanya told us she used to cut hair in Pakistan, but she doubted she could go to school and get the necessary license here.

We talked about dating. Anna was going with a policeman

and that led to the story of the lost purse. One night Shireen left a purse with all the family's money in a park. She was devastated but had the presence of mind to call the police. Fortunately, a kind policeman showed up later with the purse and all her money. We teased Shireen about the cute policeman. Jokes about dating always got big laughs.

Tanya said she had been asked out by a guy who showed up to take her to *The Perfect Storm*. Much to his surprise, everyone in the family wanted to go along. We all laughed at his surprise, but behind the laughter was sadness. All of these women had spent their beautiful youth locked in a hut in Quetta. Now they were out of step with their own people as well as with Americans. They were too sharp for many of the people they met on the job, and they had no money for the places frequented by educated Americans. Besides, not that many doctors, lawyers, or professors married women who worked in factories.

Meanwhile our food arrived, first hot-and-sour soup, then egg rolls and crab rangoon, followed by chicken lo mein, crispy fish, and fried eggplant and tofu. The sisters dutifully tried things; Shehla choked on a hot pepper and had to drink a gallon of water to recover. Meena and Shireen left most of the food on their plates. Some dishes may have been forbidden for religious reasons; some they just didn't like.

Anna offered to take the sisters "garage-saling" sometime, and they readily agreed. They were hungry for new friends. We opened our fortune cookies and laughed at their messages. Shehla would marry a rich man. Leila would soon have good news. Nasreen had a kind heart.

I snapped photos of our group. The sisters kept photo albums and had shown me pictures from their past lives. In the pictures at Imperial Palace we were smiling, with our arms around each other, the sisters were all dressed up and hopeful about the future, a good moment to capture.

A BAD DAY

At the end of March I arrived for a lesson on driving in snow. Zeenat came to the door, dressed in slippers and a housecoat, friendly as usual. But as we talked I could tell she was discouraged. She had learned a few phrases of English. She said what would become her mantra to me: "I am bored. I want to go back to Islamabad."

I felt for her. Hard as her life had been in the past, at least she had been useful. Now she was home alone most of the time. She cooked and cleaned the house, but she had no money and no friends. She missed the intensely communal life of the past. Shireen said her mother's eyes would light up when she returned from school, but then be sad again when Shireen insisted she must sit down and study.

Today all the family was sick and demoralized by the frigid weather. They spent their days assembling computer boards and pieces of electronic equipment. At best, it was dull work that required care and close attention. At worst, it involved scornful supervisors and toxic chemicals. We talked about other job options and the sisters decided to look, as a group, for a better place to work. Then they would leave this factory en masse.

The sisters were never alone. Partly this was of necessity; they hadn't had the luxury of houses with bedrooms for each person, or of separate vehicles for outings. Partly it was tradition; they came from a part of the world legendary for its female bonding. Women cooked, ate, bathed, danced, and slept together. And partly it was for protection. One of their survival tools had been to stick together.

I learned early that whenever a decision had to be made, whichever sister was involved would say, "I will talk to the family and tell you later." Nobody thought of just going off and doing what she wanted. Always the question was, "What is good for the family?"

That didn't mean there was not tension. At first I just didn't see it. I saw nothing but sharing, taking turns, and being polite. Later I would see that communal living took a toll. Sometimes it was hard to share the phone or car. The sisters had different priorities and needs. There were arguments about decisions. The older sisters were stressed by their responsibilities to the younger ones. Goals were deferred for the good for the group, but not without resentment.

Probably the most significant tension was around the younger sisters' desire to study and the older sisters' desire that they all work and make money to buy a house or a car or to send money to Iraq. Yet no one ever questioned that issues should be resolved in a group process. No one struck out on her own. Most of the time, the sisters took turns getting their needs met. Furthermore, they were best friends who went dancing together and took each other along on dates.

This snowy morning Leila brought me strong medicinal soup of spinach and beans. Perhaps because it was snowy and they were sick, the talk was a bit grim. Shireen was being bullied by an African American girl at school. Shireen made what could be considered a racist generalization and I talked about the stereotypes and media images of blacks in this country. I encouraged Shireen to try to make friends with some of the black kids at her school.

We talked about male-female relations. The sisters worried that Kurdish men expected to be the boss. But they were also leery of American men, who they'd been warned wanted to have sex right away. Shehla wanted to go see the movie *Girl, Interrupted*. She didn't know what it was about, but she liked the name.

A SPRING DAY

Another day, spring arrived and we drove to the university campus. At the campus fountain I taught the Kurdish sisters to throw pennies and make a wish, which they enjoyed very much. This was about the right level of fun. Elaborate, expensive plans could easily run amok. Small was beautiful.

I explained vocabulary words they'd heard recently. Shehla asked what *sarcastic* meant. I'd used the words *vulnerable* and *intuitive* and they wanted to understand them. After I explained them all, Meena used them in a sentence. "We are intuitive and we have been vulnerable, but we are not sarcastic." Yes, I thought, that is exactly right.

We walked to the sculpture garden. Many statues were scattered in the prairie grasses. They liked a statue of a grief-stricken daughter crying on her father's corpse. We stood a long time in front of a bronze of a buxom woman with big hips and a very small head. Finally Shireen said, "We know what the artist thought was important about women."

STATE FAIR

On a hot July night, I took the family to an outdoor musical. We carried our strawberries, naan, and goat biryani into the field that served as seating for the audience. We spread out a blanket and passed around our meal. Tanya's biryani was simple—meat, rice, onions, and cardamom pods—but incredibly delicious comfort food. Nearby, other families shared Czech runzas and kolaches. Just as the sun set and the lightning bugs appeared, the musical began.

This play helped me see how hard our language was for the sisters. I remembered reading the scene in *The God of Small Things* where the Indian narrator and her family went to the movie, *The Sound of Music*. The narrator misunderstood so much of what was happening on the screen.

The same thing happened to us at this play. *State Fair* was a total conundrum to the family. They couldn't understand the cornball, out-dated language. They didn't know what a state fair was. They had never heard of a "lickin'," a competition for prize pigs, or the game of horseshoes. They clapped at the right times, but they might as well have been watching Kabuki theater.

At one point, when the judge in the play was getting drunk from eating brandy-soaked mincemeat, Shehla asked me if he had eaten some sour pickles and was getting sick. At another point, on the fair midway, women dressed in skimpy, faux Mideastern silk pants and scarves danced erotically to lure men into a striptease show. Tanya beamed proudly to witness such beautiful Kurdish women represented in an American play. I didn't have the heart to tell her they represented the sleaze factor at the state fair.

The sisters left the musical only vaguely aware of what happened to these apron- and overall-clad farmy Iowans. Graciously Zeenat said she liked the pines in the park and Leila admired the full moon.

JULY 4

Zeenat and the sisters arrived at our house with Tanya's famous biryani. They'd bought the meat from an Arab grocer who had killed the lamb that day. It was a typical Fourth in Nebraska, about ninety-five degrees with 90 percent humidity. The air smelled of smoke and gunpowder and Lincoln boomed with a frenzy of fireworks. It was so noisy outside that we couldn't talk. Firecrackers exploded next door. Dogs barked because their ears hurt.

Leila wore cotton slacks and a simple top, but the other sisters were in fancy holiday summer wear—tank tops, short shorts, and lots of makeup. Shireen had a Madonnaesque outfit with a little porkpie hat. She carried a small American flag. Tanya wore a low-cut black silk top and blue jeans. To the sisters, one meaning of freedom was the freedom to wear American clothes. I reflected that while their clothes were sexy, their intentions were innocent: a night with Jim and me sharing biryani and homemade ice cream, then going to see our city fireworks display.

We walked through my garden looking at flowers. Shehla smelled my wild sage and said it reminded her of the spices that grew wild in the Kurdish mountains. We took photos by the trumpet vines of this new American family in sexy American clothes waving a small American flag.

Later we drove to Holmes Lake for the big city fireworks display. Thousands of people were there, but eventually we settled in below the dam on a patch of grass. We lay down on blankets, so that we were looking at exactly the right piece of sky for the fireworks.

It was a happy time, all of us lying on blankets like sparklers in a box, a breeze came up, the stars came out, and we taught each other the Kurdish and English names for the constellations. Zeenat said this park reminded her of Islamabad, her highest compliment. Shireen waved her flag at passersby.

When the fireworks began to explode, we gasped at their beauty. But between bursts, the sisters said that the fireworks made them think of the bombs over Iraq. Tonight their favorites were the gold ones, the stars, and the ones that looked like golden rain or golden tears. Afterward we held hands as we walked back toward the car. We were all tired but happy to be celebrating together. On the way home, we drove past a man holding a sign that said HONK IF YOU ARE AN AMERICAN. I said to Jim, "Honk at the guy. We all are Americans." The family clapped. Shireen waved her flag.

CAMPING ON THE PLATTE

On a September afternoon, the sisters, Zeenat, and I drove to a park along the Platte River. We drove past orange milo fields and men harvesting corn. The air smelled like we were inside a giant cereal box. It was a gorgeous day, blue sky, seventy degrees with the ten-foot-tall sunflowers blooming and red sumac and goldenrod in the ditches. It was a football Saturday with a Big Red game in Lincoln so the park was almost empty.

This was an old park with cottonwood trees and sand bottom lakes. We pitched our tents along the Platte. Nearby, coal trains passed on a regular basis. But when they were gone, we could hear birds singing and the gurgle of the Platte. The rustle of cottonwoods was hypnotic. So was watching the Platte meander toward the Missouri, its broad braided channel as slow moving as butterscotch pudding.

The geese were just beginning to move south, and occasionally overhead we would see a ragged V. A blue heron claimed a sandbar and we watched him as we talked. The girls noticed everything—a nuthatch walking down a tree trunk, the rose hips and poison ivy, the flop of a carp, and the dragonflies. Excitedly we planned our day.

Coming into the park, the sisters had seen a sign for horseback riding and they wanted to ride. They hadn't been on horses since their dramatic escape from Iran into Pakistan years earlier and I sensed this ride would be a corrective emotional experience. I agreed we would go tomorrow.

At first we were hot, but as the afternoon wore on and cicadas began to hum, the temperature dropped. Zeenat sat in a
lawn chair and watched the Platte's muddy water roll by. Most
of Zeenat's childhood had been spent outdoors. She seemed
much more at home here than she did in the family's small Lincoln apartment. She rubbed Tanya's head in soothing therapeutic motions, an ancient remedy that went all the way back to the
Stone Age. Tanya said it worked quicker than aspirin.

Meena, Shireen, and Shehla went swimming in a sandpit.
They said lake water was alive, very different from swimming-
pool water. It had layers, cool then warm, and little fish and cur-
rents. Meena said, "I wish we could stay here forever."

Shireen located my camera buried in a mound of camping
gear. When I congratulated her on finding it, she said proudly,
"I have always been good at finding things." Meena hugged me
and said, "She found you for us."

Nasreen said the Platte reminded her of the Tigris River that
flows through Baghdad. She said, "As a girl I walked along it
every day. I read poetry on its banks. It was green, not brown
like this, but it moved slowly and peacefully like the Platte."

I said that as a girl I had learned that the Tigris and Eu-
phrates Rivers were the cradle of civilization. The sisters smiled
proudly. I asked Nasreen if she read poetry now. She said no,
that she couldn't read English. I encouraged her, pointing out
that it wasn't too late to go to school. She said, "You haven't
seen my credit card bill. I will work forever to pay it off."

I asked Shehla about her studies. She said she had gone to
many schools over the years, but the schools were in different
languages with different curricula. She said, "I have big gaps in
what I know."

The sisters talked about their jobs. It was such tedious work
and afterward they felt too tired to study. Leila asked me if my

daughter had a job and I said, "Yes, she works for a nonprofit organization." Leila asked what shift she worked. I answered, "Day shift."

Tanya gestured at the beauty all around us and said, "We have spent our lives locked in little dark rooms. We love to be outdoors."

She spoke of all their journeys and losses and of the great sadness they all carried in their hearts. Shireen told of a lesson in writing class. The students were asked to make a life map, a time line with ten significant events. She said the American kids had no trouble, but she had a terrible time. The Americans listed birthdays, vacations, and maybe their grandparents' deaths. But all of her events were sad—escapes, family members being murdered, and things she couldn't write down because they were too painful to tell. She said, "I didn't do the assignment."

We prepared a beautiful ancient meal. Over the fire, using only sticks and their hands, Leila and Shireen roasted meat, corn, and potatoes. Tanya chopped eggs with some cucumbers and tomatoes. I'd brought a watermelon and an angel food cake baked by the Mennonites who sell cakes at the farmers' market. Zeenat helped me lay out plates and cups of lemonade. I served the watermelon, which Meena declared tasty. We ate under the rustling trees. It was one of the finest meals of my life.

At sunset the sun was a great orange ball with a three-quarters moon rising. We sat by the river and watched the sun go down. The river darkened and the bats came out. Shireen sang an ancient Kurdish song. We allowed our senses to feast on the scene. It is one the oldest of human pleasures, sitting by water with friends, watching the sun go down, and feeling the earth cool. Nasreen quoted a Persian poet writing about water and sunsets as "the place where gold and silver waters blend."

Later we gathered around a fire. Shehla and Nasreen had

prepared strong tea, *chai* in Kurdish, in a silver pot. I taught them to roast marshmallows on our shish kebab sticks. They enjoyed the process more than the results.

Leila said that before the Muslim prophet, Mohammed, the Kurds worshiped fire. We talked about all people's love of fire, about what an ancient experience it was to sit with your friends, full and safe, around a fire, looking at the stars and telling stories. There is no happier experience for us humans.

We fell silent watching the fire, each of us deep in our own thoughts, all of us made calm and reflective by the time and place, by the rituals of food and family. One by one we peeled off and headed for our beds.

The next morning I was up first. I made coffee and then watched as a hundred geese lifted off the Platte. They flew across the pale blue sky toward the delicate pastel sunrise. Gradually one sister after another woke up. We fixed tea and shared a simple breakfast of bread and cheese. Meena said the wind, coming through the cottonwoods, scared them in the night. When a train roared through they wondered if it was a tornado. Slowly and reluctantly we packed up. I was glad we had horseback riding to look forward to. Even so, Leila pretended to cry as we left, and Tanya looked like she could cry.

As we drove to the horse camp, everyone was talking and pointing, eager to ride. The wrangler helped the women onto their horses. The sisters looked nervous but thrilled. Shireen took all their pictures. Meena borrowed a cowboy's hat and we all laughed at her Wild West look. We rode on a well-worn trail along the Platte and under old burr oaks. We rode past a flock of wild turkeys and a meadow of sunflowers. At one point Shireen shouted, "Look at me. I am in Iran. Now I am in Turkey. Now I am in Kurdistan."

The others all pretended they were riding their horses

through the countries they had lived in. Then they had been
hunted victims, afraid for their lives. Now they were in Nebraska with new American jobs, clothes, and dreams. In a different century, they would have been mothers in arranged
marriages living nomadic lives. I would have been an Irish-
woman digging potatoes and cooking with peat. But this afternoon we were in Nebraska. Today we were free, waving to
each other and imagined crowds of well-wishers, riding proudly
past sunflowers and prairie grass, riding into a future we would
share.

HALLOWEEN

The sisters wanted to see trick-or-treaters and carve pumpkins
so we had a party at our house. It was good Halloween weather,
windy and crisp, with the leaves blowing and branches hitting
the houses in spooky ways. When I picked up the sisters, a storm
was brewing in the west. It was snowing in the Sandhills, and
Omaha had a tornado warning. Shehla was on the porch watching the sky. She ran toward me, shouting that she and Meena
had passed their driving tests. Now three of the sisters could
drive.

All the sisters came but Shireen, who worked night shifts.
Zeenat came, too, eager to get out of the house. At my house
Leila and Tanya took charge and happily cleaned and carved
three pumpkins and a squash while the others watched admir-
ingly. We put candles in the jack-o'-lanterns and displayed them
on our porch. Then we took many Halloween pictures.

We had pizza delivered, but ate a sit-down dinner with
candles and flowers. These little adornments were not much
work, but they signaled a celebration. We toasted the new
driver's licenses. We talked of school. All were discouraged by

the big classes, the hard lessons, and the difficulties in finding time to study. Just coping with America took all their energy.

Tanya said they were exhausted after a day's work and the drive across town in rush hour traffic. Sometimes one of them would be kept late, and since they had only one car, the others would have to wait in the parking lot. Tanya felt demeaned by the work and insulted by the way she was asked to do things. She asked me for help controlling her temper. Nasreen worried about her credit-card bill with its high interest. She sighed. "I work all the time and I can never pay all my bills."

The older sisters had even considered returning to Pakistan or India, but Shireen and Meena wanted to stay in America. I worried about the possibility that the family would split up. Leila said, "Don't worry. We decided to always stick together."

Everyone groaned and laughed at the same time. We moved on to other topics—the quirks of our language, the geography and politics of America. The sisters reminded me of baby birds with open mouths hungry for food, only they had open hearts and minds and they were hungry for information. Their questions never stopped. "What's the name of that flower? What's the best way to drive to work? Is that the generator for your heat and air-conditioning unit? What is the purpose of a Pap smear? When does the Immigration and Naturalization Service send the permanent residency card?" They knew what they didn't know and they knew how to ask questions. This is a set of skills not all newcomers have.

Nasreen was upset by President Bush's bombing of Baghdad during the Gulf War and also by a news story about Kurdish refugees in a boat who had washed up in France. Seeing these incidents on television made them all realize how lucky they were, but also how badly the Kurds had it everywhere.

My friend Jill had baked us a sweet potato pie and the sisters sampled it carefully. Meena pronounced it tasty. She gave me a beautiful card thanking me for helping her learn to drive.

Soon Zeenat and the sisters were dancing Kurdish dances in our living room. They stood side by side, arms behind their backs, moving their hips and feet in a vigorous dance. Tanya then did her imitation of American sexy dancing. I jokingly warned her to not do it in public.

While the others dealt with trick-or-treaters, Meena and I did dishes. We talked about time lines and I made the point that most lives alternate between easy and hard times. Meena looked at me and said with no self-pity, "Never in my life have I had one day that has been easy."

The trick-or-treaters were great fun. The sisters enjoyed every child, admiring each, discussing costumes, and laughing at the remarks the kids made. I hadn't enjoyed a Halloween as much since my kids were young.

I taught the sisters to play bingo. They loved it and happily called out, "Bingo." The prizes were embarrassingly small. I had gathered up the soaps, shampoos, lotions, and even mouth-washes from hotels I had stayed in and I'd put them in a hat. Whoever won a bingo, got her choice. The sisters agonized over their selections. They were excited and grateful for these gifts. I was almost chagrined by their gratitude, but I was having too much fun to be really upset. The evening passed, punctuated by a chorus of "Happy Halloween," "Trick or treat," "Say cheese." "Bingo."

SHIREEN'S ENROLLMENT
IN COMMUNITY COLLEGE

Shireen and I had spent hours touring local campuses, reading catalogs, and filling out forms. The process of deciding on a college, getting relevant information for enrollment, and getting moneys arranged had been cumbersome. I was struck by how much there is to know about college. For example, whom do you call for information?; how do you arrange a tour?; how do you enroll?; what are the deadlines?; what do you put in the essays?; where, when, and how do you apply for funds?; what is a major?; what are prerequisites?; and how do you read a course schedule?

I am generations deep in family with college degrees. My grandmother graduated from Peru State Teachers College in 1907. My mother was a doctor. I'd attended half a dozen colleges myself, my husband has a Ph.D, and my kids are both college graduates. But what about newcomers working in a foreign language in a system unfamiliar to them in any language? The complexity and strangeness of the system puts up many barriers.

Shireen finally decided on the community college that was cheaper and offered both short-term degrees that led to relatively good jobs and an academic transfer program that led to a college degree. The community college had an adult education program, with a more flexible schedule for factory workers than our universities.

We had turned in her family's tax records and written the scholarship applications. Finally, we were ready to enroll. I picked Shireen up at 6:00 A.M. so that we could be first in line at the 7:00 A.M. registration. She was dressed up college-girl style, with jeans, a sweater, makeup, and big hair. She was excited and nervous, with all her papers in order, we thought.

At the college we stood in long lines. Shireen told me that she had seen the movie *Quills,* about the Marquis de Sade. I grimaced and said I was sorry she'd seen it. She asked what sadomasochism was. I tried to explain the word, but she couldn't quite grasp its meaning. She had never been exposed to anything

like this. I said bluntly that mixing sex and violence was a terrible idea. I reflected on the irony that she was the war victim
and refugee and I, the middle-class Nebraskan, was telling her
about sadism.

Finally, it was our time to sign up. We found out that the
classes Shireen wanted were full. A less-experienced guide would
have given up, but I knew how to work the system and how to
plead with a dean. Eventually Shireen was enrolled. I paid her
fees. Later she would be reimbursed by her Pell Grant and could
sign over the check to me. But, again, what happens to newcomers without American friends?

We bought her pencils, notebooks, and books, and she was
shocked at the prices. As we walked out of the college and back
to my car, Shireen said, "I am the first woman in the history of
my nuclear family, in a thousand years of women, to go to college." She was beaming. Yes, I thought to myself, this paperwork and standing in lines has been worth the bother.

HOLIDAY REUNION

During the holidays my children visited and we had a holiday
feast for them at the sisters' house with gifts and lots of pictures.

Zeenat met us at the door and hugged Jim and me and our
kids. Meena made us chai and we sat in the small living room
on the couch that used to be in my therapy office. Nasreen
showed us pictures of their sister in Iraq and their home from
years ago, before Hussein. Leila asked Jim husband about snow
tires for her car. Then we opened gifts. We'd bought them a
calendar, wind chimes, origami paper, and a cookbook. Zeenat
carried them from person to person for examination. They gave
me delicate gold earrings. All the gifts were much admired and
appreciated.

Then Tanya and Shehla offered to paint my daughter-in-law, Jamie, and my daughter, Sara, with henna. This took a while. They painted brown-and-gold fish on their hands. We looked at photos of our happy year together and they told my kids stories of our many trips.

Sara mentioned she had a dream the night before, and the sisters leaped in with dream interpretation. I noted with interest that Freud was not the first to develop symbol systems for dreams. Long ago, the Kurds had one all worked out. Sara had dreamed of a dog, which in the Kurdish system meant "enemy," but at least the dog was small and white. The sisters agreed that women were good luck in dreams and men were symbols of danger. Snake and scorpion dreams were bad luck. Dreams about roads were very important and predicted the future with great accuracy.

Then Shehla read our palms. She told Sara she would have three husbands, all handsome. I was to have two, not a good fortune for me since I was happily married to my first. Jamie would have many healthy babies.

Shireen showed Jim and my son, Zeke, the college essays she had written. Jamie and Sara and I watched as Shehla taught us to make a wonderful Kurdish dessert. It involved filling French crepes with crème, folding them, and then sprinkling them with pistachios. Zeke helped chop cucumbers and tomatoes for salad.

I had brought grapes and pomegranates, and Tanya had fixed her delicious biryani. Leila showed up just as dinner was served. She worked two jobs now and I almost never saw her. She had deep circles under her eyes but, as usual, she was cheerful and energetic.

We took pictures of our families together, of my two tall brown-haired kids and my slim black-haired daughter-in-law with all the dark-eyed sisters, who by now also seemed like my daughters. We took pictures of Shehla with her pistachio treats, of Tanya with the biryani, of Meena and Shireen acting like su-permodels, of Nasreen and Zeenat embracing Sara, and of Zeke and Jamie hugging all the sisters at once.

We sat on the floor and shared the bountiful food. We ap-plauded the chefs. I was happy having my two families to-gether, my old family of Zeke, Sara, Jim, and Jamie and my new Kurdish family. There was lots of laughter and hugging. Today we all seemed like one family, the Kurdish and the Nebraska branches.

POSTSCRIPT

The Kurdish sisters are my friends. My respect for their adapt-ability has only increased. The sisters are brave, intelligent young women who have good judgment about time, money, and people. They have a thousand ways of being kind to me.

They have strong family loyalty, although that has been tested in Nebraska. In Pakistan the family all had the same dream—to come to America. Here, each sister is developing her own dream and sometimes these individual dreams collide and cause tension and anger in the family. Some members of the fam-ily want to move to India or Pakistan; others want to stay here. They all think that it is hard to pay bills in America. They argue about priorities. I think family therapy might be a good idea.

The sisters are examples of refugees whose individual attri-butes should slate them for success here. However, their jobs pay $7.15 an hour, not a livable wage. They have a great deal of ac-ademic catching up to do and not as many educational resources as they need. They are supporting family back in Iraq and have an enormous bill for their air travel to America. They drive an old clunker, which doesn't necessarily carry them where they need to go. The external environment is creating many barriers to their achievement of American dreams.

Zeenat continues to learn English slowly. She attends a group for Arabic-speaking older adults, and she is loved and cared for by her daughters. And yet she wishes she could return to Islamabad where she was surrounded by women she could talk to and where she held a central place in the family.

I visit the sisters once a week to tutor Shehla in social studies. My husband tutors Meena in math. Sometimes we all go on outings together. They all continue to love to swim. Shireen is at our community college. The sisters are slowly making a few American friends. Nasreen still has sad eyes. Meena continues to find life tasty.

BROWN NEBRASKA

Immigration is a story as old as the Pilgrims and Ellis Island and as new as the Vietnamese families that arrived last week on an airplane. What is really new in 2001 is the changing color of our nation. This century, whites will no longer be a majority. Kenneth Prewitt, director of the Census Bureau in 2000, said that the 2000 census documented a dramatic change and showed that "America is on the way to becoming a microcosm of the entire world." We have 28 million foreign-born residents, or one out of every ten people. One out of every five schoolchildren is foreign-born or has foreign-born parents. Prewitt wrote, "We are literally becoming a country made up of every country in the world." Increasingly, newcomers are being sent to cities in the Midwest and South. For example, Nashville police carry computers that explain the laws, simple requests, and commands in twenty languages. Because they are inexpensive places to live, easy places to find work, and relatively crime-free, towns like Salina, Kansas, and Fargo, North Dakota, are receiving newcomers, and Owatonna, Minnesota, has six hundred Somali refugees.

A turkey-processing plant in a small town in Minnesota was first staffed by Vietnamese and is now staffed by Somalis. A friend told me of a refugee in this plant who asked for her help with a placement test. She was trying to ascertain what he knew and wrote down a few simple math problems such as 4×2. He took her paper and wrote out a long calculus equation. He'd been an engineer in Africa for years and now was pulling out turkey guts.

Refugees and immigrants are often hidden in plain sight. Most Nebraskans aren't aware how much our population has changed. They drive down a street, see the same trees and buildings and don't realize how different the people are.

Some locals say, "We just want to be left alone." However, with 6 billion people on the planet, many of them in desperate circumstances, nobody gets to be left alone. The Dalai Lama made this point when discussing Tibet. He said, "The history of the last years shows that no place is so remote and small that it is safe from outsiders."

Environmental catastrophes, wars, and political upheavals have displaced people all over the world. According to the official World Refugee Survey 2001 of the United States Committee for Refugees, there were 14.5 million refugees and asylum seekers and more than 20 million internally displaced people at the end of 2000. Anthony Marsella in *Amidst Peril and Pain* wrote, "From a humanitarian perspective, the current international refugee problem is unparalleled in size, scope, and consequence in human history."

Many refugees arrive recently traumatized and with tragic backgrounds. Some have literally just been lifted out of a holocaust. About 40 percent of our refugees have been tortured. Many have witnessed genocide and seen family members killed. Others have been made to participate in acts of torture or murder. Many come from camps in which they were beaten or raped. The word *detained* is a terrible euphemism for what has happened to them.

People who have been in refugee camps for years have lost any sense of control over their lives. They have had years to learn helplessness, years without useful work, education, or meaningful decisions. Some have internalized a sense that they are nobody, chaff in the wind.

Refugees are sometimes portrayed as helpless victims, but the truly helpless victims don't make it here. Generally, it takes work, intelligence, patience, charm, and luck to be selected as a refugee. Arrival stories are survivor stories. However, after the victory of safe passage, years of hard work follow. And in their own way, the challenges of the United States can be as rough as the challenges of Sudan or Afghanistan.

ARRIVAL STORIES

Most of the refugees who arrive in Lincoln didn't choose to come to our city. They were handed a plane ticket to Lincoln by INS officials when they got off a plane in New York or Los Angeles. They may know nothing about the Midwest and they may have been separated from their closest friends by the assignment process. They may have bodies adapted to tropical climates or skills such as deep-sea fishing that they cannot use in the Midwest. They may be moving into a town where no one speaks their language or even knows where their country is.

Most newcomers arrive broke. In fact, I have never met a rich refugee. All arrive worried about jobs and housing, as well as about their legal status in the United States. Especially if they have been tortured or lost family members, they are not at peak mental efficiency. In many cases, refugees don't speak English and have never lived in a developed country. They have been

warned not to trust strangers, yet everyone is a stranger. They
have no way to sort out whether people are kind and helpful or
psychopaths. All of us look alike to them. They fear robbers, harassment, getting lost, or being hit by a car.

Here in Lincoln, most refugees are met at the airport by
people from their homeland and by someone from church services. An interesting thing happens at the airports. When the
newcomers and their hosts meet, they all burst into tears. The
moment of arrival has an intensity and poignancy that sweeps
everyone away.

From the airport, refugees are driven to a furnished apartment
stocked with food and used furniture. Their first day in town they
get their social security cards and their immunizations. They enroll their kids in school, and, if needed, they receive emergency
doctors' appointments. Sometimes refugees get off the plane with
life-threatening illnesses and go directly to a hospital.

Each adult is given fifty dollars per week, plus food, rent,
and temporary medical insurance. They go through an orientation that explains everything from how to use the city bus and
library to marriage laws and taxes. Adults are encouraged to
get jobs quickly. The goal of our resettlement agencies is self-
sufficiency in four months. In fact, within a few weeks, refugees
are often working. In addition to their other financial burdens,
all refugees must repay their airfares from the country they fled.

A woman from Kazakhstan arrived in Lincoln with her father. She waited three hours at the airport for her sponsor who
was at a party and had forgotten her. Later that night her father
had a heart attack from the stress of the journey. From television, she knew she could call 911. Yet even when the translation
service finally kicked in, she could give no address. Amazingly,
her father lived through this attack.

Zainab arrived at JFK Airport in New York City. Before arriving she and her husband had spent years in a camp in the
Saudi Arabian desert. They had two children in the camp and
Zainab was again pregnant. She walked off the plane, looked at
all the electric lights and the people who were walking fast and
talking loudly, and she said to her husband, "Let's go back to the
camp. At least there we had friends and family." He said, "I
don't own the plane. I don't own anything."

Telling me this later, Zainab laughed. She said, "All he had
was money for a Pepsi, so he bought me one. Drinking that
cheered me up."

Zainab and her husband had hoped they would be assigned
Lincoln, where they knew a few families, but an official sent
them to Fargo, North Dakota. They boarded another plane and
arrived in Fargo late at night. They were picked up and taken to
a hotel room. Too tired to clean up or eat, they fell into deep
sleep. In the morning they awoke and looked out the window.
They saw green trees, grass, a squirrel, and two dogs. Zainab
said, "We had spent years in a place with no plants or animals.
My husband asked me if we were in heaven."

They had never seen people in shorts or with dyed green
hair. They didn't know how to use a phone. A homeless guy
gave them thirty-five cents and dialed for them.

Soon they managed to move to Lincoln. Zainab had trouble
with our foods. In Iraq there were not many kinds of vegetables,
mostly just tomatoes and cucumbers, but they were fresh and
delicious. Zainab said Nebraskans had a huge variety, but nothing tasted flavorful.

Zainab came from an area where men and women did not
touch each other except in families. The American handshake
was a problem. When a man held out his hand to her, she had

to explain that Iraqi women do not shake hands. She learned to hug American women and say, "Hug your husband for me."

FIRST BIG SHOCKS

When I was in college, I remember reading about a tribe in Central America who thought that Americans never got sick or died. All the Americans they'd seen were healthy anthropologists, tall and well-nourished. They'd never seen Americans die.

Modern refugees often come here equally naive about us. Some have Nebraska and Alaska confused and expect mountains, ice, and grizzlies. Some think of Nebraska as a western state with cowboys, and they are ill-prepared for our factories, suburbs, and shopping malls. Many newcomers have never seen stairs, let alone escalators or elevators. Inventions such as duct tape, clothes hangers, aluminum foil, or microwaves often befuddle new arrivals.

Someone once said, "Every day in a foreign country is like final exam week." It's a good metaphor. Everything is a test, whether of one's knowledge of the language, the culture, or of the layout of the city. Politics, laws, and personal boundaries are different. Relations between parents and children, the genders, and the social classes are structured differently here. The simplest task—buying a bottle of orange juice or finding medicine for a headache—can take hours and require every conceivable skill.

Some refugees believe they will be given a new car and a house when they arrive. Some people ask government workers, "Where is my color TV? My free computer?" Others have seen *Dallas* or *Who Wants to Marry a Millionaire?* and think they will soon get rich.

This belief that it's easy to get rich in America is exploited by con artists. An Azerbaijani man received a Reader's Digest Sweepstakes notice informing him he was a millionaire. He fell to his knees and thanked Allah for his riches. A Vietnamese family called relatives in Ho Chi Minh City to tell them the great news that they had won the Publisher's Clearinghouse sweepstakes. A Siberian couple laughed and danced around their kitchen, already spending their expected pickle card winnings on a new car, a dishwasher, and a swimming pool for the kids. Later, when it became clear they hadn't won, they weren't so happy.

Some newcomers don't know the number of weeks in a year or what the seasons are. Others are well-educated but have gaps. Once when I was talking to a well-educated Croatian woman about our history, I brought up the sixties. I said, "It was a hard time with war and so many assassinations, those of John and Bobby Kennedy and Martin Luther King." She asked in amazement, "You mean Martin Luther King is dead?" When I said yes, she began to cry.

Our casual ways of dealing with the opposite sex are without precedent in some cultures. Our relaxed interactions between men and women can be alarming to some people from the Middle East. Some traditional women are suspicious of American women; it seems to them as if the American women are trying to steal their husbands because they speak to them at work or in stores.

An Iraqi high school student told of arriving in this country on a summer day. As she and her father drove through Lincoln, there were many women on the streets in shorts and tank tops. Her father kept saying to her, "Cover your eyes; cover your eyes." Neither of them had ever seen women in public without head covering.

There are two common refugee beliefs about America—one is that it is sin city; the other is that it is paradise. I met a Cuban mother whose sixteen-year-old daughter got pregnant in Nebraska. She blamed herself for bringing the girl to our sinful town, weeping as she told me the story. And she showed me a picture of the daughter, all dressed in white. A Mexican father told me that his oldest son was now in a gang. He talked about American movies and the violent television, music, and video games. He said, "My son wears a black T-shirt he bought at a concert. It has dripping red letters that read, 'More Fucking Blood.'" He looked at me quizzically. "America is the best country in the world, the richest and the freest. Why do you make things like this for children?"

On the other hand, some refugees idealize our country. They talk endlessly of the mountains of food in buffets, the endless supply of clean water, the shining cars, and the electricity. Flying into a city such as New York or Seattle, many refugees experience their first vision of America and are overwhelmed by the shining stars of light on the ground, more light than they have ever seen. One refugee from Romania captured both ideas when he said, "America is the beauty and the beast."

When I ask refugees what America means to them, many say, "Freedom." This may mean many things. To the Kurdish sisters it is the freedom to wear stylish American clothes and walk about freely. It's the freedom to go swimming and shopping and make a living. To many of the poor and disenfranchised, it is the radical message that everyone has rights, even though at first many refugees do not know what their rights are.

America means a system of laws, a house, a job, and a school for every child. In America people can strive for happiness, not even a concept in some parts of the world. They are free to become whomever they want to become. Refugees learn they can speak their minds, write, and travel. They shed the constraints of more traditional cultures. As one Bulgarian woman put it to me, "In America, the wives do not have to get up and make the husbands' breakfasts."

People from all over the world want to come here. They want a chance at the American dream. They come because they want to survive and be safe and anywhere is better than where they were. However, the process of adjusting is incredibly traumatic. The Kurdish sisters were in culture shock for about six months. After a year, they are still deeply in debt, lonely, haunted by the past, and struggling to master our language and our culture. They are overwhelmed every time their bills arrive. Nasreen and Zeenat still dream nightly of their homeland.

It is difficult to describe or even imagine the challenges of getting started in a new country. Imagine yourself dropped in downtown Rio de Janeiro or Khartoum with no money, no friends, and no understanding of how that culture works. Imagine you have six months to learn the language and everything you need to know to support your family. Of course, that isn't a fair comparison because you know that the earth is round, what a bank is, and how to drive a car. And you have most likely not been tortured or seen family members killed within the last few months.

Picture yourself dropped in the Sudanese grasslands with no tools or knowledge about how to survive and no ways to communicate with the locals or ask for advice. Imagine yourself wondering where the clean water is, where and what food is, and what you should do about the bites on your feet, and your sunburn, and the lion stalking you. Unless a kind and generous Sudanese takes you in and helps you adjust, you would be a goner.

CHAPTER 3

Into the HEART
of the HEARTLAND

LINH

"I will never see my brothers again."

A teacher who loved and respected Linh set up a meeting between us. Linh had been a straight-A student in high school and college, but this year she was discouraged with college. She had been skipping classes and had resigned from many activities, which she had formerly led.

We met at The Mill, a coffeehouse near campus. Linh was tall and thin and wore jeans, a sweatshirt, and a delicate Asian necklace. Like many Vietnamese, she spoke less clearly than she wrote. (This is the opposite of Arabic-speaking people who quickly learn to speak English, but have a hard time with our written language.)

I apologized for scheduling our meeting over her noon hour, but she said that she always skipped lunch anyway, to keep her weight down. I said, "That's a very American thing to do."

She smiled softly. "Vietnamese girls worry about weight all the time."

I thanked her for the gift of her time and asked her how long she had been in this country. She responded, "Five years." Then, without any questions from me, Linh told me about her history. She had five living brothers and one older sister, but only one of her brothers was in Nebraska. One of her brothers had died during the war when her parents were running from soldiers. The other brothers were over twenty-one and not allowed to come to America and her sister had stayed behind with her husband.

Linh was born in a small village far from Saigon. Her dad was a teacher, but because he had helped the Americans, he was sent to reeducation camp and afterward forced to farm. Because of her dad's record, Linh and her siblings weren't allowed to attend the village school. She wanted to study but couldn't afford books.

Linh smiled remembering rice harvest. She was the baby of the family, petted and spoiled. The brothers would carry her to the fields and make a little camp for her. When they could, they would stop and play with her. Her brothers might get mad at her, but no one ever really disciplined her. They would wake up in the night and make sure she was covered with blankets. Shrimp was valuable and caught only to be sold, but her brothers fed her shrimp. Still, it was a hard life, and to demonstrate that point, Linh showed me the scars on her arms from leech bites.

Her second-oldest brother awoke at 4:00 A.M. to help her with math before he left for work. She smiled remembering how he would stay up all night and work the problems so that when she awoke he would know how to do the work. This brother wrote her often, admonishing her to study. He told her he didn't believe in destiny and that in America she could become whatever she wanted. She pulled his letters out of her backpack to show me. Linh said through her tears that she would obey anything her brothers told her. She looked at me wide-eyed and said, "I will never see my brothers again."

I asked why she came to our country. Linh explained that her dad had been promised a car, a house, and a refrigerator in Nebraska, but at the last minute, her parents didn't want to come. They came only so that she could study. When her parents said good-bye, everyone in their little village cried.

The first thing they noticed here was the snow. Flying into Nebraska, Linh asked her father, "Why is the ground white?" The second thing they observed was our haste. Americans all seemed to be rushing around. Everyone had to be someplace all the time. Linh said, "I wondered if people ever slowed down and talked to each other."

They were taken to an apartment by a man who had served with her father in the army. They couldn't talk to Americans at all and they felt crazy. They never left their apartment and they wanted to go back to Vietnam. In Vietnam, they'd owned nothing, no television or books, and they'd used kerosene lamps. But in Nebraska, they were even more bereft; they didn't know how to turn on lights or use a stove or faucet.

Linh's first day of school, she missed the bus and her dad had to call his friend to give her a ride. Her father said, "You must go to school. You don't want to disappoint us; we came here for you."

Once at school, Linh made friends quickly. Some of the American kids laughed at her accent and clothes, but the teachers loved her. She was bright, hardworking, and focused. In geometry the students who had laughed at her soon wanted to copy her homework. By the end of her first year, she had made all A's. She said, "American kids have no idea how lucky they are to have good teachers."

Linh chose Vietnamese friends. American girls talked a lot about dating and boys. She said, "If I talked that way in Vietnam, I would be considered a bad girl." She explained that Vietnamese teens are more private and conservative than American teens. She asked me, "Why do Americans rush everything?"

Linh's mother worked the night shift, overtime, and weekends, whenever she could. Linh said, "Mom will sacrifice anything for the family."

Her father was sixty-five and disabled from his years in the camps. He'd tried to work, but he'd fallen down his third day on the job. He stayed home now, bored and wishing his family could go back to their village in Vietnam. He wanted to see his ninety-four-year-old mother before she died.

Linh said, "Dad wakes me at 4:00 A.M. and I study before school. He drives me to classes at the university and to my volunteer job teaching English to Vietnamese elders. He keeps all my awards and grade reports. He framed a picture of me receiving my scholarship award."

Sometimes Linh went to American movies but she closed her eyes during sexy scenes. She had been to parties but never danced or drank alcohol. The family was traditional and Buddhist and her parents didn't want her to date until she had completed college. She'd rebelled a little in junior high and had a boyfriend who was Vietnamese, but more Americanized than she was. They just talked on the phone, but she'd really liked him. Her dad and brother had yelled at her about this and finally she'd told her boyfriend not to call. After that, she'd cried, but she told me, "I am family-oriented and I made the right decision."

Her parents wanted her to be a doctor. Linh was scared of the MCAT and studied eight or nine hours a day to prepare for medical school. After she received her medical degree she hoped to marry and have children. She wanted to be able to finance her parents' retirement in Vietnam.

Now she had a case of acculturation blues. She was not fluent in any language. Her Vietnamese was not perfect, but neither was her English. There were many times when she could not express herself precisely. I suspected that part of her current malaise was she didn't have the language to express all her complex feelings.

She also struggled with identity. She moved between two cultures, selecting only what she needed from American culture, yet having to play by its rules. She was a loyal Vietnamese family member in a world where most of the people she loved were thousands of miles away. She respected her parents, but they were of little help to her in the world in which she found herself. Somehow she had to balance the freedom of America with her responsibilities to family. Sometimes she felt like "hollow bamboo," Asian on the outside, but empty within.

Linh was grateful for her opportunities, perhaps almost too grateful. She was respectful of adults and eager to become who her family wanted her to be. The trick would be to meet their expectations without feeling so much pressure that she was immobilized with anxiety. Depression descended when she sensed she might fail the brother who stayed up all night studying math problems for her or her father who gave up his world to bring her to America.

I suggested that we meet again to talk through the pressures of school. I said, "We can discuss what you want to accept and reject from American and Vietnamese cultures. You will want to build a new life for yourself based on good choices."

WHAT REFUGEES CARRY

We old pioneers dreamed our dreams into the country.
—BETH STREETER ALDRICH

Refugees may arrive penniless but they don't arrive resource-less. They carry their individual attributes, their histories, their families, and their cultures. They bring their human capital, that is, their skills and professional experience. This is a complex situation, however, because it's often impossible to transfer credentials and knowledge.

Refugees possess what Bill Moyers described as "the outsider's impatience, the gritty resolve to storm the barricades and triumph from within." They bring what I'll call newcomer zest, an initial drive to succeed that consists of hope, ambition, and trust. Research suggests that this early zest fades by the second generation and is gone by the third.

Over the course of working with refugees, I have identified twelve individual traits that contribute to success in America. I will discuss these attributes in chapter 10. For now I merely want to note their importance in determining who is able to adjust to America. The more of these attributes a newcomer possesses, the more likely he or she is to succeed. Without a certain number of these attributes, a newcomer is unlikely to make it in America. The attributes of resilience are

1. Future orientation
2. Energy and good health
3. The ability to pay attention
4. Ambition and initiative
5. Verbal expressiveness
6. Positive mental health
7. The ability to calm down
8. Flexibility

9. Intentionality

10. Lovability

11. The ability to love new people

12. Good moral character

Cultural Values

To a certain extent, a culture influences the attributes of its members. It is impossible to separate what is cultural from what is personal. (It is especially difficult to do this if one knows only one or two members of a culture. As one knows many people from a culture it is easier to distinguish between individual and cultural characteristics.) The cultural and personal are as inter-mingled as coffee and cream. But in every culture, there are people who do and people who do not have these attributes of resilience.

Refugees who come alone are much disadvantaged. Families work together, share resources, and support each other emotionally. Both tradition and circumstance encourage the closeness of immigrant families. Over and over, family is literally what keeps people alive. Some members are housed, fed, and cared for by others. And the caretakers have a sense of purpose because of their responsibilities. In hostile environments there is no greater protection and comfort than the protection of close-knit families. Our word *wretched* comes from the Middle English word *wrecche,* which means "without kin nearby."

Supportive ethnic communities also make a tremendous difference in adjustment. Nothing is as important as friends, not food, shelter, work, or even language. When I asked a man from Sudan what the Kakuma refugees most needed in our town, he said they needed to live near other Sudanese people. He was absolutely right. Newcomers need people from their own culture to orient them to America. The first family to come has the hardest time. The second family has an easier situation.

Newcomers gravitate toward places where there are others from their homeland. In fact, before we understood the importance of support, our government had a different settlement policy designed to keep local communities from being overwhelmed. Refugees were encouraged to move one family at a time into isolated communities. However, the newcomers were lonely and didn't settle in. After many failed attempts, our government changed its policies and we now encourage refugees to settle near people from their old country.

In traditional cultures, survival was a social achievement not an individual accomplishment. Pleasure and comfort were associated with being with one's tribe and with being home. One of the best places to experience community in America is in an ethnic neighborhood. The streets are lively. Generations mingle freely. People help each other out.

The American pleasure in privacy and independence is strange to many refugees. To them, our autonomy simply feels lonely. Many refugees comment on how empty our public spaces are, and, in fact, the people in those spaces are often refugees. Afghani, Iranian, and Iraqi families are the ones grilling meat and onions in our city parks and sitting on public benches talking to their friends.

The closeness of refugees to their families and communities protects, but sometimes at a cost. The ethnic community can become a feather bed, a little too soft and difficult to climb out of. To really succeed in America, refugees must learn to deal with Americans. The best way is to somehow hold on to the good from the old culture while taking advantage of the new, which is much more difficult in practice than in theory. Linh's struggles are a good example of the difficulties of combining cultures.

The age-old refugee's dilemma is whether to stay in a small, safe cultural enclave or to leave this secure place and venture into the broader culture. If they stay in an ethnic stockade, they can't really succeed in America, and if they leave, they are risking their connection with the old culture.

People from traditional cultures with no sense of clock time and languages very different from English have a harder time adjusting than do, for example, the Bosnians, many of whom come here from Germany. Older people have a harder time. Also people who are dark-skinned have a harder time. Because of racism, the darker one's skin, the harder it is to assimilate.

An important aspect of refugee culture is its similarity to American culture in terms of work ethic. Newcomers are more likely to succeed if they come from a culture whose values promote high achievement; these values include sacrifice, curiosity, enterprise, and willingness to take risks and initiate activities.

Generalizations and dichotomies are dangerous. Thomas Friedman divides the world into fast cultures and slow cultures. There are great differences between "slow" or traditional cultures. The Somalis, the Vietnamese, and the Peruvians are strikingly different from one another in many ways. Still, there are distinctions that need to be drawn. All traditional cultures share the closeness of family and neighbors. Traditional cultures value interdependence and cooperation, whereas Americans place a high value on individual autonomy. As D. H. Lawrence wrote, "America is the homeland of the pocket not the blood."

Many cultures value children who respect authority and defer to others. Linh was raised in such a culture. African and Latino children are taught to comply with authority and submerge their own needs. Traditional families tend to be big extended families with multiple adults involved in child rearing. The parent–child bond is primary. The goal of marriage isn't happiness, but rather caring for children and aged parents. Status in the family is determined by age and gender. Men are favored.

Western families are more individual-oriented. Americans want to raise independent children who think for themselves. The emphasis is on self-fulfillment and development. Rules are flexible, and status is gained by individual efforts. Families are run more democratically. The primary bond is the couple. Emotions can be expressed more directly, and in general, women have more opportunity.

In traditional cultures roles are well defined. Families are more authoritarian and there is less direct expression of emotion. Suppression of feelings and self-control are often seen as positive. Traditional cultures are fiercely loyal to insiders and wary of outsiders. They both sustain and constrain their members.

The traditional cultures tend to be much more holistic than modern American culture. There is no mind-body split, no sacred-profane split, not even a work-play split. Life isn't chopped up into neat little compartments and intervals. In fact, to succeed in America, refugees must learn to compartmentalize.

TIME

For newcomers from slow cultures, time is a river that flows through their lives. They have no abstract sense of time. Refugees who have been on sun, seasonal, or Circadian-rhythm time find the change to computer time jarring. One of the first things I teach new arrivals is time management, a very difficult skill to master but one that is essential to success in America. I bring calendars, personal planners, and watches and teach refugees how to make and keep appointments. I tell them, "Americans are very serious about two things—time and money."

Anarchist John Zerzan wrote in the *Utne Reader,* "Time is an invention, a cultural artifact, a formation of culture. It has no existence outside of culture and it is a pretty exact measure of alienation." As I wind the watches and set the alarms, I question whether I am doing the newcomer a favor. Something is gained with schedules, but much is lost. The natural flow of life is broken into units and managed rather than experienced.

Newcomers joke about how we look at our watches to decide when to eat and sleep. From their point of view, it looks like we are slaves to tiny machines that constantly interrupt us and tell us what to do next. They also notice that we are always busy. This seems weird to people who come from cultures where there is much sitting around, visiting, and watching the sunset or children at play. As one woman from Tajikistan said to me, "Americans think it is a sin to do nothing."

Newcomers sense that they are being hurried—to eat, to get in a car or out of an office. A man from Mali said to me, "I have learned that when an American looks at his watch, it means I am taking too much of his time. I had better leave quickly."

Many workers come from parts of the world where, when you are tired, you stop work and rest. You take a nap after lunch, which is provided by the employer. If you feel like taking a day off, you do it and then work harder the next day. It's a major adjustment to get used to forty hour a week jobs at which one is expected to show up on time, work all day, and take ten-minute bathroom breaks when the employer says that is okay. Discussing work in America, a Spanish man told me, "Americans invented stress. And with globalization, stress will soon be all over the world."

Many refugees are not used to efficient scheduling. They allow time to unfurl, and they enjoy however much time they want with visits, celebrations, and other events. As an Iraqi woman said, "At home if we wanted to go to the doctor, we walked to the doctor's office. If I wanted to visit someone, I just went to visit. I didn't call and ask if they could come over two weeks from Friday at three o'clock."

Daylight saving time is a hard sell. Refugees are amazed that we manipulate time this way. They forget to set clocks forward or backward and often have many frustrating experiences before they get DST down. My friend Bintu missed church her first week in America. As I helped her reset her clocks, she burst into tears of frustration because we made time so hard.

I talked to a woman from El Salvador about a conference over two years away but already set in time and place. She laughed and said, "Forgive me. I am not used to the American custom of giving away time so far in the future. How can we know where we will be in two years and what we will want to be doing?"

LANGUAGE

It takes most people from one to three years to learn social English and five to seven years to learn academic English. At first, refugees feel like children: vulnerable, dependent, and unable to express themselves. An educated man communicates only via hand signals and a few simple phrases. A doctor cannot ask for a glass of water. A teacher cannot understand her first-grade son's homework. Simple tasks, such as exchanging a pair of shoes or making a dental appointment, are complex without language. The intelligence, personality, and energy of new arrivals are submerged by their lack of English. We Americans just see the tip of the iceberg.

Language is connected to both good judgment and to forming relationships. Humans trust or mistrust others on the basis of nuances, tonal variations, and small contradictions. Without language, we miss metaphors and subtleties. We cannot read between the lines or sense what is not being said. We can't convey character or style. Imagine yourself applying for jobs, negotiating bureaucracies, and making friends with a working vocabulary of one hundred words. "Hi." "Thank you." "Where is the bathroom?" "Good morning." "You're welcome."

English isn't phonetic and has an amazing number of irregular verbs and plural nouns. It's filled with slang, academic jargon, and technical terms. Rules for prepositions and punctuation seem arbitrary. Many words sound alike, such as *writing* and *riding, a basement* and *abasement,* or *aunt* and *ant.*

And learning the language isn't enough. Certain people may speak Spanish but have limited understanding of the culture of Cuba. Likewise, one may know about the customs of a culture without being able to speak its language. To really become American, refugees must become both bilingual and bicultural. (See appendix 1 for ideas about how to speak to newcomers who have limited English.)

ACCULTURATION

I fled from despair and now each day
I find despair again and again.

—Carrie Fischer and Albert Greenberg

In their first stage after arrival newcomers briefly experience relief and euphoria. They are here and they are safe.

In the second stage reality sets in. Refugees have lost their
routines, their institutions, their language, their families and
friends, their homes, their work and incomes. They have lost
their traditions, their clothes, pictures, heirlooms, and pets.
They are without props in a new and alien environment.

They experience cultural bereavement. The old country
may have been a terrible place, but it was home. It was the
repository of all their stories, memories, and meanings. Many
times newcomers' bodies are in America, but their hearts remain in their homeland.

Ideally, the third stage is the beginning of recovery. Newcomers begin to grasp how America works. In the fourth stage,
also ideally, newcomers are bicultural and bilingual. They can
choose to participate in many aspects of the culture.

In general, there are four reactions refugees' families have
to the new culture—fight it because it is threatening; avoid
it because it's overwhelming; assimilate as fast as possible by
making all American choices; or tolerate discomfort and confusion while slowly making intentional choices about what
to accept and reject. Alejandro Portes and Rubén Rumbaut
published the results of long-term studies on newcomer adap-
tation in a book called *Legacies*. They found that this last reaction, which they called "selective acculturation," was best for
refugees.

They described two other less-adaptive ways of adjusting. Dissonant acculturation is when the kids in the family outstrip the parents. This can undercut parental authority and put the kids at risk. Consonant acculturation is when members of the family all move together toward being American. At one time this rapid acceptance of American ways was considered ideal, but now it appears that this makes families too vulnerable to the downside of America.

In *Legacies,* Portes and Rumbaut report that most immigrants move into the middle-class mainstream in one or two generations. That is the good news. The bad news is that if they don't make it quickly into the middle class, they won't make it at all. With the passage of time, drive diminishes, and by the third generation, assimilation stops. If two generations fail to make it into the middle class, the following generations are likely to be stuck at the bottom.

Failure to succeed will drive refugee families away from mainstream culture into what Portes calls "reactive ethnicity." Newcomers will revert to enclaves and see failure as inevitable, thus, in many cases, dooming their children to fail.

Portes's research obviously has implications for social policy. We need to help refugees and immigrants early with job training, education, language, and business loans. It's hard to study physics when one is sick and hungry, or to attend GED classes when one has worked all night at a factory. If we miss our chance to help them, we miss our chance to create well-adjusted, well-educated citizens.

I will discuss our environment and the ways we do and do not help refugees in the next chapter, but first I want to tell an archetypal success story. The family arrived here badly traumatized after wandering across many countries looking for a home.

But they were a strong family with many attributes of resilience. In Nebraska, their community helped them survive and their hard work enabled them to build a life for themselves. Thirty-seven million people watched the last episode of the TV show *Survivor.* This family's story and the stories of most refugees are much more compelling than any contrived reality-television program could ever show.

KAREEM AND MIRZANA
"I could smell freedom in America."

I interviewed Kareem and Mirzana at their high school. Mirzana was small and blond. Kareem was heartbreakingly handsome, with thick eyebrows and black hair. But he was shy and let his older sister do most of the talking.

Their family had lived in a village in northern Bosnia. Their father was an engineer, and their mother worked in a store. They were a hardworking middle-class family. Mirzana said she and Kareem had an easy life, consisting mainly of school and play. Their grandparents lived nearby. Kareem said, "We had everything we wanted. We were never lonely."

Nearby there was a war in Croatia, but their parents didn't think the war would come to Bosnia. One day the Serbs came and put their father and all the men in their village into a concentration camp. The siblings and their mother fled to Croatia.

Mirzana told me about her father's camp. She said, "Many men were in a small, empty room. They had nothing to eat, no papers, and no money."

Their father developed a lung infection. Still, he was lucky—he was only there for a month and not too badly beaten. He suffered most hearing the pain of others when the soldiers took them out and beat them. He listened to men scream for hours.

Their father saw many bad things, most of which he didn't tell them. He did tell of a drunk soldier who came into their cell and shouted, "Run to the corner. The last one there will be shot." One man didn't run and was killed by this soldier. Mirzana shook her head sadly as she said, "This man was deaf."

Eventually their father was released. Before he could escape the country, he was ordered to fight the Serbs. He didn't even have a weapon and, as Mirzana put it, "He was there to be shot." After a while, he managed to run away and find his family in Croatia. When he came to their door, none of them recognized him. In the two months he had been away, he'd aged ten years.

The family lived in Croatia for two years. Eventually a friend helped them get into Germany. They spoke no German and lived in one small room, which Kareem didn't like. He said no one could ever be alone and there were fights about space and sharing.

Mirzana and Kareem learned German, but their family couldn't become German citizens and they had no hope of improving their situation. In 1998 the Germans kicked them out and they came to the United States.

They were optimistic on the plane here, but when they arrived in Lincoln they were taken to a small dirty apartment. They were exhausted from the thirty-hour flight, but they couldn't sleep. Their mother was in shock. She cried, "I want to go back." The father said, "You forget, we have no choices. We have no country to return to."

They had no car and they didn't know anyone. No one in the family spoke English. But after five days they moved into their own apartment and they discovered next door a family that the father had known as a child. The two families cried with joy to be reunited. Now the family knows all of the Bosnian community. Bosnians in Lincoln share meals and throw parties. The men help each other find jobs and the women help each other learn English and shop for bargains.

When I met them, Kareem and Mirzana had been here only three months, but already they were speaking pretty good English, their fourth language. They laughed as they talked about early experiences in Nebraska. A neighbor gave them bananas, but they thought they tasted like soap and threw them away. They missed European bakeries. In America everything supposed to be sweet was salty and vice versa. Here herring was sweet and butter was salty.

Kareem and Mirzana like it here. Mirzana is making A's and, after school, she is a stocker at a supermarket. Mirzana laughed as she explained. "The staff teaches me a new word each day." Kareem is too young to work, so he cleans the house, does laundry, and studies after school. Both Kareem and Mirzana want to go to college and get good jobs. They want to care for their parents.

Their parents are ambitious, too. They have difficult factory jobs because their English is still poor. They work from two until ten. But in the morning they study English. Mirzana said, "In a year or two they will have better jobs."

This family is lucky. They have each other and a supportive community. Everyone has many of the attributes of resilience. The family carries with them a great deal of human capital. The external environment has been pretty harsh, but most likely, they will eventually transcend it.

Sometimes Mirzana wishes that her life these last few years

were just a dream and she would wake up in Bosnia in their old house. Her grandmother would be calling her to come work in the garden. There would be no war. Kareem disagrees. He is filled with newcomer zest. He said, "I could smell freedom in America."

ALL *that* GLITTERS . . .

THE WIZARD OF OZ

Recently I visited friends from Northern Iraq to celebrate their daughter Noora's tenth birthday. They live in an apartment complex run by Lincoln's most notorious slumlord. Shady Acres is a stucco building with six units on the outskirts of town. Just west of the building is a trailer park, infamous for its tornado deaths, and next door to the east is a triple-X dance club featuring a dancer named Anna Mal. As I walked toward my friend's place, I passed an empty unit with its door open. Piles of beer bottles and magazines, trashcan liners filled with old clothes, and unfurled rolls of toilet paper filled the place. I wondered if someone called this unit home.

My friend's place was clean and neat, an oasis of order in this chaotic universe of sleaze. Zena, her husband, and four kids lived in a two-bedroom apartment. Zena greeted me with a big hug and led me into the living room where a small television blared cartoons. I asked about the new baby and Zena said she was sleeping. I asked about her husband, a gentle man hurt in the war, and Zena said he was at an ELL class at the library.

Zena's daughter Noora carried her stuffed dog, Toto, over to show me. Her two younger brothers ran by in Spiderman underwear. I called the three oldest kids Snap, Crackle, and Pop, because their favorite food was American breakfast cereal—the more sugary the better.

The living room was dark and bare with no curtains on the small windows, no pictures on the walls, and only one saggy couch. Like many refugees' homes, it was a weird amalgamation of Disneyesque cutesy stuff, goods from the old country, used furniture, and discount-store toys. Video games, Pokémon figures, and plastic motorcycles were piled everywhere. I noted a pack of Marlboros and an ashtray, new since my last visit.

Zena looked at me apologetically as she lit up. "My job makes me smoke. Since I work there, I do many bad things." Zena worked for a food-processing plant that used up, then discarded, its workers. I had been trying to get her a better job, but she had limited English and couldn't read or write in any language.

Zena was a small, almost fragile, woman who worked eight-hour shifts lifting heavy buckets in the frozen-food locker. Her arms were always tired and were growing weaker. She knew of workers who could no longer lift bags of groceries or their own babies. Tonight, even though it was hot outside, Zena was dressed in several sweaters. In the food locker she wore three jackets, a wool cap, and two pairs of gloves. Still, she was always chilled there and she told me, "I can never get warm. Not even on weekends."

While we talked, her sons banged action figures into each other and zoomed their motorcycles around us. Noora watched an animated version of *The Wizard of Oz*. Zena said the kids had memorized the five cartoon videos they owned. As if to prove this, when the video reached the scene where Dorothy clicks her ruby slippers together, Noora jumped up, clicked her heels together, and recited Dorothy's speech. I laughed and clapped but felt a twinge of sorrow at this young Kurdish Dorothy looking for home.

This family had come from a very different world than they now inhabited. Zena was sixteen when her marriage was arranged, and like many brides from her country, she first met her husband on her wedding day. Now Zena was twenty-eight, caring for four kids and an ill husband and supporting the family. She had many more burdens and far fewer resources than she ever imagined would be her lot.

She hadn't been able to attend ELL classes and was learning English from television. It was amusing, but unnerving, to hear Zena express herself in cartoon language. "Yikes. We run for our lives."

Noora was dressed in a long pink dress and her hair was curled and adorned with barettes. I handed her my gifts, two books, the first books the family had ever owned. Noora examined them happily. I offered to read them to the kids and they gathered around eagerly. First I read from *A Light in the Attic,* then from *The Cat in the Hat.*

As I read, Zena prepared our dining area. She lay a tablecloth on the floor and carried out cans of Coke and bags of generic chips. I hated to see her spend her hard-earned money on junk food, but refugees learn what to love and value in our country from advertisers. The best minds of our generation are writing ad copy. In America, it's a rule of thumb that what is least necessary is what is advertised most. Refugees often buy expensive junky toys before they buy toothbrushes, and sugary treats instead of fresh produce.

Clearly Zena had spent all day and most of her food budget fixing us a beautiful meal. She proudly carried in a plate piled high with homemade flatbread still warm from the griddle, a tray of roast chicken, and another with chopped tomatoes, cucumbers, and green peppers. We sat on the floor, passing dishes and eating with our fingers. I loved her Kurdish cooking but the children preferred the chips and Cokes.

As always, I was touched by Zena's kindness to me. She had so little and yet whatever she had was shared with grace. But I was also struck by the limited information the family was receiving about our culture. They had come from a rural area and had never had consumer goods. Now they had no antidotes to our consumer society. They bought some of the worst junk America has to offer—cigarettes and soda pop, violent video games and cartoons, and easily broken "action figures."

Television tells newcomers lies—that most Americans are rich, that most African Americans are gang members and drug dealers, and that happiness comes from buying consumer goods and unhealthy foods. There are no ads for the joys of quiet time, gardening, looking at sunsets, visiting with neighbors, or reading to children.

All refugee families are given televisions and encouraged to "improve their English." But television doesn't improve English so much as foster shopping. In most refugee homes, televisions are always on and become virtual primers of acculturation. Families learn about America from the *Jerry Springer Show* and the *Simpsons*. They observe a monoculture with only three elements—sex, violence, and consumption.

Of course, Americans are much more complex and interesting than our media suggests, and we are not as violent or obsessed with sex, money, and power. I wanted to tell Zena, "Most of us lead quiet lives, and not necessarily of desperation. We spend much more of our time planting flowers then we do robbing banks, more time calling our mothers than we do having sex."

Over and over I have noticed a certain innocence in refugee families who have not lived in a world of media—their children are quieter and more respectful; everyone is less cynical and more content; hedonism is tempered with a strong sense of social responsibility; and people take pleasure in small, quiet events. It is an innocence that rapidly fades.

Refugees often come from places where money isn't very important. Trade is by the barter system and food is caught or grown. Clothes are made at home and entertainment is other people in the village. Travel is walking or boating. Healers work for a good meal. Some refugees come from Soviet bloc countries where everything is paid for. A Russian woman told me, "In my country everything was free unless otherwise specified. In the United States everything costs money unless it's specified free."

After dinner, Noora went back to *The Wizard of Oz*. The boys ran out into the parking lot to play soccer. Zena worried about them outdoors in such a bad neighborhood, but they couldn't be indoors all the time. However, she wouldn't let Noora outside at all.

She asked me about a letter offering her a MasterCard. She didn't really understand what that was and asked, "Can I buy whatever I want with this free card?" I explained interest and service charges and advised her to tear it up. This time she would, but would she tear up the Discover card application she receives next week?

When we give refugees charge cards long before we give them green cards, we set them up to be debtors. Newcomers experience a lethal combination of poverty and bombardment with ads. They don't understand the American way and almost immediately are into trouble with money decisions.

I wished I had more time to be this family's cultural broker and to show them our library system, our parks, and our free entertainment for families. They were in a magical country, bright and shiny with possibilities, but they needed someone to teach them that children need toothbrushes and beds more than action figures. I felt a responsibility to help them to see that all that glitters is not gold. Courage, heart, and brains are necessary to survive in this new land. Otherwise, for new arrivals, our magical country can quickly turn into a barren landscape.

CULTURAL BROKERS

One does not discover new lands without consenting
to lose sight of the shore for a very long time.
—ANDRÉ GIDE

The United States is a series of paradoxes for newcomers. Every plus is married to a minus. It is the land of opportunity and yet the opportunity is often to work in a meatpacking plant. Newcomers have fled war zones for the safety of our country but, in the United States, they often find themselves in our most dangerous neighborhoods. They are in a country with sophisticated health and mental health care but often cannot afford even the most basic treatments. They come for our wonderful educational system, but often their children are educated by television and learn all the wrong lessons. And finally, they come because of the generosity of the American people, and yet once here, they must deal with an unfriendly and grossly inefficient INS.

From the moment refugees arrive they are offered ideas about how to spend their time, energy, and money. There are two main ways refugees are educated. One is through the media and ads that are omnipresent. The second is through cultural brokers—schoolteachers, caseworkers, public health nurses, and American friends who may teach them to make intentional decisions about what to accept and what to reject in America. Cultural brokers help ease people into each other's cultures. Foucault wrote that "information is power." Cultural brokers give newcomers information that directly translates into power.

This chapter will discuss both kinds of American education as well as examine the conditions in our host environment. Right away, refugees must deal with housing, transportation, and legal status, as well as work, health, and mental health issues. These external factors have a great deal to do with a refugee's later success in America. Cultural brokers can make a tremendous difference.

The most important cultural brokers are schoolteachers. Schools are the frontline institution for acculturation, where children receive solid information about their new world. Almost all refugee families have a tremendous respect for education and educators. And our schools do not let them down. I have met many heroic teachers who, among their other responsibilities, become the antidotes to media and ads. One ELL teacher told me, "We're all there is between them and Howard Stern and Eminem."

Cultural brokers can teach the difference between *need* and *want* and also the meaning of the word *enough*. They can teach, as Bebe Moore Campbell said, that "Everything good to you ain't good for you." They can teach, as Paul Gruchow put it, that "Labor saving machines delivered not so much freedom from drudgery as enslavement to creditors." Gruchow also wrote, "Wealth is fully as capable of corrupting the soul as is poverty. What makes people happy in small doses is not necessarily good in large amounts. Too much candy, alcohol, leisure time, and shopping choices all make people miserable."

Cultural brokers encourage families to read, go to museums, draw, learn to play an instrument, and to find a place of worship or a community center. They encourage them to walk on our prairies, fish in our lakes, and ride bikes on our trails. If refugees learn only from television, they will end up unhealthy, stressed, rushed, addicted, and broke.

Cultural brokers teach Budgeting 101. In their home countries, many refugees have not had to manage their desires because never before has there been enough. Cultural brokers try to teach intentionality, that is, thoughtfulness about choices. Intentionality requires a moral center, accurate information, and the skills to implement good decisions.

A cultural broker has information on everything—what schools are the best, where to go fishing or buy lemongrass, where to find work or buy a used car, and how to change a tire. A cultural broker knows whom to call about INS problems and where to get free legal aid and tax assistance. Cultural brokers understand local resources and have a commitment to helping newcomers avoid mistakes that can slow down their adjustment. Below is a list of things that, as a cultural broker, I have taught newcomers.

How to order food in a café
How to use escalators, stairs, elevators, and revolving doors
How to cross streets with traffic lights
How to feed a traffic meter
How to drive—what signs and signals mean, how to start a car,
    defensive driving as a concept
What is the length of a human life in America

How to use a water fountain

How to tell time and use an alarm clock, a watch, a calendar, and an appointment book

How to work a bike lock and a combination lock

How to put on a bike helmet and why helmets are important

How to check the oil and put gas in a car

How to write a check and balance a checkbook

How to peel an orange and eat watermelon

What to put in a refrigerator

How to bake a frozen pizza and use Shake 'n Bake to cook chicken

How to mix juice

That most Americans shower daily

What a doctor is doing—taking a temperature, blood pressure, drawing blood

What are dangerous situations—don't ride with strangers and don't walk around alone at night

Why we don't give money to phone or door-to-door solicitors

How to use hand lotion

How to swim, folk dance, and go on a picnic

How to read the want ads

How to read the entertainment section of the paper

What to do if the tornado siren sounds

How to shop at a grocery store

How to fill out a job application

What are vitamins

How to interview for a job

How to enroll in school

How to apply for Pell Grants and other financial aid

How to make a doctor's or dentist's appointment

When to call a lawyer and how to find one

Who to go to with INS problems

That cut flowers need to be put in water
How to buy shoes and to learn one's shoe size
How to buy clothes and learn one's waist size or dress size
How and why to take aspirin
How to call Ask a Nurse
Where to find bargains
How to get around town
What a United States map looks like and where Nebraska is
How to drive on the interstate
How to read a map
What elections are
What political parties are
Who is president, mayor, and governor
What happens when people break laws
Where parks, prairies, and state lakes are
The names of animals, trees, birds, and flowers
Where the bike trails are
How to walk on snow and ice
What to wear outside in winter
What animals Americans eat
That many mushrooms are poisonous
Why drinking water in hot weather is important
What a birthday is
What cake, cocoa, and pie are
How to roast marshmallows and make s'mores
What American holidays are
How to carve a pumpkin
That Christmas trees must be put in water
How to brush teeth
What Band-Aids, sanitary napkins, dental floss, and deodorant are
How to do math and how to read

How many weeks are in a year
That the length of day varies according to the season and dis-
    tance from the equator
How long a fetus grows in its mother
What a time zone is
What a buffalo is
How to check out books from public and school libraries
How to use a cell phone
What a snow day is
That some stores stay open all night
What various slang words and phrases mean, such as *noogie, okay,*
    TLC, screw up, and *keep your fingers crossed*
How to make grilled-cheese sandwiches and toast
How to wear socks
How and when to call 911
What Easter eggs are
How to get a prescription and get it filled
How to play cards
How to put together a jigsaw puzzle
That police can be helpful
How to use cleaning products
What to do for acne
Why young clerks cannot sell liquor
What kolaches, muffins, runzas, and corn dogs are
What asparagus and rhubarb are
How to change a lightbulb, a battery, and a furnace filter
How a flashlight, a microwave, and a can opener work
Where to get air for bike tires
Where to play basketball
What dry cleaning is
What fabrics need to be dry-cleaned

What happens if you don't pay your bills
Why I don't beat my children
Why we wear seat belts
What sex offenders are
Why we should wash our hands after going to the bathroom
What germs are
What *homesick* means
What a washing machine is
What aluminum foil is
Why American parents talk to babies
What animals pork and beef come from
What a tissue is
What a rocking chair is
What a dinosaur is
Why we shouldn't litter
How to eat an ice-cream cone

One aspect of being a cultural broker is being an introducer. Cultural brokers can attend every first meeting between a refugee and a caseworker, doctor, banker, or employer. Just being present as a supportive friend helps these first meetings, often filled with anxiety on all sides, go more smoothly. If a local person accompanies newcomers to their first Jazz in June, contra dance, or GED session, the newcomers may later return alone. Without a guide, certain things never seem to happen on their own.

Having a cultural broker can make a tremendous difference in how successfully a new family adapts to America. People come here traumatized, and the trauma doesn't end with arrival. Without guidance and support, it's difficult to survive.

Every newcomer needs someone who knows how to get

things done locally. Communities are nuanced cultures, and the nuances are precisely what newcomers need help with. Songwriter Greg Brown might have been speaking of cultural brokers when he wrote, "Your hometown is where you know what the deal is. You may not like it, but you understand it." (See appendix 2 for ideas on how to help.)

LIFE'S NECESSITIES

Housing

Because of their poverty, refugees often move into our slums, what Eleanor Roosevelt defined as "inhabited, uninhabitable habitations." Slums are filled with desperate people looking for their first chance or settling for their last resort. Refugees move into neighborhoods with meth labs, crack houses, sex offenders, and gangs. Some landlords take advantage of newcomers and overcharge. A woman from Nigeria lived in a small, dark basement with poor ventilation, for which she paid more rent than would be charged for a reasonable student apartment. Some landlords will not rent to people they regard as "foreigners." I once called a landlady about housing for a refugee family. I made the mistake of telling her that they were from Macedonia. Over and over, she demanded, "Are they clean?" She wouldn't tell me what the rent was. Rather she said, "Have them come by and we'll talk about it. It's negotiable."

I have visited refugees in places where it wasn't safe to stand on the porch because the roof was falling down; in places with snakes, roaches, and rats; and in places that were hot in summer and freezing cold in winter. I've been angered at greedy, indifferent landlords. However, I've also met good landlords, eager to welcome newcomers and conscientious about charging reasonable rents and keeping things fixed up.

Many refugees live in extended families or have many children. They want to rent a unit for as many as fifteen people. Lincoln has few three-bedroom apartments, let alone six-bedroom apartments. Often the family needs a place to live before the adults have any savings. Deposits necessary for rentals are difficult to acquire. Finally, even if a place can be found and money garnered, the rents are just too high for a family living on minimum-wage salaries while sending money home to relatives.

A cultural broker can help a family locate a safe neighborhood near their ethnic group. Cultural brokers can help determine what is a reasonable rent. They may need to read the lease and cosign, or write a check for the damage deposit. Later they can mediate between the newcomers and their landlord and show newcomers how to take care of their places. This can include everything from lending them tools for fix-up jobs to explaining American cleaning products.

Orientation, Transportation, and Driving

An American city is a complicated place with stores, houses, schools, places of worship, different kinds of thoroughfares, government and business offices, hospitals, emergency services, transportation systems, public and private property, parks, and recreational facilities. And yet, almost from the first, people must get around. They need doctors, schools, and groceries.

Most American cities are designed in ways that make a car necessary. Soon, most newcomers want a car. Buying a vehicle involves evaluating, comparing, and then selecting a car. Many times the purchaser must secure a loan, demonstrate a credit rating, be employed, and have references. Then, he must buy insurance, which is not even a concept in many parts of the world.

Driving is a complex skill, requiring the ability to read maps and street signs, as well as an understanding of vehicles, laws, and traffic. Newcomers must pass a written driver's test and drive with a state employee. Many refugees are very anxious about being alone with a large American wearing a uniform. For many Middle Eastern women, this is the first time they have ever been alone with a man not in their family. After obtaining a driver's license, there is the risk of accidents, speeding tickets, and injuries, all of which can ruin the life of a refugee.

In fender benders, refugees are often at a disadvantage. They don't know the laws or the language and they panic around police. Consequently, newcomers often are unfairly ticketed. I have known refugees to be ticketed when they were rear-ended or even when they were hit while sitting in a parked vehicle.

Certain car dealers have taken to defrauding refugees. They buy an old clunker, clean it up, pour oil treatment in its engine, and sell it for far more than it is worth. A few weeks later, the newcomer, who has spent his life savings on the vehicle, discovers the car needs a new engine or transmission.

Ideally, locals help newcomers shop for cars. They ask questions of the dealers in English, test-drive the vehicles, check on warranties, and get second opinions. Local people know who are the honest car dealers. Furthermore, dealers are more accountable when someone is involved who knows how to call the Better Business Bureau and write letters to the editor.

Cultural brokers can also help with maps and orientation to the city, with all the legal procedures involved in licensing and registering cars, and, if necessary, with paying traffic tickets, which are frightening and confusing to refugees.

Work

Refugees have always done the work that other Americans didn't want to do. But there is a big difference between the work environments of the past and the present. In the past, immigrants and refugees could slowly work their way up the ladder to better jobs. They might be on the killing floor of the packing plant. But their sons would be shop stewards and their grandsons union organizers.

Portes and Rumbaut document this new situation. Whereas job distribution used to look like a triangle, it now looks like an hourglass. There are many jobs at the top and at the bottom, but the jobs in the middle are gone. These intermediary jobs are now handled by computers or other machines. There is no job ladder to climb. Refugees must somehow leap from the bottom half of the hourglass to the top. It's a giant leap, even for the second and third generation. Many don't make it and end up permanently locked in the underclass.

Refugees are much more vulnerable and controllable than other workers. Hence, they work in the places where their ears hurt from constant noise or where they get headaches or throw up because of noxious materials used in production. They work in factories that have poor ventilation and no windows, and that insist upon split shifts and forced overtime. Even though these conditions are unhealthy and unsafe, there is little anyone can do to protect workers. By now OSHA exists only theoretically. It's virtually impossible to obtain a workplace inspection for any reason.

Many Nebraska refugees work in meatpacking plants. People fall down on the bloody floors. Knives slip while slicing meat.

Carcasses hit workers when they are not watching. Many of these plants were built for brawny Swedes and Germans, and most of the workers now are smaller people, Mexican, Laotian, and Vietnamese, who are the wrong size for the equipment. Lack of orientation, long hours, language problems, and pressure to work faster increase the danger.

Rules at many of these plants are draconian—no breaks, no talking to others, and no calling in sick. Most do not complain for fear of losing their jobs and/or their work permits. Some workers get sick from dehydration because they don't have time to drink water or because they are afraid to drink for fear they might need to use a bathroom. Injury rates in our packing plants are as high as 50 percent. Some places have an injury rate of 80 percent for workers the first year on the job.

Educated newcomers suffer the most from their drop in status. A Romanian pediatrician works stuffing envelopes. A director of a hospital from Hungary drives a taxicab. A Nuba woman who was a great leader of her people in the Sudan now sorts mail. A judge from Haiti works as a janitor. Lawyers become doormen; teachers assemble computer boards or sell fast food. A distinguished writer fries doughnuts for a fast-food chain. He can speak no English and is treated in a demeaning way by some staff and customers.

Many people come from places where one person could work outside the home and support the family. In America, all the adults must work just to pay the rent and buy groceries. Women from traditional cultures hate to leave their children and move into the labor market, and when they must do this, they feel impoverished indeed.

But status issues are complex. Without money, people have limited control of their lives. And while money doesn't buy happiness, neither does poverty. As a Latino man told me, "Nobody listens to a poor man." Work outside the home is not just the source of income; it is the source of dignity. Without dignity, people are powerless.

Still, in the rather dismal scene, there are points of light. A local man serves as a cultural broker by running an employment service that connects refugees with jobs. His staff speaks many languages and they know the bus routes and who works where. Dave tells companies, "I can get you workers, but I expect them to be treated well and given benefits and good wages."

Dave acts as an intermediary for people who cannot do interviews and who don't have cars or money for required work uniforms. He knows which factories use up their workers and which offer good benefits, including dental care and education. He encourages workers to speak English whenever they can and to not just talk to people from their homeland. He tells workers, "Ask questions; ask your supervisor if you're doing a good job. Ask if there is more you can do."

Dave told me of one woman from the Ukraine who called him up after she got a job and said, "Tell my boss he pays me too much. My English not so good. I don't deserve seven dollars an hour."

Thanks to people like Dave, we have a kinder, gentler employment scene than we would otherwise. He's a big-hearted guy who is on a mission to find work for desperate people. He has a sense for what refugees have been through and are going through but he also understands the very practical needs of employers. When my refugee friends are in trouble with work they call and ask, "Will you talk to Dave?"

Health Care

In our country health care is wonderful for the people who have access to our modern medical system. However, access is difficult for people without cars, money, or English. Services are available only during hours when refugees must be in factories. Doctors often schedule appointments two or three weeks away, even for very sick people. Furthermore, while refugees are urged to show up on time, the doctors may keep them waiting.

Although there are some praiseworthy exceptions, many of the doctors who will take Medicaid are overworked and schedule short appointments. Many newcomers feel rushed and, especially if a translator is involved, there isn't time to handle things. They feel rebuffed by a doctor who doesn't take the time to visit.

Many refugees must have their children interpret for them. It's convenient to use kids as translators but not generally a good idea. Kids often don't know the words for medical terms, and having them translate upends the family hierarchy by putting them in a position of power and responsibility.

Gender issues complicate the situation. Many women come from cultures where only their husbands will ever see or touch their bodies. Many will not go to a male doctor and our city doesn't have enough female physicians to meet their needs.

The book *The Spirit Catches You and You Fall Down* by Anne Fadiman tells of the great cultural misunderstandings that occurred between a Hmong family and American doctors. For example, each believed that the other ate human flesh. When the Hmong asked for the placenta, which they bury as a "soul jacket" under their hearths, the American health professionals thought this was so the Hmong could eat it. The Hmong, who knew that doctors cut open their people during surgery, thought that the doctors removed internal organs and ate them.

Serious mistakes happen when people are not bicultural. Vietnamese parents who have used coining, which is rubbing their children with hot coins to draw out fevers, have been arrested for child abuse. In many traditional cultures, there is the belief that to predict something is to wish it. To say "You will die if you do not get treatment for cancer" is tantamount to wishing for that.

Of course, our medical practitioners predict and diagnose all the time. A man from Iran wanted to sue his doctor because the man had told his mother she had cancer and would not live much longer. He said, "In Iran we would never handle it that way. The doctor would merely tell family members to be very good to their mother. He would say that she was fine, just be good to her."

Because of language differences and cultural misunderstandings, some diseases are missed or misdiagnosed. A Croatian child who had significant learning disorders wasn't identified because his language skills were not good. All his teachers just thought he was quiet. A Caribbean woman was diagnosed as psychotic because she spoke with her dead husband at night. However, in Caribbean culture people believe in ghosts, and many non-psychotic people converse with them.

Women who have been raped are often ashamed to speak of it. In some parts of the world, if a woman has been raped, she and the rapist will both be executed. Even in less-punitive cultures, women who have been raped are regarded as unmarriageable. So rape is kept secret, which means such women who have been raped don't receive physical or psychological care.

Many new arrivals come from places with unhealthy diets, bad water, and no preventative health care. After years of neglect, their teeth are often in terrible shape. Refugees may have chronic health conditions. They also may have been bombed, tortured, or hurt while escaping. Many have untreated injuries from work or prison. Women often have gynecological problems caused by female genital mutilation.

Many newcomers are from areas with absolutely no public health information. They do not know that alcohol can be addictive or that cigarettes cause cancer. They may not know how to cook or understand even basic information about a healthy diet. Some new arrivals have never seen a toothbrush; they do not know what germs are or that it is important to wash their hands.

Many people who have been tortured have injuries they are ashamed to discuss. An older Vietnamese man had a very bad shoulder. He had been yoked like an ox to a plow for years in a POW camp. A Cambodian man had his hip broken under torture. It was never treated and now, of course, it was too late. Many Middle Eastern refugees have been beaten on the feet. Their feet are in perpetual pain and they have trouble walking. Others who have been tortured by electroshock are frightened of EEG machines. Many are brain damaged from head trauma or from nerve gas.

Some refugees come from places where to admit you had a physical or mental problem was to be killed. They are ashamed of these experiences and do not share them with others. But they have physical and psychological scars. Some withdraw from their families. Others are violent or suicidal. Given their histories, it's hard to talk such people into hospitals, which cost a lot of money and involve paperwork and dealing with strangers and unfamiliar treatments. One woman from Mali had chest pains for a week before a public health nurse stopped by for a routine visit. The nurse told me, "She could easily have died of a heart attack."

Mental Health

Every culture has its own ways of expressing and repressing emotional pain. Many complaints that we would consider mental health problems are expressed somatically. Often refugees say they are sick when they really mean "I am incapacitated by stress." People don't sleep well, are always tired, or their back hurts. Middle Eastern people frequently express emotional pain by talking about pain in their arms or legs. A woman from Liberia complained about blurred vision and eye pain. The doctors could find nothing. Finally I said to her, "I imagine you must have seen terrible things." She answered, "They shot my husband in front of me."

It's more acceptable to speak of physical pain than mental pain. A doctor with training and experience working with refugees will understand that some of their physical problems are stress related. A less-experienced doctor may order expensive and scary tests.

Psychology is irrelevant to most newcomers. This doesn't mean refugees don't have mental health problems. They have high rates of depression and anxiety. But in their hierarchy of needs, these are not their most pressing problems. It's hard to do therapy with someone who is hungry. In fact, it is silly to sit and talk to someone about their need for a ride to the grocery store. It's better to just take them.

Every culture has its own system of healing. All over the world, healing involves calmness, beautiful places, kind people, simple routines, rituals, and temporary protection from everyday problems. Laughter is a part of many healing systems. There is really no period in history when humans didn't laugh. Even during war there is laughter. Music, touch, dancing, food, and prayer are part of healing all over the world. But psychotherapy is a hard sell.

BUREAUCRACIES AND QUESTIONNAIRES

Even before refugees arrive in the United States they must go through interviews to determine their refugee status. Many say this interview, conducted in a foreign language and consisting of odd questions that must be answered precisely, is more stressful than being tortured. Even the smallest mistake can condemn their families to permanently live in a refugee camp or return to a situation that will get them killed.

Assuming the family establishes refugee status, they begin a lifetime of dealing with bureaucracies. America is awash in paperwork. There is a form for everything from going to the dentist to signing up for a field trip to checking out a library book. These forms are an annoyance if one knows the language, but they can be an insurmountable barrier to adults who cannot read or write in English. There are other barriers as well. Many refugees don't know their age or birthdays. They may not have other vital information about health history and vaccinations, about school and employment, or about dates and places of residence.

Often our categories don't even fit native-born Americans, but they really collide with the cultural traditions of refugees. For example, the Kurdish sisters tried to fill out a scholarship application to the YWCA. But all six sisters were in their twenties and thirties and lived with their mother. The sisters supported her and their sister in Iraq. Who was the primary wage earner in a family when all resources were pooled?

There are privacy issues. Refugees are leery of revealing confidential information about family members. This makes it stressful and sometimes impossible to fill out intake forms at a mental health center, a hospital, a school, a social welfare agency, or a bank. Refugees feel alarmed when they see questions about domestic violence or mental health. These are personal matters, not to be shared with strangers on paper. Questions about education, employment, income, religion, and health problems can also seem invasive.

Many refugees come from places where written information and signatures have gotten people arrested and killed. When they arrive here, they are warned to be careful what they sign. They are leery of signing forms they do not understand, which is prudent, but this wariness makes transactions difficult.

Any procedures that involve the police, such as dealing with a minor traffic offense, reporting a robbery, or even answering questions about a barking dog next door, can frighten refugees. Many come from countries where police are corrupt or associated with repressive governments. As a Siberian woman put it, "In Russia a policeman means trouble is coming." A Kurdish woman said, "Back home if a policeman knocks at your door, it means death."

All of the problems with paperwork and bureaucracy come together in their worst form when newcomers deal with the Immigration and Naturalization Service. The INS is the great American dragon that all must slay to enter the gates of the promised land. It angers, terrifies, and discourages newcomers. Some the INS drives back home; others it drives to suicide; most it eventually grants permanent residency status.

As one lawyer told me, "The INS is the mother of all bureaucracies; compared to the INS, all other bureaucracies are rank amateurs." The INS is incredibly understaffed. For the last few years Congress has funded enforcement but hasn't funded routine service and processing of documents. A recent newspaper article reported that of the 115,000 calls made to national INS offices daily, only 500 are answered.

In Nebraska we create illegals, then arrest and deport them. The INS in Nebraska doesn't have adequate staff to help newcomers secure legal status. People wait three years for routine papers to be processed. Yet, the INS raids meatpacking plants to round up illegals. Refugees live in fear of the INS. It's a Kafkaesque situation. People must cooperate with the INS or they will be deported, but they cannot cooperate because the INS doesn't respond to their attempts.

I know of only one positive story about the INS. It demonstrates that at least some employees are better than the institution. An INS official asked a man from a camp in Saudi Arabia if he wanted to come to America. He said sorrowfully, "I have no one in America." The official held out his hand to him and said, "May I have the honor of being your first American friend?"

SADIA AND THE INS

One night Sadia, a woman from Afghanistan, brought me a letter that ordered her and her fourteen-year-old daughter to report to Hastings, Nebraska, on a certain day to be fingerprinted. She was frightened by the letter and unsure how to comply with the order. She didn't have a car and couldn't drive to Hastings. There was no bus. She asked me if she could walk there and if it was bigger than Kansas City. I said it was small but one hundred miles away. Sadia wept, certain that she would be deported. I told her I would try to make arrangements to have her fingerprinted here in Lincoln. But if necessary, I would take her and her daughter to Hastings.

As I left, I reflected on Sadia's hard life, most of it spent on the run and in prison camps. Now she worked at a factory and had barely enough money for a small apartment for herself and her daughter. Sadia's daughter was fatherless and learning her third language. She'd missed a lot of school during their years of flight and really didn't need to be pulled from high school to be fingerprinted.

The next day I sat at my phone for two hours rapid-repeat-dialing the INS. The line was always busy. I double-checked the number and called to make sure it was in order. A telephone company supervisor told me that every day she received many complaints like mine. She sighed, "We tell customers to consider that line inoperative." This was frustrating enough for me, but it creates an impossible situation for refugees who have only ten-minute bathroom breaks and a pay phone at their factories.

In despair, I called my senator's office. A special staff member whose sole job was to deal with the INS said he would look into things. Two days later he called back to say there was no way for the prints to be done locally and that the lines in Omaha were even longer than the ones in Hastings.

He said Sadia was being sent to Hastings because there had been a glitch in the computer program that assigns fingerprinting locations by zip code. Many refugees were told to go to faraway stations rather than to the one nearest them.

Two days before we left for Hastings, I called to make sure we would be received. There were no phone numbers on Sadia's letter so I called directory assistance and asked for the Hastings INS. No number was listed. Then, because the stationery also had a Department of Justice insignia, I asked for a Department of Justice number. None was listed for Hastings. I called the toll-free Customer Service number on the letter and was told by a recording that the number was no longer in service. Eventually I reached the Omaha office of the INS. I spoke to a grumpy man who said there was no Hastings office. When I tried to read him the letter, he hung up on me. I had now spent the entire morning on the phone trying to track down this Hastings office. Not only had I been unsuccessful, but by now I was unsure if we were even supposed to go to Hastings.

I called the Department of Justice in Lincoln and finally reached a live human being. She said she would give me a phone number if I promised not to give it to anyone else. I

thanked the woman profusely and hung up, feeling hopeful for
the first time that day. But when I called the number, it was out
of service.

I had entered the twilight zone. This was a mess for me and
I am a native-born, English-speaking clinical psychologist with
a telephone. What was it like for a desperate refugee with no
cultural broker? I again called my senator's office. They must
have some secret number because someone called me later and
said, "Go to the Hastings police department tomorrow."

So we went. When she heard that we had to go the police
department, Sadia immediately associated the place with torture
centers. But she got off work and pulled her daughter from
school. We drove the three hours to the Hastings police department. It was anticlimactic. A kind middle-aged woman helped
them. In one half hour the fingerprints were taken and we were
on our way home. I had learned something about how our government works and Sadia was grateful she hadn't been tortured.

REFUGEES *across the* LIFE CYCLE

PART TWO

CHAPTER 5

CHILDREN *of* HOPE,
CHILDREN *of* TEARS

Home is where you hang your childhood.
—WRIGHT MORRIS

In southwestern Minnesota, there is a quarry for pipestone, the rock used by all the Plains Indians to make peace pipes and many other sacred objects. It is a soft, carveable rock that glows red at sunset. Pipestone quarry was a sacred site where all the tribes came together in peace. While they were there, a truce existed; all the tribes mined side by side, then parted to fight on other ground.

Pipestone is a good metaphor for schools. Schools are the sacred ground of refugees, and education is their shared religion. At school, the Croats and Serbs study together, as do the Iranians and Iraqis and the southern and northern Sudanese. Outside school, groups may feud, but inside school, they will be respectful so that they can all quarry the American educational system.

Before their first day of school, many children from traditional cultures have never been away from their mothers for even an hour. At school, they may feel far from home. Everything may be different—the language, customs, the colors of the people, the clothes, the foods, and even the play. Developmental levels of children are not uniform either. Five-year-olds from one culture have very different skills, relationships to family, and comfort levels with strangers than do five-year-olds from another culture.

Schools are often where kids experience their first racism and learn about the socioeconomic split in our country. There is the America of children with violin lessons, hockey tickets, skiing trips, and zoo passes, and there is the America of children in small apartments whose parents work double shifts.

English as Learned Language classes are taught by teachers who are responsible for everything from cultural orientation to teaching English and basic academic skills. The students are grouped according to their ability to speak English, and kids from as many as twenty different language groups may be in one class.

School may be overwhelming at first, but it is school that will enable children to make it in America. School offers students the freedom to develop and to dream big American dreams. In spite of their disadvantages, refugees have lower drop-out rates and better grades than native-born kids.

A determining factor in kids' success is the quality of their family lives. Well-loved, well-nurtured kids from all over the world have a tremendous advantage. Mothers and fathers who carefully select the best from both the new and old cultures have the best-adjusted children. Parental involvement in education varies. In general, refugee parents have high expectations, but limited contact with the schools. They feel that education is the job of the teachers. Parents may want to be involved, but may not understand how to be involved. Also, work schedules, transportation, and language problems make contact with schools difficult.

Schools are therapeutic environments. Half the world's refugees are children and adolescents, many of whom arrive in the United States malnourished and with health problems. Many students have lost siblings, parents, or other family members. Teachers may not deal with trauma directly, but they are part of the healing process. They give their students order and predictability. After the chaos and confusion of their lives, nothing is more comforting than routines. Kids like the same things to happen at the same time with the same people. Students need to receive the message that school is a safe place. Order, ritual, and predictability are part of this reassurance.

Relationships with kind, consistent adults are deeply healing. Good teachers, to quote Nellie Morton, "hear people to speech." They give children lap time, pats, and nonverbal reassurance that they are going to be okay. Physical affection and smiles can occur in the absence of a common language. A hug has a universal meaning.

Teachers connect the dots between the world of family and of school, the old culture and America, the past and the future. They help children understand how their worlds fit together and they teach empathy and good manners. Children become moral beings, not through lectures, but through countless daily encounters with moral people. They learn how to be good through stories about honesty, kindness, responsibility, and courage. Moral behavior is essentially a set of good habits. Good teachers help children form those good habits.

The class story that follows is about ELL students and their teacher, who is a cheerleader, an instiller of hope, a cultural broker, a therapist, and an occasional comedian. I worked in elementary schools and summer ELL camps. Over the course of my research, I met hundreds of children, all of whom had interesting stories. However, for the purposes of this book, I will limit

my discussion to one classroom at one school, which I'll call
Sycamore Elementary School.

The class actually had twenty-five kids, too many for one
teacher. Grace was an excellent teacher, but there wasn't
enough of her to go around. Many kids who were eager to
work couldn't get the help they needed. For this story I chose
to describe only ten of the kids. I picked both kids whose parents were doing a good job making choices in America and kids
whose parents were choosing all the wrong things. And I picked
kids who varied in resilience and overall adjustment to America.

SYCAMORE SCHOOL
The number one thing is to care for children.

CLASS ROSTER:

| Abdul | Ignazio | Ly | Trinh | Deena |
| Pavel | Khoa | Mai | Walat | Fatima |

September 6, 1999

Sycamore Elementary School is a three-story redbrick
building just off a busy street that is lined with a McDonald's,
Arab and Mexican markets, liquor stores, pawnshops, and a Vietnamese karaoke bar. The houses around the school are small,
close together, and dilapidated. Police cars cruise the area. Unemployed men stand on the corners and in the alleys. The
school was built for the children of Czechs and Germans, but it
now welcomes students of all colors and ethnic groups.

Walking in the first day, I admired a sycamore tree with its
sheltering white branches and big greeny gold leaves. There is
something about the shape of a sycamore that reminds me of
embracing arms. On the playground, a Latino boy scored in a
vigorous soccer game and his team shouted and high-fived each

other. Soccer is the universal solvent in Lincoln—Vietnamese, Mexican, Haitian, Romanian, and Serbian kids all like soccer.

Inside the school, a boy who looked like a biker's kid, wearing black jeans and a black T-shirt, watched a girl with dreadlocks twirl in circles, singing to herself. A teacher listened to an Arabic-speaking mother in a hijab. The mother was surrounded by her four wide-eyed kids, the youngest of whom clung to her skirt. The teacher imitated talking on a phone, then she wrote down a phone number and handed it to the mother.

I walked past a sign that said YOU HAVE ONLY ONE CHANCE TO HAVE A CHILDHOOD. I examined pictures of houses from all over the world—a Thai houseboat, Panamanian hutches, a Somali camp—and a display of macaroni-and-cereal necklaces, some of which had been nibbled on.

I signed in at the front office and a third grader named Judy Running Wolf escorted me to a portable classroom, a trailer outside the main building beside the clothing and food distribution center. My new class was a ragtag group, dressed in Salvation Army clothes, with an amazing array of bad haircuts. Most of them looked between eight and eleven, although some might have been small twelve-year-olds.

They were holding Village Inn menus and practicing how to order. The kids giggled and pointed at the glossy pictures of cheeseburgers and blueberry pie. In a dozen languages they discussed the pictures as if they were rare objets d'art. These kids came from many religious traditions and had food taboos and preferences. Some kids don't eat lettuce. Others didn't like milk. But today several ordered pretend hamburgers and boasted they had eaten before at McDonald's. Others ordered the most expensive dishes on the menu and bragged about how much it cost.

Their teacher watched them converse. Grace was a pretty woman in her late thirties. She didn't miss much and nothing rattled her. She spoke softly, laughed easily, and kept the room reasonably calm without making threats. As the kids ordered pretend meals, she told me a little about each of them.

Grace's biggest worry was Abdul, a beautiful kid with nut-colored skin and deep dimples. He was an Iraqi boy who had watched his younger brother freeze to death in the snow when his family walked barefoot across mountains into Turkey. Possibly he was brain damaged from gas attacks during the Gulf War. Abdul rarely did his work and he didn't seem to connect with anyone. Other teachers thought he should be in special education classes, but Grace wanted to give him a chance to adjust. She said many of the ELL kids look like special education kids at first, but then they adapted.

Pavel sat beside Abdul. He was a big awkward kid from the Former Soviet Union (FSU) with tangled blond hair and his shirt half tucked in. Grace said he was much indulged by his parents. Pavel was good-natured, but restless and lazy. He preferred playing with Nibbles the rat to doing his studies.

Ignazio was a good-hearted Mexican boy whose parents worked long hours at a sugar beet refinery. Nobody at home seemed able to help him with his studies. He was lovable and well behaved, but not very focused. Grace worried that Ignazio might be picked on because he was chubby and innocent.

Khoa was skinny and wore tight polyester pants that didn't reach his ankles. He wore a torn Star Wars T-shirt and his shiny hair badly needed a wash and a cut. He was clowning and hamming it up, making everyone laugh at his outrageous order of four hamburgers and three malts. Grace said his family had experienced great trauma getting to this country from Vietnam. In Lincoln, he lived in a rough neighborhood and his older brother had been in trouble with the law. Khoa was a fan of violent video games and twice Grace had confiscated nunchaks from him. Still, she felt he was essentially a good person.

Beside Khoa sat three Vietnamese girls. Grace said, "I put them beside Khoa because he can make them laugh."

Ly was a Vietnamese girl from a big hardworking family. Her parents were strict and Ly had extremely good manners. Her schoolwork was consistently A-plus.

Mai was a small angry-looking girl on the edge of the group. She had lost her mother when she was three, just before she and her father came to America. Her father had remarried and Mai lived with her father, stepmother, and new baby brother. Mai was troubled and had few ways to deal with her troubles. She scratched her arms or pulled her hair when she was upset.

Beside Mai, Trinh stared at her glossy menu. Grace said, "Trinh will not answer questions. I haven't heard her speak yet." Her parents had drowned crossing from Vietnam into Thailand. She lived with her grandparents, who had told Grace that Trinh spoke occasionally at home.

Walat was a handsome, self-contained, and competent boy from Iraq. His family was part of the close community of Kurds. His dad had been an engineer in Kurdistan and, even without credentials, he had found related work in America. Walat's mother was able to stay at home, study English, and help the kids with their homework.

As Grace told me about Deena's life, the small blond-haired girl ordered an imaginary ice-cream sundae. She had seen her grandparents and uncles killed in Bosnia, then she and her parents had been herded into an internment camp. Her mother was depressed and her father was incapacitated by stress. Solid, energetic, and intelligent, Deena spoke the best English in her family and was often kept out of school to translate.

Next to Deena, Fatima held up her menu and, like Deena, she ordered a pretend ice-cream sundae. Fatima was a Kurdish girl who'd been burned on her face and arms when Iraqis bombed her village. Grace told me that her scars had caused her some trouble at school. Some ELL kids came from cultures where deformed people are shunned. These kids did not want to hold her hand. "In America," Grace had explained, "We treat all people with respect." Fatima's father could not work, and her mother supported the family of five by working at a food-processing factory. Grace said, "Fatima can wear me out asking for validation."

Grace tapped on her desk and the kids stopped ordering food and looked up. She introduced me as "Miss Mary" and the kids stared at me with interest. Ly smiled. Khoa loudly declared that I looked old, very old. He kept saying this and finally I said to him, "Yes, I could be your grandmother." After that, he stopped.

Grace picked the name of a helper out of a hat. Today it was Fatima, whose job it would be to feed Nibbles and distribute supplies. Grace had the class look at a calendar and take turns saying, "It's Tuesday, September 6, 1999." She asked what kind of weather it was. "Clear," shouted Khoa, and Grace smacked a yellow plastic sun on the calendar board.

As Fatima, Deena, and Ly worked at their spelling, Khoa talked about poop and eating boogers. He looked like he needed everything—a bath, a good meal, a full night's sleep, and lap time with a patient adult. He watched me as closely as I watched him, and he winked whenever our eyes met.

Pavel twisted in his seat as if he were being tortured, broke his pencil, and wrinkled and smeared his papers. But like Khoa, he somehow managed to be disruptive and sociable at the same time. Together they gave the class a certain energy that wasn't all bad.

Grace went over the spelling words: "father," "mother," and "uncle." Then she began a discussion of what people needed to do at home. She wrote down phrases on the board such as "sew clothes," "mow yard," "cook food," "change baby's diapers." When she said this, Khoa shouted out, "Change the diapers or the baby will get a stinky butt." He laughed uproariously at his own joke. Grace cleared her throat and asked what else should families do at home.

Ignazio shouted, "Buy food." Deena said, "The number one thing is to care for the children." Ignazio elaborated, "Without food you might die." Fatima said, "Buy clothes. Without clothes you can't go outside." Mai said, "Take care of the baby."

Grace asked what chores were not so important to do. Pavel shouted out, "It's not important to pay the bills." Grace said gently, "In America that is pretty important."

Grace asked the class to write a story about a family who forgets to do some jobs. I pulled my little chair up by Abdul. He bristled and turned away as if he were allergic to me. However, for the first time that day, he did some work. He hunched away from me, working on his assignment so that I wouldn't stay with him. Grimly, I reflected that I was helping him, but it wasn't much fun. When he finished, I checked his work. Then I turned to Pavel who had been waiting impatiently for help. He was a big teddy bear of a kid. He wrote, "Good dads take their sons fishing."

I asked him if he liked to fish and his eyes brightened. Stupidly, I said maybe the class could go fishing sometime. Pavel was riveted by the suggestion. He asked, "Tomorrow? Where? How would we get there? Could I bring my own pole?"

I realized what I had done and tried to put the rabbit back in the hat, but, of course, I failed. Other kids also got excited. We never finished the spelling words.

It was time to go. Fatima picked up papers and pencils. I helped Ignazio with the broken zipper on his coat. Ly flashed me a smile and said, "I'll see you next Monday, Miss Mary." Trinh and Deena slipped out, but Fatima waved shyly at me. I gave Abdul a hug, but he shrugged it off. Pavel had one last fishing question and I smiled sheepishly at Grace, remarking, "I've created a monster." As Khoa dashed out the door with his shoelaces untied, he asked me, "Will you come back tomorrow?"

As I watched Mai walk across the yard into the main school building, I thought about her complex situation. I wanted to help her with her feelings about her baby brother, her step-mother, and even about her mother's death. She was raised in a culture that teaches the suppression of negative emotions. It was unlikely she knew what to do with her troubled feelings.

Her scratches were a call for help. I recommended that Grace do all she could to feature Mai in class, to give her some power and visibility. I suggested a Big Sister from the YWCA so that she could have one person who cared just for her.

These children had many complicated needs, including the need to heal from great sadness. Some dealt with the sadness by withdrawing, others by clinging. Trinh, Deena, Mai, and Abdul needed therapists, but they all came from places where mental problems are unacceptable. Many students came from cultures where creative expression in children isn't valued. Yet, they had great needs to understand and share their experiences. Group storytelling would be great, and art and music therapy might work because children don't need verbal skills for them. Play and laughter are therapeutic. I had never been around kids who loved to laugh as much as ELL kids.

The ELL kids needed help with self-definition. I wanted to put their birthdays on the calendar and take their pictures. I wanted to identify what each child did best. Question games might help. What was their favorite food? What games did they like? What was the scariest thing they ever did? The bravest thing? What was their earliest memory?

With ELL classes, I really understood the value of classrooms small enough that each child could be given individual attention. The kids were at very different developmental and acculturation levels. Some kids were precocious from war experiences but had missed kid experiences. Some children cared for younger siblings, cleaned and cooked, or even did factory piecework at home. A few had no play in their lives.

There were differences in intelligence, motivation to learn, energy, confidence, and likability. There were differences in the amount of trauma the kids had experienced and in the amount of family and community support they received in America. They all had much in common—they were strangers in a strange land, eager to be accepted. They liked games, music, puppets, and cookies. And they had a thousand needs. Compared to American kids, they tended to be better behaved, more respectful of adults, and less spoiled. Grace said the longer they were in America the more likely they were to act up.

It helped me to remember that these kids had simple needs as well as complicated ones, needs to be hugged, helped with spelling words, smiled at, and read to. Even small acts of kindness made a difference.

I had been in class three hours and was ready for a nap. How do teachers do this five days a week, eight hours a day?

September 22, 1999

I approached Sycamore on a crisp morning, with the sky blue, the leaves red and gold, and the light hitting the sycamore just right and turning its trunk silvery. When I walked into the classroom, Khoa jumped up and hugged me in an exaggerated, self-mocking way. He was both affectionate and embarrassed to be seeking affection. Pavel shouted out that there would be a fishing trip next week. I looked at Grace and she shrugged. I apologized, and she said, "Don't feel bad. The kids are really excited about this."

Ly plopped on my lap. Today she wore a Yum-Yum T-shirt and faded bell-bottom jeans. She weighed about forty pounds and reminded me of a hummingbird, light as air, but pure energy. She had a cough and twice I offered her cough drops from my purse. I invited Mai to join us and I read them a Laura Ingalls Wilder story. Ly snuggled in. Mai sat stiffly, but she listened carefully to my voice.

Today Walat was student helper. As he handed out paper and pencils, Grace wrote tool words—"hammer," "nail," "scissors," "screwdriver"—on the board. Walat looked at pictures of these tools with great interest.

Abdul and Pavel scuffled over a pencil. Pavel wore a green sweat suit from Goodwill that left a few inches of skin between his shirt and pants. Instead of watching the board, Pavel doodled and scratched his stomach. I moved over and sat between him and Abdul.

Trinh looked exactly as she had last week, with the same outfit and the same inscrutable expression. Beside her, Deena leafed through a picture book on animals of the jungle. Twice Deena tried to show Trinh a picture and start a talk, but Trinh ignored her.

Whenever Grace asked a question, Fatima raised her hand with ready, but not always right, answers. Fatima and Deena were both from Muslim families, but they were being raised quite differently. Fatima's family was more traditional. She wore long flowery dresses and a head scarf. Deena dressed in a sweat suit and wore her hair in a ponytail.

Ignazio wandered in late. The ELL students were often tardy and Grace was casual about time. She permitted table talk and interruptions in the lessons for side discussions. She limited her discipline to a soft "Let's use our quiet voices now."

Deena and Fatima argued about a book. Grace stayed out of it until Fatima called Deena stupid, then she said, "In this class we are kind to each other." Ly, who had been watching anxiously, smiled to herself.

Abdul had his head on the desk and wasn't even pretending to work. I sat by him and gently prodded him into picking up his pencil. His body language shouted, "Go away," but I persisted.

Grace asked the students to write a letter to members of a sorority to thank them for a fund-raising project for the school. She wrote a simple letter on the board as an example. Walat and Ly followed the format exactly and soon had good letters ready. Pavel's letter was covered with smudges and cross outs: "Thank you for caring about our school. We want you to stay our friends." Deena's letter was neatly written and flowery: "Thank you with all of my heart for your great efforts. I wish you long lives and many great times."

Abdul and I labored over his letter with me doing most of the work. But when it was time to sign his name, Abdul suggested that we sign it, "From one of the kids who learns the best, Abdul."

Mai struggled with handwriting, spelling, and even the sentiment. I had the feeling she had heard few words of thanks herself. But when she finished, I praised her work. She shyly told me she had a Big Sister now, a young woman named Amy who came over Saturday afternoons. Next week Amy was taking her to the park. Mai spoke of Amy as if she were a fairy godmother.

Grace demonstrated simple tools: a lever, a pulley, and an inclined plane. While she talked, the kids passed around Nibbles, a docile black-and-white rat. Except for Trinh, all of the kids appeared to love Nibbles. As Deena whispered and stroked Nibbles, she seemed to relax a little and her blue eyes softened.

We sang "Farmer in the Dell" and used the tool names. Then Grace led the class in a patriotic song, "Columbia, the Gem of the Ocean," which many sang as "Columbus Jump in the Ocean." Still, it was a rousing version that had us all clapping at the end.

I had read of children in a refugee camp in Angola who were singing and dancing as a way to learn their lessons and heal from the trauma of war. I wished we could do more teaching in song.

September 29, 1999—The Fishing Trip

It was a good day for the trip—blue sky, seventy degrees, and still. Pavel ran up to me when I walked into the classroom. He had a pole and a brand-new tackle box filled with lures and a can of government corn labeled for distribution to low-income people. But that corn was for the fish—his mother had packed him a Big Mac and candies. Khoa was jumping up and down like a jack-in-the-box. Deena in her red cape with her blond curls looked like Little Red Riding Hood. She asked if we could bring Nibbles along. Grace said, "No, I'm sorry."

Ignazio unzipped his jacket and slipped Nibbles in by his stomach, but Grace gently lifted Nibbles out and put him away. Fatima held up her arms and said, "Carry me." Grace said, "Our arms are full of equipment." We marched everyone to the special vans and drove to Holmes Lake.

At the lake parking lot, we passed out poles. While I baited hooks, Grace gave instructions on casting and reeling. Abdul,

Ignazio, and Walat had fished before, but Trinh, Ly, and Deena watched what was clearly a new lesson. Pavel proudly prepared his pole, while Khoa cast blithely at the picnic table. Mai hung back, but I took her hand and helped her select a fishing spot. Before he began, Pavel ate his Big Mac; "For energy," he said.

With much shouting and bragging about skills, the other kids spread out along the shore. It was a nice tableau—red and gold trees, silver water, and happy children. Trinh cast once then set her pole down and stared across the lake. Deena's red coat shone against the blue water. She walked over to Trinh and asked her if she needed help. Trinh shook her head no, but Deena stayed beside her anyway. Ly danced along the shore, pirouetting from rock to rock.

Mai found some broken glass and scratched at her arm. I went over and took the glass away. I said, "It isn't good for you to hurt yourself when you do not know what to do."

Ignazio tossed his line, snagging, then ripping, then snagging again. Soon I was retying a hook for him, untangling other lines, rebaiting hooks, and then, miracle of miracles, taking off a fish. Ignazio shouted out, "*Gracias a Dios!*" and held up his five-inch catfish for all to see. Just then Walat caught a little sun perch, which he expertly took off himself. I took his picture holding his fish up. Then he gently put it in our bucket.

Pavel was upset that Walat and Ignazio had caught the first fish and he positioned himself in their area. Meanwhile, Khoa cast his entire pole into the water and jumped in after it. By the time we got him out of the water he was soaked and had lost a shoe and his pole. But he had achieved what he wanted, which was to steal the show from Walat, who had now caught a second fish.

With what sounded like Russian cursing, Pavel redoubled his efforts. Fatima grew discouraged and sat down on a pile of rocks. Soon Deena and Trinh joined her, and the girls watched a green caterpillar crawl across the grass. Fatima wanted to pick it up, but Deena said firmly, "Leave her alone."

Meanwhile, Abdul had also quit fishing but he noticed that Ignazio's line was all tangled up and he worked to unravel the bird nest of tackle. For the first time since I'd met him he seemed interested in something. Walat caught another perch and then Ly pulled in a small bass. She danced around with her fish, looking like happiness personified.

Watching kids fish was a good way to learn about them. Some like Walat and Ly were patient and methodical; others like Pavel and Khoa couldn't settle down. Ignazio was enthusiastic but clumsy. Trinh and Fatima were indifferent to the sport, while Deena, an animal rights activist in the making, kept asking Grace if the fishes' mouths were hurt by the hooks.

With her pole still in the water, Mai wandered off alone. She sat under a willow tree, her hands folded in her lap. The natural world is a great healer and her body looked more relaxed.

Soon we had twenty perch and the small catfish—Walat caught seven, while Pavel hadn't caught any. Pavel's frustration had built, making him a less and less competent fisherman. He wouldn't stay in one spot but ran to wherever anyone else had caught a fish and wrestled for their place. Then, when nothing happened, he would try a new piece of tackle or eat his candies.

Meanwhile, Abdul fixed Fatima's pole and untangled Ly's line. He messed with Ignazio's broken reel. I wondered if we could find him a shop project or even let him follow the maintenance staff around.

Ignazio held a fish up to his lips and kissed it, talking to it as if it were a little pet. Then Deena and Walat released all the fish. As they swam away, Deena asked, "Will they live?"

Grace got out Five Alive and Goldfish. The kids liked those

little cracker fish, but they didn't like the bees that gathered around the juice. Still, Pavel and Ignazio managed to drink three cups of juice each and then needed a bathroom.

Abdul bragged to no one in particular, "I fixed three poles and I'd fix Khoa's, too, if we could find it." Khoa shouted unapologetically, "My pole lives with the fishes now."

Walat, Ly, and Deena gathered and stacked the poles. All the kids looked happy today, the way people do when they are lucky enough to be outdoors in beautiful weather. I thought how rich our country is, and yet we are all inside toiling on gorgeous days. It is hard on everyone, but especially on children.

We took more pictures, passed out the rest of the Goldfish, and then, alas, headed for the vans. Pavel said, "If we could just stay a while longer, I could catch a big fish." I didn't say, "We'll come back soon."

October 14, 1999

It was a blue-sky day and the leaves were turning on the sycamore. There is something about a crisp fall morning, walking into a school, the voices of children, the smell of sunshine on leaves, that brings back my own childhood. I could see Beaver City Elementary, smell the chalk and the cereal breath of my classmates.

I'd been sick for a week. And several of the students had colored get-well cards for me. Khoa was an origami master and his card was large and elaborate. Ly had written, "Miss Mary, you are so nice. I missed you." Deena had drawn fish and flowers and written, "Please get well, Miss Mary." But Mai wouldn't look at me, and Pavel asked accusingly, "Were you really sick?"

These kids had said too many good-byes and they didn't like feeling abandoned, even for a few days. I made a point to state loudly that I was healthy now and would be returning regularly. I passed around pictures of our fishing trip. Pavel asked if he could keep the one of him with his new tackle box. I handed it to him but reflected that Pavel always wanted more attention, more food, and more time with Nibbles. Many of the kids were like him, filled with needs of every kind. Yet there were also kids like Trinh who appeared to want nothing from any of us. Today Trinh moved like a duck on water, movement without motion, gliding.

I watched Mai draw her baby brother, then beside his crib, she drew a giant red Stop sign. I asked her if she had gone to the children's museum with Amy and she nodded. "Amy is good," she said soberly.

While Grace gave a spelling test, Abdul fooled with two video games—Nitro and War Zone. Grace said, "Put them away or I will have to keep them." She whispered to me, "I wish we could ban these games. Yesterday I confiscated Mayhem and Deadly Arts from Khoa. These kids have enough problems without violent role models."

As if to demonstrate her concerns, at just that moment, Abdul and Pavel got into a scuffle. Grace sent both boys to quiet corners to think about their behavior. She said to me, "It's been a rough morning. Khoa was teased on the playground about his purple pants. Ignazio was called a wetback." She sighed. "Many of these kids come from war zones where violence is the first thing people do when they are upset. I want them to learn they have choices."

She called the boys together and talked to them. "Pavel, what else could you have done when Abdul took your backpack?"

Pavel said, "I could have asked him, 'What do you need, buddy?'" Grace hugged him and laughed. "That's right."

Deena wrote her numbers along one side of the paper and

diligently began to spell out words. Ly and Walat did the same. Ignazio, who had some egg yolk on his shirt, kept rubbing his eyes, and I suspected he had stayed up late to see his parents.

Amazingly, Abdul asked for my help and I went to sit by him. With me almost doing his work, we completed the spelling test. He never looked at me, but he smiled when I helped him, and afterward, he showed his paper to the other students.

Deena asked me to feel her forehead. She was hot and said her head hurt. Grace wrote out a slip and sent her to the nurse. She told me that Deena had been stressed lately. Twice this last week Deena had stayed home to translate for her mother's medical appointments.

Khoa handed me a drawing that said, "I like you. Do you like cats?" The words were enclosed in a heart surrounded by small drawings of cats and of me. He'd given me big eyes, a big smile, and very curly hair. I smiled to think that might be how he saw me.

Today's work was a unit on grooming. Fatima wore a long silky pink dress covered with red roses. She had blue nail polish on her fingers and toes. Trinh almost never took off her jacket. Today Ly wore a white corduroy dress with a faux leopard-skin collar and Mary Jane shoes with white lacy socks. Khoa and Pavel looked like they should exchange clothes. Pavel's T-shirt didn't cover his round belly while Khoa wore a Big Red T-shirt that looked like a blanket on him. Only Walat was always carefully groomed in new Kmart clothes.

Ignazio had protruding teeth and Fatima's teeth were very crooked. I wondered if their parents would be able to afford orthodontists later. Many of the kids had bad breath and I wondered if they came from countries without toothbrushes.

Grace explained that Americans brush their teeth two times a day and that we take showers daily. The kids were amazed by this fact. Ignazio said, "In Mexico we took a bath on Saturdays." Ly said, "You will get sick if you take baths when it is cold." Grace said, "Not really. But in the winter you must dry off very well and put on warm clothes right after your bath." Khoa asked, "Do you put on your underwear?" Everyone laughed.

The spelling words—"toothbrush," "toothpaste," "soap," "comb"—were to be used in sentences. Khoa called toothbrushes "toothbutts," and everyone laughed. Grace said, "No more nasty stuff now, Khoa." Deena returned from the nurse and I asked about her family. She whispered, "My mother wants to go back to Bosnia."

Grace showed the class health books. One about hair was entitled *Mama, Do You Love Me?* Khoa joked about flakes in hair and about Ignazio's cowlick. Fatima explained that in her country women wore veils when they went out. She said that only little girls could wear shorts. Older girls must wear dresses.

Ignazio explained that it was hard to stay clean in Mexico. Some mornings there was water and sometimes there wasn't. He said there were rats, not like Nibbles who loved to play, but rats that bit and stole the family's corn. Mai said that her mother had gotten sick in Vietnam because of dirty water. Fatima said that it was the same in Iraq, not enough water and big mean rats. For some reason this got Walat thinking of Iraq. He told the class that in Iraq his dad was rich, but his enemies had threatened to hurt them. They had to move. Abdul had been drawing dolphins. But as he listened to Walat, he switched to sharks.

Grace said the kids could draw something from their old countries. Trinh drew a river with black water. Mai drew a picture of her hut in Vietnam. In front was her mother, a stick figure, holding the hand of Mai, also a stick figure, but with a big smile.

Many refugees yearn for connection with missing or dead parents. Grace encouraged them to bring pictures of their family to school and to look at or kiss the picture whenever they felt like it. She recommended they bring an object from the missing parent. Kids are concrete thinkers and can more easily imagine a parent if they are touching something that stands for the parent.

Ly drew a plane that looked like a silver bird. She told me the villagers thought that she rode on this silver bird to her home in the clouds. She giggled, "We thought America would be in the sky."

Khoa drew a rice field with an old man in it and said, "That is my dead grandpa." Walat drew his fancy home that was burned down by his father's enemies. Pavel drew a picture of his family at a dinner table with empty plates and he said, "In Russia people had no money to buy soup." Deena drew a street filled with dead bodies.

I marveled at these kids' resilience. Many had only been here a few months. They had been starved, shot at, and terrorized, and yet here they were drawing and talking. Some seemed more mangled emotionally than others. Walat and Ly were in good shape; Ignazio and Pavel were basically comfortable with their lives. However, Khoa's constant hyperactive chatter suggested a bad case of nerves, and Trinh and Abdul seemed almost mute from the stress of living in war zones. It is not surprising that traumatized kids who don't speak much English have trouble learning. What is surprising is given their circumstances how much and how quickly most kids learn.

Grace and I talked about rituals—lighting a candle in memory of relatives who died in a war or making a toast to what one most appreciates—small acts that can have great power. I suggested a flower day in the spring when everyone could bring flowers for the people they loved who were no longer with them.

November 4, 1999

The day was cool and cloudy, the sycamore's brown leaves blew in the wind. A few swirled to the ground. When I arrived at the classroom, Walat was drawing a map of train tracks with switching stations and overpasses. Deena looked at a book on horses as she caressed Nibbles. When she smiled at me, I noticed her two front teeth were missing. Mai read a book about a girl who ran away from home. Khoa was reading *Curious George*. Grace whispered that Khoa's oldest brother had just been arrested on drug charges. Pavel proudly showed me his Pokémon toys. His parents might walk to work and have holes in their shoes, but Pavel had the stuff he wanted from television. Ignazio looked at a book on giant cobras. He had a bandage over his eye. Grace thought it was pinkeye and gave him a slip to see the nurse.

The class worked on spelling. Today Grace taught them words for winter clothes—"mittens," "boots," "caps," and "coats." Many of the kids had never lived in a cold place before and were unprepared for winter. Mai asked, "Please, Miss Grace, what is snow?"

Grace wrote the words "wind chill," "sleet," "ice," and "blizzard" on the board. Every time Ly got a word right she yelled out yes. Two months ago, Ly had been quieter, but now she was one of the most enthusiastic students.

Abdul would not do his spelling today. When I offered to help him, he turned away from me. "Abdul," I said, "I would like to be your friend." He smiled, but not at me. Progress with Abdul was like that of the frog climbing up a wall, two inches up and then one back down.

Grace led the class in a song about good grooming. To the tune of "London Bridge" the class belted out, "Here we go to wash our hands, wash our hands." To the "Hokey Pokey" song, they sang the words, "Germs are really mean. But they can't be seen. They will make you sick. Then you're gonna feel ick. Use some soap and water, Scrub your hands to get them clean, Clean's what it's all about." Khoa howled, yipped, and barked creatively instead of singing. Grace ignored him. Ignazio's stomach growled and Abdul and Pavel laughed.

Mai had her shirt on backward. I could see some scratch marks on her arm. I asked about her Big Sister, Amy. She said, "Amy has tests at her school." I said, "Don't worry, Mai, she will come back."

Ly signaled me to sit by her and watch her draw. I thought how hard it was to give these kids all the attention they needed. Indeed, as I watched today, the kids seemed wilder and all wound up. Deena and Fatima were fighting over colored markers. Trinh was zipping and unzipping her jacket. Only Walat seemed on task.

When Grace read *The Crocodile's Toothache* by Shel Silverstein, Ignazio forgot his rumbling stomach and clapped when the crocodile swallowed the dentist. Deena and Ly laughed out loud. Even smart-mouthed Khoa and dreamy Abdul listened. For a few good moments we were all together.

Then it was time to work on silent *e* vs. long *e*. Mai sighed and jabbed her pencil into her desk. Ignazio scratched his belly. Abdul didn't even pick up his pencil. Pavel crossed out a sentence and began another, his nose almost touching his pencil as he strained to write. I made a note to suggest to Grace that he get his eyes checked.

As he scribbled with his stubby pencil, Khoa hummed the "Star-Spangled Banner." I took him a new pencil and realized that, like Grace, I was hooked on this kid. He was mouthy and coarse, but he held our hands on the way to assembly.

I was also falling for Ly with her bright smile and happy talk. I respected Deena's work with her family although she was way too young to be so burdened. Mai's palpable loneliness touched the place in my heart that remembered loneliness. They were all getting to me. I wanted to capture Abdul's attention. I wanted to elicit a look of interest from Trinh, something I vowed I would accomplish before the year was out.

November 17, 1999

When I got to class, Fatima reported that Nibbles had died the day before. Two days ago the class had noticed he had a little blood on his nose and that he wasn't moving around too much. Then yesterday when they came to school he was dead.

Deena had immediately developed a headache and had to go to the nurse for a Tylenol. Mai had pulled her own hair. Ignazio and Abdul had punched each other. Fortunately Grace had channeled their grief into a service for Nibbles. She'd allowed Pavel to run home for a special rock to bury with Nibbles and she'd put Khoa in charge of the funeral. The kids had added a candy cane and a blue crystal to his shoe-box coffin. Ignazio had said a prayer. They all had helped dig the grave in the flower garden of the school. Ly and Deena had cried. Grace had led them in a good-bye song.

The funeral had been well handled, but I could see the grief today. We had a story circle and each student shared one happy memory of Nibbles. Deena remembered one day when Nibbles slept on her lap. Ignazio remembered how much Nibbles liked bananas. Khoa made spirited comments about Nibbles's poop. Ly remembered a day she had drawn Nibbles. Walat recalled the fun Nibbles had with his exercise wheel. Pavel said Nibbles tickled him when he crawled all over his back. Mai and Trinh refused to tell a Nibbles story, but they liked the other kids' stories. Telling stories never fails to produce good in the universe.

Grace whispered that there had been other troubles this week. Khoa was upset that his brother was in jail. Deena had missed several days of school translating for her family with the INS. On the bright side, Pavel would be getting new glasses. When the class was ready to work, Grace suggested we do family drawings.

I circled the room as the students worked on their drawings. Pavel drew his parents in their car with his brother, himself, and his sister in the backseat. He told me, "They are on their way to work and we are going to day care."

Ly drew herself surrounded by family—her mother and father were sewing and her siblings were studying. Ignazio drew himself in the middle of his extended family, which included cousins and grandparents. Fatima drew her parents and siblings giving her presents. Deena drew her mother in bed and the others watching television. Walat drew his house in Iraq with a star on top. He said, "Our house in Iraq was nicer than the one we have here."

Abdul smiled his Mona Lisa smile and drew fish with teeth and wheels where they should have had fins. Khoa's drawing was the biggest and most colorful. He had drawn his siblings around his parents with a big red heart in the center of the picture and everyone holding hands. He pointed to the tallest brother and said, "My dad hired a lawyer. We'll get his butt out of jail."

Mai drew a picture of her father, stepmother, and baby brother. I asked her why she was not in the picture, and she said,

"I am in Vietnam." I asked if she had a picture of her mother and she nodded yes. I said, "Carry that picture with you and whenever you look at it, your mother will be smiling at you." She looked at me carefully and then nodded again.

Grace explained the Thanksgiving story and suggested a game with Thanksgiving words. Normally games animate this class, but today even Ly and Khoa were low-key. When Grace called on Walat he was under the table looking for his eraser. Deena had a headache and lay her head on her desk.

Abdul and Khoa picked at each other, trying to start a fight. I remembered something Grace had told me earlier about Abdul. She had described him as not following rules. But she said, "He recently arrived from a war zone and there were no rules. No good rules anyway." She told me about a Bosnian boy whose dad had taught him, "Always attack first," which may have been a good rule in Bosnia, but it didn't work well at Sycamore School.

Grace took out a picture book and told them the story of the *Mayflower*. The pictures were from a book entitled *A Better Life*. The best students paid attention, but unfortunately, the kids who most needed to pay attention didn't. Khoa was listening a little because when Grace talked about the Pilgrims' hard times he shouted out, "Boohoohoo." Grace asked what was the name of their boat and Deena answered, "The *Titanic*."

Fatima was impressed with the fact that there were no bathrooms on the *Mayflower*, a fact that generated a host of raucous remarks from Khoa. Ignazio was most impressed that the Pilgrims had only cold food and not much of that.

Grace showed them pictures of the *Mayflower* landing and of the Indians helping them plant corn by burying little fish by each plant. When Grace showed a picture of Massasoit, the

Indian leader at the first Thanksgiving, Ly said, "He looks Vietnamese."

Khoa shouted with great enthusiasm, "Let's all meet at school for Thanksgiving dinner."

Pavel said, "I will go shoot rabbits for our food."

Deena said, "Please don't kill a rabbit."

Ly announced that last night someone had thrown a rock in the window of their home. Grace asked if her parents called the police and she nodded. The children discussed robbers and getting hurt. Deena, Mai, and Pavel seemed especially anxious during this discussion. Grace tried to make good things happen but the tone remained somber. We kept returning to themes of loss. Nibbles's death had cast a pall over the class. When I left, even the sycamore was in shadow.

November 24, 1999—Thanksgiving Day Celebration

The sycamore flamed in the morning light, and this morning the blazing tree made me philosophical. I wondered if this was what amazed Moses, a tree backlit by sunrise, and made him feel God spoke to him.

As I walked in, Khoa carried over a white rat with a brown head and a mark down his back. After much deliberation, the kids had named this rat Sunny, because of his happy disposition. As I patted Sunny, I noticed that the kids seemed perkier. Deena was handing out hard candies. All the others clustered around us, laughing at Sunny's movements and explaining the process of selecting this rat from the psychology lab at the university.

Pavel came up to show me his new Coke-bottle glasses, which he felt made him look smart. I thought they gave him a rather comedic, Dickensian look, but I didn't challenge his opinion. Instead, I ruffled his hair and offered to help him finish his homework.

Mai approached me shyly and stood by my side as I helped Pavel. When I finished, she pulled out a black-and-white photo of a woman in a cotton dress in front of a flowering bush. The woman was squinting into the sun and her face looked like Mai's. I said, "You look like your mother." She hugged the picture to her chest.

Grace beckoned me to a corner of the room and told me that Khoa had been assigned to a class for behavior-disordered students for two hours each day. He was learning to be more compliant and proper in class. That was good for him and for the others, but Grace missed the old Khoa.

The school custodian, Mr. Trvdy, had agreed to let Abdul shadow him a couple hours a week. Abdul started yesterday and seemed proud of his new job. He'd told Grace, "From now on I'll be fixing up this school."

Grace reminded the class of the Thanksgiving Day story and read a book on the arrival of the Vietnamese boat people in America. Trinh listened with interest. Mai looked closely at the pictures of Vietnam and twice whispered something to Khoa. When he examined the cover to the book, Khoa said happily, "That boy was my friend in Vietnam."

A few minutes after nine, we marched to the next-door classroom. The students from the other ELL classroom had prepared a tablecloth on the floor with hand-decorated paper napkins. Grace handed every student an Indian headdress or a Pilgrim's cap. They put on their costumes and giggled at each other.

Grace led the class in songs. As they belted out the songs "The More We Get Together the Happier We'll Be" and, of course, "Over the River and through the Woods," all the random energy became group energy.

I reflected how fitting it was that this class celebrate Thanksgiving, the refugee's holiday, the holiday that said we came to a new land and endured hardships, but we survived. The Native Americans said to the Pilgrims, "Welcome, there is room for us all. We will help you until you can take care of yourselves."

The Sycamore students' stories were unique to their places and times, yet universal to the American condition. The refugee kids had tales as harrowing as that of the Pilgrims, but now they were warm, well-fed, and safe. Of course, there was sadness and poverty in the room, but there was also the sweet glaze of hope.

With her red jacket and blond curls, Deena sang and clapped, as exuberant a Little Red Riding Hood as I'd ever seen. Ly showed me her tattoo of a dragon on her left wrist. Then she jumped on my lap and nestled in.

While Walat and Fatima passed out slices of bread and pumpkin pie, Grace served cups of chicken soup. Then she said, "Let's all go around the table and say what we are thankful for." Ignazio, his mouth full of soup, said, "Food," and everyone laughed. Trinh whispered, "My house," so quietly only a few of us heard her. Walat said, "I am thankful for books." Khoa shouted out, "Toys and pizza."

Abdul didn't want to answer, but when Grace pushed he said shyly, "My teachers." Mai said, "I am thankful for Amy and my baby brother." Deena said, "For our church that gave us clothes and furniture." Fatima said, "I am thankful to the hospital that treated my burns." Pavel said, "I am thankful for Sunny." Everyone cheered. Ly said, "I am thankful for Miss Mary." I asked myself, How did I deserve this honor?

We ate the healthy soup in silence. Unlike many American children, these children don't take food for granted. They came from places where food is respected and where people had been hungry. But today's meal was more than vitamin supplements designed to keep humans alive. Food celebrated the soul of our little community. It is our most ancient and beautiful ritual of connection.

While the kids ate, Walat took pictures with Grace's camera. Khoa, Pavel, and Ignazio got into a contest to see who could drink the most cider. The tables were cleared and the music games began, "Itsy Bitsy Spider" was first, followed by "Head, Shoulders, Knees, and Toes," then the "Chicken Dance." Only Ignazio and Trinh didn't seem to like dancing. Trinh didn't have the energy and Ignazio just didn't like to move much.

By noon the music was Cuban music, easy to dance to any way we liked. Deena passed out temporary tattoos. Walat took photo after photo of the singers and dancers. Khoa mugged for the camera, sticking out his tongue and then his behind. Abdul twirled a hula hoop in time to the music. Mai, usually so serious, did a mean belly dance. Ly and Fatima held hands and twirled in a circle. Deena joined in on the choruses, softly, but with us. Only Trinh was in a corner watching.

It takes so little to make a party with children—a little food and permission to dance and sing. I was happier than I usually felt. The energy and the joy were infectious and I started thinking of all I was thankful for—my health, my family, my work, and finally my time with these kids who brought into my life something I hadn't had for a long time—the strong, fresh energy of childhood.

January 4, 2000

We made it into the new year with no Y2K disasters in our town. As I walked past the bare sycamore I thought that a new century had commenced and that the new century belonged to these children, not to me.

I arrived in the cold classroom to the news that Fatima had broken her arm. She had a cast covered with Snoopys and was playing Uno with Deena. It was below zero outside and Deena was wearing sandals and socks decorated with reindeer and Christmas trees. She had only her red cloak for a coat. I sat down beside the girls, watching the game and smelling their familiar garlic breath.

Pavel came over and allowed me to stroke Sunny. Ly jumped in my lap and showed me a puzzle she was working on. But when I unthinkingly asked about her holidays, she changed the subject.

Grace was worried about Deena, who had made low scores on standardized tests that require fluent English. Her parents felt she should have made a hundred percent on this test. Grace had tried to explain that no one made a hundred percent, but Deena's father felt Grace was being too easy on Deena. They had ordered Deena to her room from after school until bedtime every day for a month. Still Deena didn't seem too much the worse for wear. At least she knew her parents considered education important.

Grace said Abdul had been placed in a special education class first period and would come in at 9:00. She had fought this placement all first semester but had now acquiesced. Abdul wasn't even trying to learn to read.

Grace announced that she would be gone the next day because of a funeral. Mai twisted around in her seat and looked as if she might cry. I put my arm on her shoulder and asked, "Do you feel sad that Miss Grace will be gone tomorrow?" She nodded miserably but calmed down a bit.

Fatima asked, "Can I come with you, Miss Grace? I'll be good." Ignazio said he wouldn't come to school if Grace couldn't be there. Walat asked me if I could come and be the teacher. Deena worried the new teacher would be mean. Grace said, "No. The substitute teacher will be kind."

Khoa arrived late. His hair was still uncut but he wore a new warm coat. He sat down quietly and participated appropriately. Only once did he speak out of turn and that was to whisper to me that his brother was home. Otherwise, he was preoccupied with whether he would get his name on the list of students who caused trouble.

Ly was more restless this morning. As she had assimilated, she'd grown louder, more assertive, and more American in her actions. Today she'd rapidly finished her seatwork and she rolled her eyes impatiently that others were so slow. Ly had blossomed into a confident, loving girl, who also could be mouthy and impatient.

Ly sat gratefully by my side, not so much listening to my reading as absorbing me. She told me her family was Buddhist and didn't get a Christmas tree. She had wanted a tree—it's understandable in a country where Christmas is on TV from October until January.

We were all happy to be back together. Even a cold room with a wheezing heater had clean paper, sharp pencils, and a teacher to suggest that the universe was a bright, well-organized place that smelled like books and chalk.

Abdul came in at 9:00. He had grown taller in the two weeks since I'd seen him. He showed me his key ring with a key to the tool room and the furnace room. He reported that he had been checking the pipes with Mr. Trvdy, "his boss." He could have been president, he was so proud.

Grace had a clear plastic globe for the lesson, and she found the countries of her students and asked them to tell about their homelands. Deena said, "Bosnia used to be a beautiful place with many forests." "There were floods in Vietnam every year during our rainy season," Ly said. Khoa added, "There were cobras and rats in the rice fields."

Ignazio told of the flooding in Mexico near his home. He said, "The river was filled with frogs, and after the river went away, the frogs stayed in our yard." Pavel said, "It snows all winter long in Russia."

Grace asked what the big chunks of land were on the globe. The kids had various answers—"cigarettes," "islands," "cabinets." Grace was gentle with the wrong answers, "No," she said tentatively, as if the answer were almost good enough to be correct. "The right word is *continent*."

While Grace read a book with pictures on the history of the earth, Khoa played with Sunny, and Pavel pulled some toys out of his backpack. Grace had to reprimand both boys. Ignazio asked for my help and we struggled with the scrambled spelling words.

Abdul put his feet on a chair and didn't even pretend to work. I went over to sit by him and asked about his job. He said, "I like it, but they don't pay me."

Khoa's father was coming for a conference. Khoa wriggled in his seat and looked at the clock every few minutes. He showed me a report that had half happy faces and half sad faces and asked me if he had enough happy faces to stay in school. I explained that he wouldn't be kicked out of school. I said, "We want and need you at this school."

Grace decided to give the kids a pick-me-up. She taught them all twelve verses of "Hickory Dickory Dock." Ly smiled ear to ear as she sang. Mai couldn't carry a tune, but she belted it out anyway. Ignazio drummed on his desk. Not yet fully socialized, Khoa added a few nasty words here and there. Deena swayed to the music. Everyone but Abdul and Trinh sang.

Singing warmed us up. Some kids soloed, other kids didn't want to and Grace didn't make them. I remember a mean teacher who made me sing in front of the class when I was in second grade. I was so frightened when I tried to sing that nothing came out. Thank goodness, Grace was kinder. I couldn't bear to watch these kids get pushed around.

February 4, 2000

It was a gray, cold day, the kind of day that induces epidemic seasonal affective disorder. I was glad I had these kids to cheer me up. But this morning no one jumped up, as they sometimes did to shout, "Miss Mary, sit by me."

Grace looked tired. She had a bad cold and had been at the school every night with conferences. Fortunately, the class was getting ready to celebrate Tet. As students filed in, I filled red-and-gold paper envelopes with money and notes. Then I sat by Mai and Fatima and we looked at a book filled with pictures of flowers and butterflies, a good book for February.

Almost all the kids were talking; only Ly and Trinh's table was quiet. Ly was drawing ballerinas and Trinh quietly stared into space. Deena brought over Uno cards and she and Trinh began a game. Fatima still had her cast on and all the kids had written or drawn on it. By now I could recognize Ly's and Khoa's excellent art.

Mai told me her father's factory was having layoffs. As she chatted with me, I realized that we had a friendship of sorts. I liked and understood this tiny, angry girl, and she liked me, a gray-haired psychologist. It was a proud moment.

Grace read a story about Vietnam called *The Lotus Seed*. The kids listened, but afterward, they wouldn't do their seatwork. Usually, this class liked group work; they were a collective culture and floundered when they were left on their own. I wondered how they would change as they moved into the American system.

Abdul poked Walat and generally disrupted the class until, with a sigh, Grace wrote his name on the board. However, when I asked Abdul about his job, he said that he had earlier looked at the heater in the school's basement. Mr. Trvdy had asked him to carry the crescent wrench because he was so strong. As he told me this, he calmed down.

Ly wandered around the room, first to the bathroom, then to sharpen her pencil, and then to check on Sunny. Ignazio tilted his chair so far back that he fell over backward. Khoa laughed uproariously. Ignazio, who wasn't hurt, smiled sheepishly. Pavel farted loudly and the laughter started up again. Deena asked to go to the school nurse. Grace looked as if she would prefer to be home in bed. It was not this class's finest hour.

When all else failed, Grace encouraged stories. Khoa said, "When we flew to America we came across a great ocean." Abdul told how his family had been airlifted by helicopter from a place in the desert. Deena said they had dinner on the plane. "Very delicious. Ice and noodles."

Khoa told of Tet in Vietnam at his grandmother's house. He had burned incense sticks on a shrine to his relatives. He showed us some incense sticks. Almost all these kids carried totems of their former countries. Mai had her mother's picture. Ignazio wore a leather belt made by his uncle, and Pavel still had his favorite toys from Russia. Fatima carried a twig with one green leaf that her grandmother sent her from Iraq. Walat spoke of the Turkish delight that his family saved for special days. Deena's grandmother sent her spinach gum that she passed around.

I asked about the future. Walat announced he would be an engineer. Fatima said she would like to be a bride in a beautiful

white American dress. Ly said she would be a doctor in Vietnam. Khoa said he would be a criminal, but when nobody
laughed, he changed his future career to fireman.

Grace and Walat pulled the shades, turned off the lights, and
turned on the video. We got to see a movie of *The Lotus Seed,*
which began with a poem.

> *Nothing that grows in a pond*
> *Surpasses the beauty of a lotus flower,*
> *With its green leaves and silky yellow styles*
> *Amidst milky white petals.*
> *Though mired in mud, its silky yellow styles,*
> *Its milky white petals and green leaves*
> *Do not smell of mud.*
> —ANONYMOUS

In the film, women in traditional gowns sell flowers along
the Perfume River in Hue. But the hero is a young girl who
tells the story of the lotus. All of the kids were spellbound, but
especially Khoa, Mai, Ly, and Trinh. The lotus seed could survive cold and fire, last a hundred years, and still grow all over
the world. The lotus was a good symbol for Ly. She had been
through so much, in so much metaphorical mud, and yet, she
was emerging clean and beautiful.

Khoa loudly said, "When this movie ends, I will explain
everything to you." Mai said, "I come from a town like that
one." Twice Khoa shouted out, "I know her." Once Ly said,
"That is my friend." For the first time all year, Trinh's eyes were
sparkly and her face shone.

I thought how rarely Trinh saw a face like hers on TV, how
rarely the hero of any story was a ten-year-old Vietnamese girl.
This was too bad since many girls like Ly and Trinh were heroes
and deserved to be recognized. Also, it helped all girls to see

themselves reflected in that great mirror of life, the television. Being represented signaled the girls that their story mattered. As I watched Trinh become animated, I realized how badly she needed to hear that message.

We need to hear refugee stories; they are more interesting and hopeful than many of the stories we do hear. We Americans watch more movies about space aliens and serial killers than we do about Vietnamese children. But today Trinh blossomed. She spoke for the first time in class. She said, "That little girl looked like me."

As the children left, I handed out "lisi," the special red-and-gold packets with dollar bills. Grace was smiling. I was temporarily cured of my seasonal affective disorder.

February 16, 2000

Before all the kids arrived, Grace talked about Abdul. She was thinking of getting a translator for a meeting with his parents. She wanted to ask how Abdul was at home and if he was different since the family had been bombed crossing the mountains.

As we talked, Abdul arrived wearing a new blue-and-white-checkered shirt. With his creamy skin and big liquid eyes, his appearance was perfect but his psyche had been damaged. The pathology of the world had injured this boy. How different the Gulf War must have looked to Abdul than it had to me.

In fact, all the historical events these kids had experienced seem different to me now. I am much more aware now that many Vietnamese paid a terrible price for being our friends during what they call the American War. The wars in Croatia and Bosnia seem much sadder now that I know children from those countries. Now, every war has a human face. Nothing is abstract and faraway anymore.

Ly raced into the room and handed me a beautiful hand-made valentine that said "I love Miss Mary." I almost wept.

This week the spelling words were about feelings. Grace read them out: "Happy," "sad," "mad," "surprised," and "scared." The word "sad" triggered Pavel to bring up the rat's death. Deena said quickly, "We are happy to have a new rat." Fatima said, "I was scared to fly to America."

I asked about anger. Abdul said, "I'm mad at my father for shouting at me." Grace and I exchanged looks. Ignazio said, "I am mad when we don't have enough to eat." Mai said, "I am mad when my father doesn't come home from work."

Grace read a book entitled, *What Would You Do?* The first question was, "What would you do if you went home from school and were locked out?" Khoa joked he would pee in the bushes. Deena said, "I would be scared and sad." Ly said, "I would pray for my mother to return." Pavel said, "I would break in."

This led to another animated round of robbery stories. The kids thought that in America all robbers were African Americans. Grace worked to dispel this myth, but there was a big issue here. Fatima said she had seen blacks stab people on television, and Abdul said his parents were afraid of blacks and wouldn't go out at night for fear black people would rob them. This fear came mostly from watching television and movies where so often African Americans are portrayed as criminals.

Grace explained 911 and also what to do if your parents are not home after school—look for a Neighborhood Watch house sign in a window, go to that house, and call the police. The kids were clearly skeptical. Many came from countries where the police were associated with violence against ordinary people.

We moved back to "sad." Deena felt sad in Bosnia whenever she heard gunfire. Mai said, "I felt sad when my mother died." Grace hugged her and said, "I am glad you told us that." Khoa said, "I would feel sad if a dog barfed on me." Everyone laughed.

Pavel said, "I am sad when kids pick on me." That led to a discussion of bullies and prejudice, which all of the kids had experienced. It was hard to sort out which were usual school bully stories and which were stories of prejudice. These kids, like the African Americans they feared, were sometimes unfairly pegged as having a host of undesirable qualities.

Grace talked about prejudice, about how it came from fear and ignorance and about how it could hurt people's feelings. She asked the class to promise her they wouldn't be prejudiced and hurtful of others. They solemnly nodded.

She said that if the kids were picked on, they should tell a teacher. Abdul made his fists like boxing gloves and said, "I would fight the bullies." All of the boys loudly agreed. Ly said, "I don't think a teacher could help." Silently, I had to agree with Ly.

Khoa said that he had bad dreams after he stayed up watching horror movies with his brothers. I wished his brothers were a little more protective of him. Better role modeling at home could make a big difference. Pavel and Ignazio also had been frightened by "bad movies." The kids interrupted each other with stories of scary things. I thought of Adrienne Rich's line, "That which cannot be spoken becomes unspeakable." Better to speak here where the kids had Grace, myself, and the pets to calm them down afterward.

Grace handed out paper and crayons and asked the kids to draw pictures of bad dreams they'd had. Trinh drew a picture of a car following her home from school. Ignazio drew a picture of big dogs chasing him and wrote, "A dog chased me." Then he said to Grace, "That's me. I have a gun." Grace said, "I hope it's a tranquilizer gun."

Mai drew a house fire with her baby brother and stepmother on the second floor looking out a window and she and her father standing outside. After all his statements about having no fear, Abdul could think of nothing to draw. I reflected on the irony that he'd been bombed and seen his brother freeze to death. Yet, he insisted he had no fear. Walat, who had been quiet during the discussion, drew a picture of airplanes with bombs dropping from their bellies. I wondered if he, like Abdul, had been bombed.

Khoa, the best artist in the class, drew himself in bed with two ghosts and a glittery disco ball above him. He drew himself sleeping with a sword by his side. He said, "I'm not scared. I boogie with the ghosts." Then he danced salaciously for the benefit of us all.

Grace looked through the drawings then said, "Before you go today, I think we should draw a happy picture." All the students spent a few minutes drawing something that made them smile.

March 15, 2000

It was a gorgeous spring morning. The sycamore hadn't yet leafed out, but soon it would. Fatima waved her cast-free arm at me. Ly came over to hug me and she kept hugging me. Khoa asked me to sit by him. Much to my surprise, Trinh smiled at me. She must have had a wild bout of spring fever.

I asked Abdul how he was. He said proudly that he was working on pipes in the boys' bathroom. He said, "I don't have time to come to class. I should be helping Mr. Trvdy."

Grace whispered about the conference with Abdul's mother,

who had come with a translator. The mother was pregnant, due in May. Grace told her that Abdul wasn't ready to pass into the next grade. The mother told Grace that in the old country kids were beaten if they didn't learn and she recommended that the school whip Abdul. When Grace explained that we don't do that in America, the mother hadn't been pleased.

When the mother talked about the war, she broke into sobs. When Grace gently asked if Abdul had experienced any toxic chemicals, his mother beat her breasts and tried to run out of the room. Grace apologized for upsetting her and told her about Abdul's work with the maintenance man. The mother asked if the school was working her son instead of teaching him. As Grace told me this story, she rolled her eyes.

That morning Grace explained about St. Patrick's Day and reminded the kids to wear green. Mai had heard that if they didn't wear green they would be pinched. Deena had heard that boys chased the girls and kissed them. These rumors led to whispers and worried looks. Grace said that she didn't think they would get pinched or kissed, but to wear green just to be safe. The scared looks reminded me just how vulnerable these kids were. Everything here was new, and until they experienced events, they had no way to know they were safe.

Grace gave the kids the assignment of unscrambling their spelling words. Abdul asked for my help. Even though we spoke very little, I was starting to feel a connection with him. I would be hard-pressed to explain why. It was something about the way he smiled at me, a more connected smile. Together we finished ahead of some of the others.

He lifted his paper high above his head and announced loudly that he was finished. It was the first time all year he had truly completed work early. Grace made him an award that was covered with ribbons and stars and said, "To Abdul, for paying attention in class and doing his work." Abdul held the award up for all to see. In fact, he held his award all morning.

Trinh worked slowly and twice Deena leaned over to help her. Ly wore new glasses today. They made her look more serious; still, when she saw me looking at her, she broke into her usual grin. Neither Ignazio nor Pavel finished their work. Abdul lorded his finished piece over them. Khoa gave up halfway through and poked at Pavel. Pavel almost punched him, but then he just made a joke and looked away. Grace said, "Thank you, Pavel, for using your head not your fists." Fatima, Trinh, and Deena worked together and soon had their papers done perfectly. Abdul bragged to Walat, "I got a hundred on that paper."

Class ended with the kids inviting me to the St. Patrick's Day party. I suspected they wanted a protector in the event they were attacked by kissing or pinching kids.

As the class left, Grace told me sadly that Sycamore had "lost points" because the students didn't score well on standardized tests. Resources would be cut and they'd lose their media specialist and their music and art staff. Grace said that she'd have to teach to the tests which she hated to do, especially with these kids who needed practical knowledge, socialization, and help with trauma.

May 3, 2000

It was a beautiful spring day. Today the sycamore had lime green leaves rustling against its gold-and-white-streaked trunk. As I walked into school, I thought, where has the year gone? How could it have disappeared so quickly?

Class began with our flower ceremony for those we loved who were gone. The kids had brought locally blooming flowers—lilacs, daffodils, tulips, jonquils, and forsythia. Everyone had someone they wanted to remember and Grace asked each child to say what they liked about that person. Then they could put the flowers in a communal vase.

Deena said, "My uncles carried me whenever we went to the market." Mai said, "My mother would be happy I have a Big Sister." Trinh said, "My parents took good care of me." Ignazio said, "My grandmother made great tamales and dulces." Khoa said first, "My grandfathers had lots of girlfriends with big boobies." Grace frowned at him and he changed his story: "My grandfathers worked hard so that we could have rice to eat."

Abdul's eyes were faraway and when it came time for him to put his lilac in the vase he plopped it in without saying anything. He spilled some water from the vase. Grace put her arm on his shoulder and said, "That flower was for your brother. I am sure he was a good boy like you."

Afterward the class was silent. Pavel was reading a book about a steam shovel. Abdul noticed this and bragged to no one in particular that he could drive a steam shovel. Ignazio was wearing an Outback Steakhouse T-shirt. I wondered if he'd actually been there or if this shirt showed up in a Goodwill barrel. Ignazio's English was only marginally better, but only Abdul would be held back in the same classes next year. Even Trinh would move forward, thanks mainly to Deena's tutoring.

To celebrate Cinco de Mayo, Grace read about Mexico. Ignazio interrupted her constantly to say that his family celebrated with a fiesta. When she finished the book, Grace located Mexico for the students on her big wall map. Ignazio described the delicious food—pineapple, ceviche, and enchiladas.

Abdul began pounding on his desk. Walat said loudly, "Excuse me, Abdul," and he stopped.

Grace asked Ignazio to tell about Cinco de Mayo. Before he could begin, Khoa asked in a way that made kissing sound naughty, "Do you kiss your girlfriend on that day?" Ignazio ignored him and said that in Mexico the boys play basketball and light firecrackers. The grown-ups have a dance at night. Khoa shouted, "Do you dance dirty with girls?" Ignazio looked at the floor, embarrassed.

Grace asked Ignazio to teach the kids a few Spanish words. Ignazio wrote the word for "cow" in Spanish, and Grace asked about this word in Vietnamese and Arabic. Everyone was eager to share information about their cultures of origin. They liked knowing things the teacher and the other kids didn't know. As I said good-bye, Ignazio shouted, "*Adios,* Señora Maria."

May 23, 2000

My last day I walked past the sycamore, with its crown of new green leaves, and entered the school. I brought all the students pencils as good-bye gifts. As I passed them out, I said, "If you see me on the street, come over and give me a hug." Even Trinh smiled.

The class had prepared me cards. Ly's was ornate with heartfelt statements of feeling: "You help us. We love you." Khoa's card said, "Marry me." Mai gave me a card covered with flowers that said, "I hope you will come back next year." I asked if she would see Amy over the summer. Mai nodded happily and I thought how much difference a college student had made in the life of this child.

Khoa was still a troublemaker. Trinh wore the same clothes, but with Deena's help she had crawled a little ways out of her shell. Fatima's English was much better and she had learned to read. Deena was more confident now. Helping her own family and Trinh had given her courage and maturity. Still, I worried about all the school Deena missed while she translated for her family. I remembered a line I'd read: "No one gets ahead in America without leaving people behind." Deena wasn't leaving anyone behind, even fish and rats.

Today Ly again said to me, "You are so beautiful." I believe that she really thought this. There had been some kind of deep, almost mystical, connection between us, as if we recognized each other's souls.

Grace announced three more days of school. She showed the kids the peonies she had picked and taught them to spell *peony*. Ly said they looked like lotuses. Yes, I thought, Ly is the lotus of the class, the truly strong and resilient one.

The kids looked nervous and uncertain about the long summer ahead. Some would move. Many would spend the summer in cheap day-care programs or at home alone, latchkey kids with few of the advantages of middle-class kids. No tennis camps or family vacations for them. A few, like Ignazio, might get to visit relatives in their home countries. A few would go to the community action program's day camp. As Grace read a story about summer, I realized how important school was to these kids. It's where they play, see their friends and teachers, get food and clothes.

Grace explained about sunburns, suntan lotion, and Lyme disease. Then she told the kids about city soccer, baseball leagues, and swimming lessons. She warned them to be careful around water. Grace suggested swimming lessons and the summer reading program at the library.

Then Grace handed out a word puzzler based on summer words. Abdul asked for my help and I sat down beside him. He told me he had helped paint some of the pipes in the basement of the school. As we worked together, I remembered our first meeting, how he had turned away from me so that he wouldn't have to work with me.

Khoa drew a picture of surfers and bragged that he had surfed in Vietnam. Abdul worried that somebody in the class might drown in the summer. Grace changed the subject and told them she would bring some seashells to school tomorrow. Abdul whispered to himself, "I'll take them from her. I'll steal those seashells."

I realized he was trying to tell me he was upset I was leaving. I hugged him and said, "Don't worry. I will see you again, Abdul."

Grace handed out papers with seashells on them. The kids were to count and color them and sort them by kind. Most of the kids liked sorting and classifying. We graphed the seashells. I helped Pavel, who had some trouble getting organized. I told him I hoped he could go fishing this summer.

Deena carefully put a sticker tattoo of an American flag on my arm. She used her own spit to wet it and pressed it warmly against my skin. When Fatima whined, "Why can't you come tomorrow?" I regretfully announced my last day.

Grace picked up on the anxiety and sadness and suggested singing some songs. We started with, "On the first day of summer my true love gave to me a robin in a maple tree," and sang on through two ducks, three bees a buzzing, four watermelons and more. I watched each face as Grace led them in song. Most of the faces were so open and sincere that it broke my heart.

Deena belted out the words. Trinh was quiet, but she smiled at me twice. She seemed less wooden today, more comfortable with herself and with the other kids. Mai was better, too. She no longer scratched herself, and she talked more positively about her stepmother and baby brother. She was reaching out for love, and her family and Amy were reaching back. Khoa was still mouthy and unkempt, but he had learned English. Since he started in the behavior-disordered class, he was less impulsive and more subdued. Eventually Khoa would fit into the school system better, but I'd miss the Curious George of our group.

I wanted to believe that all was not lost with Abdul, that given enough time and love, someone could connect with him and he could be a mainstream student and a healthy person. Mr. Trvdy and I had made some progress. Maybe together, next year, we could love him into relationships with us and with other Americans.

Ly had blossomed. She had a big smile and her hand was always up with answers. She was wise, loving, and confident—a Willa Cather heroine. It speaks well for our species that we can produce a Ly now and then.

Walat had come to us strong and he was leaving strong. I had great respect for his inner strength. He also had an intact family and parents who were rapidly becoming bicultural. Pavel was struggling with his academics, but he was happy socially. His parents were loving but not particularly sensible. I wished they had a good cultural broker.

Deena was that strange mix of strong and vulnerable that kids sometimes are. She had healed herself by healing others. Ignazio was no mental giant, but his English was improving. If only his parents could be home evenings.

To say good-bye, Mai gave me a shy wave. Ignazio handed me a root-beer lollipop. Abdul didn't hug me, but he stood almost on top of me. I hugged him and said, "I will miss you, Abdul."

Fatima said, "I will miss you, Miss Mary."

Mai said, "You promised to come back."

Deena's tattoo stayed on my arm all day. It was hard to scrub off in the bath. Even the next day I could see its shadow on my skin. Whenever I looked at it, my heart ached.

CHAPTER 6

TEENAGERS— MOHAMMED MEETS MADONNA

LIEM

"My parents have two rules for me: No trouble and all A's."

Liem's dad had been a prisoner of war in Vietnam. During the day he'd been given Sisyphean labors; he was forced to build houses, then forced to tear them down. He'd performed both jobs diligently or he would have been killed. At night he slept in a small cage like an animal.

Liem was born about a year after his father was released from the camp. Although the family lived in a village of fishermen, they couldn't afford to eat the fish his father caught, and Liem often went to bed hungry. His parents had to borrow money to send him to school, and the teachers were harsh.

In 1992 the family came to America. On the plane, the family didn't eat; they had never seen Western food and didn't know how to use the utensils the airline provided. They were frightened of the airport's elevator; they didn't know how to work the controls and felt as if they were locked in a moving box. In Lincoln they were met by Liem's uncle, who had a one-bedroom apartment for his family of six. The first few months fifteen people lived in that apartment.

Eventually Liem's dad found a job as a janitor and his mom was hired at an electronics plant. His dad learned a little English, but his mother gave up and Liem spoke only Vietnamese with his parents. The family rented their own small house in "Little Vietnam" and joined the Buddhist temple. Liem said, "My parents have two rules for me: No trouble and all A's."

The third day in Nebraska, Liem walked to middle school. It was a sleety day and he had no jacket, but mostly he trembled from fear. He spoke no English and worried the American kids would make fun of him and beat him up, both of which they did. He knew that his parents had sacrificed everything so that he could be educated and he was determined to be an A student.

He met other Vietnamese students and kind teachers. Soon he was playing soccer and making good grades. Any word he didn't know he wrote down and looked up in the dictionary. He memorized these word lists conscientiously.

After school he helped with chores, studied, and cared for his younger siblings. In the summer he hoed beans and detassled corn. He'd been invited into a gang but he declined. He was friendly with Vietnamese gang kids, but not too friendly.

Liem was an expert at cultural switching. He said, "I'm an American teenager at school, but at home I am Vietnamese." He was horrified by how American kids talked about their parents. He would never drink, smoke, or disobey his family, and he wouldn't date until after college.

One day when it was very cold, Liem had walked to Holmes Park and snapped a picture of the frozen lake. He'd sent this picture to Vietnam where it had utterly confused his relatives. They couldn't figure out the milky hard water with people skating on it.

Liem had gone back to visit his grandmother for a month. He'd fished, played soccer, and savored his grandmother's cooking. He sighed as he talked about that time. He was grateful for Nebraska's economic rewards and educational system, but he missed the communal life of Vietnam.

Liem wanted a college degree, a high-paying job, and a quiet life helping his parents. He was worried about his ACT scores and his essay writing. His only goal was to be a good son. He had many of the attributes of resilience and a strong family and community. Even with their limited English and scant understanding of American culture, his parents were managing to keep him on a good course and away from gangs. Because he was bright, studious, and young when he came here, Liem was likely to make it into college. But it would take every calorie of energy he and his family had to make this happen.

ANTON
"I saw my father and grandfather shot in our living room."

Anton was a tall and well-dressed Bosnian boy with big brown eyes. Superficially, he had good social skills, but underneath he was immature. He had had no childhood. He'd had too many dislocations and witnessed too many murders. He was constantly in over his head.

I saw Anton for an evaluation. The referral said Anton was struggling with grades. That was a kind way to put it; I saw no evidence he was actually struggling. His teachers were worried about suicide or that he might provoke the gang kids into hurting him. Anton had no common sense and a kind of manic energy that constantly had him in trouble.

He had a terrible history, a fractured family, and little contact with the Bosnian community. His mother couldn't get along with anyone, even her own people. Neither Anton nor his mother had many attributes of resilience. Indeed, he had no ways to calm himself down.

Anton was born in a small town one hundred miles from Tuzla. He was fifteen now, seven when the war began in 1992. Of his life before the war, he said, "It was a good life, an ordinary life. I played soccer, watched television, and screwed around with my friends."

At first Anton was reluctant to talk about the war, but when he started he couldn't stop. He said, "I saw my father and grandfather shot in our living room."

Then the soldiers set fire to their home. He, his grandmother, and his mother ran for their lives. While on the run, Anton witnessed bombings and rapes. He saw corpses in the streets and he heard the screaming of injured people. Eventually the three made it to Germany. Even there, life was traumatic. In his neighborhood, the police often came around to warn them to stay inside, that thugs were beating up refugees. In some cities, refugees were killed by skinheads. They were in Germany three years, then, as Anton put it, "The Germans kicked out the Bosnians."

He and his mother decided to come to America, but his grandmother returned to Bosnia. She didn't think she could learn a new language. Anton said, "She wishes she were here with us. Life is very hard for her."

Anton smiled when he recalled that, in a stroke of luck, he and his mother accidentally had been assigned first-class seats on the flight from Munich to Chicago. In Nebraska they rented a small apartment. He said, "I like it small. I don't want us to be in different rooms all the time." His mother worked at a noodle factory and studied English at night. She and Anton kept to themselves.

Anton said, "We don't trust anybody." I asked him about his grades and he said, "It is hard to learn everything at once."

I gently asked Anton how he slept. He said, "I dream of my father and grandfather's death. I try to save them, but I can't." We talked about what calmed him. He said American movies made him feel better. He had bought a video of *The Mask* and he watched it over and over. He also liked *Halloween, Scream,* and *I Know What You Did Last Summer.* He said, "It feels good to see someone else in trouble."

He had many complaints. He felt the ELL kids gave him a rough time and the American kids ignored him. He said, "I believe I am an American, but the American kids do not." He loved soccer, but had to work after school and couldn't play. He didn't like the Bosnian kids in Lincoln. His only praise was for his teachers—"They do everything they can for us"—and for his mother: "She won't let me eat American food. She cooks me good Bosnian food."

He didn't like how Americans waste food. He said, "Whenever I see someone throw away food, I wish I could give it to my grandmother."

I asked Anton how he would feel about seeing a therapist. At first he shouted, "No way," but by the end of our talk, he was willing to give it a try. Later, with the help of a translator, I gently broached the subject of therapy with his mother. She was so upset she threatened to pull Anton from school.

After all his loss and trauma, she couldn't bear to see him reinjured by what she feared was treatment for crazy people. These last few years she had fought to keep him alive and she wasn't going to let down her guard. Maybe after what had happened, she couldn't.

To Anton's mother, love meant protecting him from the

outside world. She had lost her husband and father, her work, and her language, and she wasn't going to lose Anton. She had lost everything but the power to say no to an American who wanted to help.

I wondered what she had been like before the war. What had she been like when she had a nice house, a husband, and a flower garden? How do we evaluate a woman who has seen her husband and father killed, and who has walked past bombed villages with a hungry, traumatized son at her side? How do we judge a woman who has seen all systems fail?

She had a highly aroused flight-and-fight system that wasn't adaptive now. But her protectiveness and her fierce intensity had kept Anton alive. Seen from her vantage point, her behavior was understandable. She and Anton weren't crazy, only reacting to a crazy world. The irony was that they could really use someone to help them understand they were in a new place and could calm down.

ADOLESCENCE

While puberty is a biological event, adolescence is a cultural phenomenon. American adolescence is about individuation, risk taking, and experimentation. It's about wildness and freedom. Our concept of adolescence is discordant with the values of many cultures. While American children often are raised to be independent and antiauthoritarian, children from traditional cultures are raised to have great respect for adults. In Middle Eastern, Latino, Asian, and African cultures, elders are venerated. Old and young enjoy each other's company. They all enjoy the same activities; they work together and play together.

Refugees are amazed by how American teenagers treat their parents and grandparents. Many of the ELL teens plan to live at home until they are married. Some hope to live all of their lives with their families. And yet, at school, like all American teenagers, they learn to think for themselves. In fact, the major identity struggles of refugee teens involve finding the balance between independence and their obligations to family and community.

As discussed earlier, for refugee families in America, the power often shifts radically from parents to children. Children of refugees frequently become bicultural and bilingual more rapidly than their elders. As teens, they learn how to drive and get around town. Some even support their families. Parents no longer have superior knowledge of the world and they no longer have a village helping them raise their kids.

When teens become surly and disobedient, refugee parents often don't know how to respond. Their traditional means of discipline—shaming from elders, reprimands from the extended family, or physical punishments—may not be possible. Furthermore, the parents may be dependent on their child's goodwill in order to have a ride to work or even an income. This parental lack of power allows teens to rule the roost in ways that hurt the whole family and especially the teen. Many parents feel they lose their children to America.

At the high schools in Lincoln teens must call home for permission to do many things. However, since these teens speak English and their parents often don't, the school must trust them to explain problems to their parents and accurately report their parents' reactions. Parents often cannot read grade cards or talk directly to school personnel about their concerns. One boy told his parents that the school required all boys to wear expensive black leather jackets, and his impoverished parents scraped together the money to buy him one.

And yet, in spite of the many problems, I was struck by the love and loyalty refugee teens feel for their parents. When I asked teenagers, "What is your dream now?" many answered that they wanted to buy their parents a house.

Teens are caught between their families and the larger culture. They are expected to meet demands in school that vary significantly from what they experience at home. At school they may not be considered American and at home they are considered too Americanized. The most resilient kids do a lot of cultural switching. They act American at school, traditional at home. They are bicultural, or in many cases, multicultural, and they know when "to wear each culture."

Adolescents are identity-seeking organisms. They try on different identities for size and fit. Nothing is yet fixed. This experimentation is intensified for the ELL students. They hunger to be defined, to be told, "this is who you are or who you could become." Eleanor Roosevelt's definition of success is, "To cultivate and express one's talents and powers to the utmost and to use those powers for the good of the community." That is a good definition for the ELL students, many of whom want to use their gifts to serve their families. They really appreciate cultural brokers who take the time to notice what they do well and help them see how they might develop their gifts.

Most students take great pride in their home countries. They bring pictures of their countries to school. They like to talk to Americans who have visited their country and know a few words of their language. They love to share information about their home countries. One of the best things an American can do is ask about their homelands.

A Vietnamese boy told me he felt sorry for white teens who had no ethnic group to identify with. He said, "They are really unlucky. They have no real culture. They go around trying to steal other people's groups—blacks, Asians, just so they can find some identity."

HIGH SCHOOL

Refugees are allowed to attend our high schools until they are twenty-one. Many have to drop out and work, but those who can stay feel lucky to be in high school. Many of the students work after school, both part-time and full-time jobs. Others go home to clean, cook, and care for younger siblings while their parents work. One Guatemalan student, who was in Nebraska without parents, worked all night at a factory. A Croatian student supported her family by working in housekeeping at a downtown hotel.

The teachers' biggest challenge is helping students with English vocabularies of two-year-olds to feel respected as adults. These students can express so little of what they are thinking and feeling. Mainstream classes are hard. Often students don't have prerequisites. Some teachers talk too fast and won't repeat.

The students make small but significant mistakes. A Bosnian girl, assigned a report on Stokely Carmichael, misunderstood and researched Hoagy Carmichael for her political science class. One Kurdish girl liked the flower-covered packaging of a box of raspberry douche. She thought it was perfume or lotion and bought it for the school gift exchange. Fortunately a teacher intercepted this gift and found something less personal for her to give her seat mate.

ELL students are often smart and eager. They speak several languages and possess many life skills. However, because of language problems, many have low ACT scores. The older students are at the time they start American schools, the more difficult it is for them to catch up. Sometimes students surmount all the academic hurdles and are accepted to college, but then they do not have the right INS paperwork to qualify for loans or grants.

Many of the students feel tremendous pressure to succeed. Their parents have literally risked their lives so that they can go to school. And yet some start from far behind their American peers—some students don't know that the earth revolves around the sun. They've never heard of gravity, of germs, or of fractions.

Between past traumas and present stresses, students are often upset. Many report headaches, stomachaches, tiredness, or dizziness. During class, students periodically "check out." Their teachers touch them gently and say their names to bring them back to the classroom. Other times, students are so anxious they run out of the room or burst into tears. Small changes in the classroom trigger anxiety. A loud noise or a chair falling can make them jump. The regular Wednesday 10:15 A.M. civil defense siren upsets students. Many are fearful of thunderstorms and tornadoes.

These students are expected to have a lot of emotional stretch. A Bosnian student whose father was killed two weeks earlier came to his first day of school. He had no friends and spoke no English. At the same time he was grieving his father's death, he was learning the states and capitals and how to work American machine tools.

Some students express their emotional difficulties with cruel practical jokes, bullying, and harsh teasing. Many come from places where homosexuals are feared, reviled, and even killed, and hence many are homophobic. Once some ELL students made fun of a special education student who couldn't talk. Their teacher dealt with that by teaching them about mental handicaps. She encouraged students to befriend handicapped students and learn more about their experiences. Some refugees come from places where handicapped people are not respected.

Their teacher said, "We are in America now. At school every-one deserves respect for trying to learn."

Refugee students in high school seem more affected by poverty than do younger kids. They are more sensitive about class and status differences. Except for the gang kids, the ELL students can't afford the designer clothes many American kids wear. Most wear Goodwill clothes, although some kids do amaz-ingly well with what they pull from used clothing boxes. Other kids have parents who spend their meager salaries buying them a pair of designer jeans or Doc Martins. One particularly cold year a teacher bought all the ELL kids hats and gloves for the holidays. Several marveled that they had something actually new to wear.

Some teens learn all the wrong things about America. In-stead of listening to their teachers, they listen to their peers, the media, and ads. Sometimes when parents realize they have lost control and that their children are in trouble, they return to their old countries to save the teenager from American problems.

Boys, especially, are trapped in a weird bind. Their peers teach them that "to act white" is to be disloyal to their ethnic group. Studying, making good grades, being polite, or joining school clubs are all defined as "acting white." So the boys must choose between social acceptance by peers and meeting parental expectations. Many conform their way into being rebellious at school. They learn not to learn.

The Vietnamese gang boys are a good example of the perils and complexity of cultural switching. They are an odd combi-nation of playful and tough. They often take on a "tough guise" in class. But they don't date and many work after school and hand their mothers their checks. When a community celebra-tion occurs, they show up with their families and act like good sons, but some are dealing drugs, stealing cars, and robbing their own people.

There are Bosnian gangs, Kurdish gangs, and Latino gangs as well. The gangs meet two legitimate needs—the need for a peer community and the need for power. Gangs are default communities that exist because there is nothing better.

However, in spite of some sad stories, results from the National Longitudinal Study of Adolescent Health show a remarkably high level of general adjustment in refugee kids. They tend to make grades that are equal to or better than those of American kids and they are less likely to drop out of school. They are physically and mentally healthier. As teens they are less likely than American kids to use drugs and alcohol, to be obese, or to have asthma. This study found a high level of self-esteem compared to native-born kids. In fact, with acculturation, the well-being of refugee students actually decreases. The longer kids are in America, the less time they spend on homework and the more likely they are to be sexually active.

On the surface, it seems as if American teens would be happier than refugee teens. They generally have more money and fewer obstacles in their paths. However, American kids have much more exposure to a toxic media culture then do most of the refugee kids. They don't necessarily have the newcomer zest of refugee kids. Also, being useful gives humans great pride and satisfaction. Overcoming obstacles and transcending difficulties builds self-regard. Refugee students know they are vital to their family's functioning. American kids sometimes feel like they are a drain on family resources.

Few American students in Lincoln were interested in the ELL students. Schools often have what Jesse Jackson called "the illusion of inclusion." There are bright posters on the walls of kids of all colors, but there is little real mingling or appreciation of differences. At school, American kids never suspected that the Dinka student they passed in the halls had walked from southern Sudan to South Africa to find a safe haven. Or that the girl next to them at lunch heroically had led her family to a safe house after her father was shot in Colombia. Instead, the American students passed the ELL students in the halls for years and never spoke.

I spent a year at a high school in Lincoln, sitting in on classes, doing therapy, and interviewing students, including Liem and Anton whose stories open this chapter. I befriended students and their families and became part of their lives. I taught a few students to drive. I have tried with these stories to remain true to the spirit of the school. I have changed names and identifying details of the students. At the high school, I worked with many of the ELL teachers but, for simplicity's sake, I will refer only to one composite teacher I'll call Mrs. Kaye.

I first visited on a crisp fall day. I parked in the crowded parking lot and walked through students of all shapes, styles, and colors toward the enormous high school. On the front steps of the school, Vietnamese young men, wearing baggy pants, silky shirts, and gold chains, with their hair slicked back in a gangster look, danced to Vietnamese rap music. The young women, tiny and delicate, wore skintight pants and high heels. They alternately flirted with the boys and yawned at their antics. The girls were a funny combination of sophisticated in their dress and innocent in their behavior. They giggled and blushed but managed to look seductive as well.

Inside the big doors hung flags from twenty countries. The language rhythms of Arabic, Vietnamese, Spanish, and Bosnian jazzed up the halls. Young Iranian women in long black robes hurried past African American and Latino kids. There were lots of white kids here, too, some from poor families but many from middle-class and even wealthy families.

I walked up two flights of stairs to Mrs. Kaye's room. Her classroom had many welcome signs and a quotation by Teilhard de Chardin: THE FUTURE BELONGS TO THOSE WHO GIVE THE NEXT GENERATION A REASON TO HOPE. She had only one rule posted: BE POLITE. IT'S MORE IMPORTANT TO BE NICE THAN TO LEARN ENGLISH. The walls were covered with maps, piñatas, Buddhas, paper flowers, posters from various countries, and photos of "great students through the years."

Mrs. Kaye greeted me warmly, and as the students filtered in, we chatted about the ELL program and about the students I would soon meet. She spoke about how scary it was to walk into this giant building with no English. Many of the kids arrived jet-lagged and in severe culture shock. For the first few weeks everyone had a "deer in the headlights" look. New students could hardly comprehend what was happening to them. They drifted through the day, trying to stay out of trouble.

Mrs. Kaye was an excellent teacher, gentle and low-key. I sat in on her cultural orientation class for most of a year. I'll report on just four classes: day 1, which was my introduction and orientation to the class; day 26, which was a discussion of family differences across cultures; day 75, which was a class for young women on health; and day 170, a day in which students discussed identity poems.

CLASS ROSTER:

| Liem | Khoi | Alberto | Velida | Faisal | Nadia |
| Patti | Cahn | Zlatko | Tharaya | Anton | Homera |

Day 1—September 9, 1999

Mrs. Kaye introduced me and asked the students to tell me about themselves. In halting English, and with both laughter and embarrassment, the students responded to her request. The Vietnamese kids went first. A young looking guy dressed in slacks and a dress shirt introduced himself as Liem. He had a reserved manner and kept his eyes on his papers or the teacher. When a flashier Vietnamese boy nearby made a joke, Liem ignored it.

Liem sat next to Patti, who was dressed in leather slacks, a shiny top, and high-heeled sandals. She was femininity personified, delicate and shy. Patti looked like a pampered princess, but she was a steel magnolia. She worked an eight-hour shift after school to help support her family. She was a good daughter, but on the edge of trouble at school. Because she was so pretty, the gang boys were all after her. Lately she had been flirting back.

Khoi introduced himself in a flamboyant way, standing and bowing as if he were before a crowd of thousands. He was good-looking and cocky, with dyed red hair and dragon tattoos all over his arms. He wore a silk shirt and baggy pants that almost slipped off his bony hips. He carried a CD player and CDs of Jay-Z, OutKast, and Snoop Dogg.

I'd met Khoi's parents the first day of school. His father had been forced as a POW to clear land mines from the fields and he'd seen several of his friends blown up at this job. In Vietnam the family had been so poor that, as Khoi's mother put it, "cockroaches couldn't survive in our kitchen." As a boy, Khoi had prayed that his father wouldn't be beaten and that his mother would not cry from hunger.

Whatever trouble Khoi was in wasn't because of family dysfunction. His was a loyal family, well connected to their community, but the parents didn't have control of Khoi. His father worked two factory jobs to support his big family. He hadn't been able to learn to drive or speak English. Khoi was the oldest son of an oldest son and the family had pinned their hopes on him. He was smart but had twice been suspended from school. He'd been arrested for petty theft and he sometimes came to school stoned on pot. Clearly, he was in a gang. Still, Mrs. Kaye felt he was a good kid. However, his virtues wouldn't be of much use if he ended up in our state penitentiary.

Cahn, the alpha male of the class, wore baggy pants, a shiny jacket, gold chains, and three gold watches. However, his flashy clothes couldn't mask his basic homeliness. He had huge ears and an uncorrected cleft palate. During class he challenged Mrs. Kaye constantly, but he backed down when she dealt with him respectfully and firmly.

Cahn's father had shoulder and back injuries from being a beast of burden in a POW camp after the war. His father was a broken man, whipped first by the communists, then by a country he couldn't master. He stayed home and drank beer all day. As Cahn developed problems and rebelled, his father had tried to control him with threats and beatings. For the last year Cahn and his father hadn't spoken to each other.

At school the Vietnamese homeboys sat together, speaking Vietnamese and laughing at whatever happened in class. Cahn and Khoi sparred, poked, hooted, and generally created quite a ruckus.

Next to Cahn sat Alberto, a quiet kid who seemed ill at ease in school. Alberto looked down and said softly, "I am from Mexico. This is my second year in America."

Zlatko was an Ichabod Crane look-alike with a confident manner. He was a Russian Baptist from Siberia whose English was already very good. His family had moved here because they were persecuted for being Christians. In Russia they'd lived in a condemned building. The brick stove was falling apart and they fastened it together with wire. They had no running water and only an outhouse. He laughed sadly. "At that time, except for the Mafia, no one in Russia ever had hot water."

When his family came to America, they had many misconceptions. Zlatko laughed, explaining, "We thought money grew on trees here. We thought all American women would be beautiful. When we got to Lincoln we were shocked to see Lincoln looked like Siberia. The trees were bare of dollar bills, it was freezing, and not all the girls were pretty."

Anton interjected, "The girls in this class are all pretty."

"Of course," Zlatko responded gallantly. "I was referring to girls who do not go to this school."

Zlatko stayed in good touch with Russians. After school, as he cleaned a bank, he listened to CDs from Russia. He e-mailed his Russian friends, many of whom were in the army. He said they hated it. They had no money and the army shaved their heads. Older soldiers beat them. He said, "I am happy to be in America, far from the clutches of the Russian military."

Zlatko hoped his family could someday buy a home. He had great optimism about our country. He thought American police and government officials were honest and that there was less alcoholism and fighting in America.

Next Velida introduced herself. She said, "I am from the Ukraine. I live here with my parents, cousins, aunt, and uncle." She said her family was happy to be in Nebraska. They had a little house with a garden. Her parents had jobs. She said cheerfully, "How surprising are God's pathways. He blessed me with his wonderful blessings."

She had bandages all over her head from a recent surgery for a brain tumor. Now she was taking chemotherapy. The doctors were hopeful. Velida refused to be defined by her illness or her past trauma.

Although Velida had seen her home burned and her family scattered across the globe, her belief in God kept her positive. Velida called her mother "mamochka" and spoke glowingly of her family. She said, "We have many of life's problems yet we love each other and are blessed."

During the year I knew her, Velida missed school often, but the only time I saw her unhappy was when she had talked on the phone to her family in the Ukraine. She told me, "They were crying. They were so hungry they were going into the fields and eating grass." She paused, then repeated in disbelief, "My relatives were eating grass."

Mrs. Kaye whispered to me, "Thanks to globalization we can now talk on cell phones to people who are starving to death."

I could tell Velida was much loved by Mrs. Kaye and the other students, Even Cahn and Khoi listened respectfully when she spoke. She was tenderhearted, the kind of person who would cry at the death of a cricket. It was simple really: she loved people and they loved her back.

Tharaya, Velida's closest friend, seemed very unlike her. While Velida was a plain country girl, Tharaya was a true beauty, with strawberry-blond hair, porcelain skin, and stylish American outfits. But as Velida put it, "We are friends of the spirit." Tharaya said of their relationship, "When we met, sparkles of friendship flew between us."

Tharaya is the name of the brightest star in the Pleiades and means "she who illuminates the world." This was the perfect name for this idealistic young woman. What Tharaya and Velida had in common was core gentleness. Tharaya worked at Old Country Buffet and was horrified by all the food people threw away. She had lobbied her boss to save leftover food for the city mission, and she formed a club to help hungry people in Lincoln. From their own hard experiences, Tharaya and Velida had learned the importance of kindness. I never saw either one of them treat another person badly. They were even kind to Anton when he was frenetic and difficult.

Next to Tharaya sat Faisal, a handsome Kurdish kid who wore his hair in a spiky Statue of Liberty style. Faisal's grades weren't good, but he was a survivor. He had street smarts—what I've heard called Mafia smarts. Once Mrs. Kaye told me, "Kurdish boys can get rowdy, but they have experienced everything." She said, "If I were stranded on an island or lost in a desert, I would want a Kurdish boy to help me survive." Faisal struck me as fitting those remarks perfectly. He was a terrible reader, but he knew what was happening in the halls of school.

Faisal was born in Iraq. Before the Gulf War, his father had grown cotton, rice, and grapes. After the war, his family hid in the mountains where they witnessed many deaths. They lived in a tent and almost froze. In 1991 the Americans brought food and allowed the Kurds to go home. Eventually, Faisal's family flew to Guam and later to Nebraska. Faisal's father was disabled by the war. His mother now worked as a cook's helper for the university's food service.

Faisal was a big flirt. He liked both Tharaya and Patti and he competed with Anton for their attention. But he was barely polite to me, a middle-aged woman. He simply told me his name and that he was from Baghdad, here because of the Gulf War.

Beside him, Anton was young and brash. He seemed frenetic and haunted, someone in fresh pain. Anton had a punk haircut, nice clothes, and good English, and he should have been more popular than he was. The other kids called him crazy, or loco, and shied away from him. Some days he laughed, talked loudly, and hugged every girl he could. Other days he withdrew and was irritable with everyone.

He'd seen too many things for a boy his age. He knew both too much and too little about the world. His mother could not control him and he stayed out late with his friends, drove the car without a license, and took his mother's rent money for pizza and video games.

Anton, more than any other boy, challenged the Vietnamese gang boys. He was in some sort of weird contest with them to be the most manly. Once Alberto whispered to him, "Are you crazy man, those guys will kill you if you don't chill out." But Anton seemed incapable of controlling his impulses, or of acting on the basis of reason.

Anton didn't want to be seen as a refugee. He wanted out of ELL and he wanted some American friends. He desperately wanted to be seen as normal and as masculine. But his very desperation belied how abnormal and vulnerable he felt.

The last two students in the class were Middle Eastern girls. Nadia was small with long dark hair and tiny hands that moved in graceful, birdlike ways. She was fifteen and spoke four languages—Arabic, Kurdish, English, and Hindi. Nadia said, "I am here because of the Gulf War. I have said too many good-byes. Sadness has built a nest in my heart."

Her father had been a doctor at a hospital in Iraq. Like Faisal's family, her family was evacuated to Guam, then sent to Nebraska. The first year, her father did factory work, but now he worked in a hospital emergency room. His coworkers said he was a better doctor than many American doctors.

Nadia wanted to be a doctor. She told me that her father didn't let her talk to boys and would choose her an Iraqi husband when the time came. She lived to please him and after she'd failed a geometry test, she sobbed. She said, "I was crying for my father."

Beside her sat Homera, almost completely covered with a

veil and long black gown. Homera had a round face and dark heavy eyebrows. She barely whispered her name and kept her eyes down as she spoke. She was eighteen and she had come to this country three weeks ago for an arranged marriage to a man she'd never met. Her husband brought her to school every day and picked her up when it was over. She seemed overwhelmed by America, the loss of her family, and the marriage.

With introductions complete, Mrs. Kaye showed the class the day's newspaper and made points from front-page stories. One story was about a drunken driver who killed a teen. She said, "Promise me you will never drink and drive." Anton asked if the drunk driver would be executed. Mrs. Kaye said, "No, but he may go to jail." Velida said, "I will pray for her family."

Mrs. Kaye read the students a story about consumer fraud. She told the students never to sign anything without discussing it with a trusted American friend. She said some students had accidentally bought things they couldn't afford. One student from Bosnia, in Nebraska for only two weeks, signed an agreement to buy a swimming pool. Another student was arrested after he signed papers confessing to crimes he didn't commit. A Vietnamese student ended up in drug treatment because he filled out an evaluation form incorrectly. He'd checked yes to everything to be agreeable.

She warned students to walk away from trouble at the school. She said, "If someone gives you a hard time, talk it over with a teacher. Don't get in fights or you will be in trouble, too."

Faisal said, "I saw a guy in a T-shirt that said, 'Iraq sucks.'"

Mrs. Kaye asked, "What did you do?"

Faisal answered, "I asked him, Hey man, why do you think my country sucks?" He made a gesture like a boxer with his gloves on. Everyone laughed.

Khoi said, "Yeah, Faisal is Bruce Lee. A mean mother."

Mrs. Kaye said, "Khoi, watch your language please."

Anton said, "Faisal thinks he is a tough guy. He thinks he is Ahhnold." Everyone laughed at Anton's imitation of Arnold Schwarzenegger.

Mrs. Kaye said, "Let's laugh with Faisal not at him."

The bell rang. Everyone bolted but Homera. She asked Mrs. Kaye if she could change classes and have only women teachers.

Mrs. Kaye said, "In America, men and women work together; you must get used to it. We don't have classes just for girls."

Homera looked upset and Mrs. Kaye hugged her. "It will get easier. I'll help you whenever I can."

Day 26—October 21, 1999

Class began with a stern lecture on politeness. The day before, a policeman had visited to answer questions about how the law worked. He was a friend of Mrs. Kaye who was interested in helping ELL students. But the Bosnian and Croatian kids were afraid of him. Tharaya said, "In our countries, the police cut off your ears." The minute he walked in, the tough guys had something to prove. They refused to tell him their first names. Khoi and Cahn treated him rudely. Faisal and Anton had mouthed off as well.

Mrs. Kaye said, "He was my friend and our guest. We don't treat guests that way in Nebraska."

The kids were silent during her reprimand, heads down and bodies slack. She said, "I want your promise that the next guest I invite will be well treated." Of course, the polite kids immediately promised, but she had to call on the troublemakers one by one.

"Faisal?" Without looking up, he mumbled, "Yeah, sure,"

Mrs. Kaye said, "What?" He repeated it slightly louder and she passed on to Cahn.

Cahn said stubbornly, "I didn't do anything." Mrs. Kaye said gently, "Cahn, this is about the future. Will you be polite next time?"

Khoi said, "I'll respect guests if they respect me." Mrs. Kaye said, "I want you to be polite no matter what."

Khoi muttered something under his breath and Patti giggled. She had on elaborate makeup and in the middle of each silvery nail was a gold star.

Mrs. Kaye asked Anton if he understood her. Not to be outdone by Khoi, Anton said, "The police are pigs."

Mrs. Kaye said sharply, "My friend is not a pig. It isn't polite to call anyone an animal's name."

Mrs. Kaye asked, "How is school different here than in your home country?"

Tharaya said, "For the last few years there was no school in my country. Parents helped their children learn to read in basements." As usual, Tharaya looked fashionable today. It was hard to believe she put her outfits together from the Dollar Store and Goodwill baskets. But her surface appearance was deceptive. Her values were not the values of most Madonna fans. She was not a material girl.

Alberto continued the discussion about school. "My teacher was good, but we didn't have any books or supplies."

Zlatko said, "In Russia, there was better discipline. I learned to multiply in second grade. My brother is in fourth grade here and still cannot multiply."

"Maybe your brother is stupid," Cahn said.

Mrs. Kaye said, "We don't use the word *stupid* in this class."

He grinned and looked out the window at the falling leaves.

Cahn was such a heartbreaking mixture of tough and shy. One day there was a very telling incident. When the class played charades, Cahn refused to play, claiming it looked boring. But when Anton and Faisal teased him and Khoi called him a chicken, he sauntered to the front of the class. He looked sure of himself, until he looked at his charades assignment. Then he froze; he was too nervous to think and his voice wouldn't work. Mrs. Kaye had to gently signal him to return to his seat.

Zlatko continued, "The American educational system is designed to make students stop thinking."

"I love the teachers at our school, especially the ELL teachers," Velida said.

Tharaya added, "The teachers are our American mothers."

"The teachers are okay, but I don't like school," Faisal said. Alberto and Anton agreed.

Mrs. Kaye asked Homera how she felt about American teens.

Homera said in very broken English, "I want them to understand our culture. American girls see my scarf and ask if I am a slave. I tell them I choose to wear this. I need something to believe in."

Faisal said, "One time a boy asked me, Why should we care about Iraq?"

"I would tell him that the more he cares about other people, the happier he will be," Velida said.

"Americans have bad ideas about Muslims. We are not all terrorists. Islam is a religion of peace," Nadia said. "We offer food for anyone who comes to our home. We treat others as if we were all one family."

Anton said, "American kids ask me how to say dirty words in my language." He laughed and said, "I tell them the words for 'butterfly' or 'flower.' They think they are cool, but the joke is on them."

Mrs. Kaye said, "Good use of an idiom, 'the joke is on them.'" She explained it to the class.

Nadia was amazed by how disrespectful American students were—talking to their friends in class, mouthing off, and sleeping. She could not imagine interrupting a teacher or calling an adult by a first name.

Zlatko had been taught to help his friends, and he didn't like the competitiveness of American kids.

Anton was shocked by American kids kissing in the halls or shouting, "Fuck you."

Everyone looked at Mrs. Kaye when he said that. She only said, "Swearing in public isn't good manners."

Tharaya said, "I hate how teenagers here talk about their parents. My mom is my best friend." She choked up a bit. "My mother works all the time, then she bakes bread on her days off."

"American teens are always talking about sex and alcohol," Velida added. "In the Ukraine, virginity is more respected. The music here is too sexual and has many bad words. Eminem would never be allowed in my country."

"American kids brag about getting drunk," Liem said. "In my country, alcohol was no big deal. Here teens are desperate to drink."

"American kids are superficial. They have too much freedom, especially sexual freedom. Russian kids respect their parents and never talk back," Zlatko said. "My parents told me to never use alcohol or drugs and I will obey them."

"In Vietnam we were taught that if kids talked badly about their parents, we must walk away immediately," Patti said.

Velida protested, "Some American kids are nice."

"They are nice to their friends," Tharaya agreed. "But not their parents."

"How can they be rude to their parents?" Velida asked. "Parents gave us the gift of life."

The talk moved from teenagers to American media. Zlatko said he hated American TV. He liked a few American movies— *Patch Adams, Contact,* and *Deep Impact.* But he'd walked out of *American Pie,* which he said was filthy. His family rented Russian movies.

Nadia said her family only watched Iraqi movies. Homera had never even seen a movie. Once Tharaya had watched the *Jerry Springer Show* and she wondered how the show found people who would talk badly about their own families. Faisal defended *Springer.* He said, "That's where you learn what America is really like."

Mrs. Kaye said, "America isn't as bad as that, really."

Anton said he liked the court shows. He joked he was learning to be a judge. Khoi said, "Are you sure you are not learning to be a criminal?"

Alberto said, "At first I was shocked by Americans, but now I like them." Cahn pointed at Faisal, "He likes X-rated movies."

Faisal looked embarrassed. Recently, he'd been caught in the media center on a triple-X web site. As the year had progressed, Faisal had become contemptuous of women and less respectful of authority.

Once when Mrs. Kaye had said that a heart filled with goodness was important, Faisal sneered that he preferred a house filled with money. In an earlier class, while discussing *Driving Miss Daisy,* Mrs. Kaye had asked the class about the feelings of Miss Daisy in a particular scene. Faisal had asked scornfully, "What do the feelings of an old woman matter?"

Mrs. Kaye was angry at Faisal, but she felt for him, too. He couldn't read; his parents were not learning English or becoming bicultural, and he had no real adult guides. Previously, he had worked with a mentor and he had been happier. One glorious day he had come into her room and shouted happily, "I am learning to read." But the school had to cut funds and the reading mentors were gone. Faisal had become angrier and more misogynistic.

By now Faisal seemed to be inhaling the worst influences in our culture. He was losing his cultural values and gaining gangster values. Tharaya and Velida, by contrast, seemed to know what was good and beautiful. They made good choices about everything—friends, studies, even leisure activities. Patti liked Vietnamese movies. Cahn and Khoi loved Jackie Chan. Velida loved *Titanic* although it made her cry for hours. Actually, all the girls loved *Titanic*.

Nadia's family got cable television so they could receive stations from the Middle East. In fact, many of the students' families watched shows from their home countries.

Alberto said, "TV is boring and stupid, but it passes the time."

Mrs. Kaye said, "Don't watch too much TV. It isn't a good way to learn English. It's better to learn by making friends with Americans and by studying. TV rots your brain."

Cahn said, "Drugs have already rotted my brain." Nobody laughed.

Day 75—March 23, 2000

On a spring day, Mrs. Kaye separated the girls and the boys for lectures on health issues. I stayed with the girls as the health educator arrived with her handouts and a box of props. Many of the girls were a strange mixture of ignorant and traumatized. Most had never experienced anyone talking about sexuality.

They knew almost nothing about reproductive health or normal sexuality, but many had been raped or seen their mothers and older sisters being raped.

Homera seemed most upset about the topic. She wore a black scarf that completely covered her face except for her eyes. Today she shut her eyes when the health educator put up the first overhead slide. Even though Homera was married and presumably had been sexually active, she obviously didn't want to discuss sex in public. I could tell she would rather be anywhere than in this class.

Patti was the biggest contrast to Homera. She was dressed in a tight mustard-colored sleeveless shirt and overalls. She wore long dangly earrings and a bored expression to disguise the fact that she was paying close attention.

Velida had missed the last few weeks of school, but today she was here. She had a shaved head now, but she didn't seem to mind. She wore a little pink ribbon around her head and laughed easily as always. She was interested in all aspects of health and not embarrassed by the sexual discussion.

The health educator explained that Americans are obsessed with cleanliness and she talked about the need to shower every day and to shampoo regularly. She passed around samples of deodorants and talked about body odor. Patti passed the deodorant on without looking at it, but Nadia and Homera examined the deodorant as if it were a piece of the space shuttle.

The health educator had an overhead that showed stick people washing their hands and getting immunizations. She spoke about dental hygiene. Most of the girls knew about brushing teeth, but no one had heard of dental floss.

The health educator explained what it is like to go to the doctor. She first mentioned the need for a Medicaid or insurance card. She explained that it wasn't personal, but that American doctors wouldn't treat you if you didn't have these cards. Now it was my turn to sigh and look uncomfortable, ashamed of our rich country that wouldn't help a sick baby without making sure there was money.

Velida said, "To see the doctor here, you need many papers. But my doctors are kind."

The health educator covered generic versus brand-name medications and why it is important to finish a bottle of antibiotics. She warned against mixing medications. Here, for the first time, the girls had a few questions. Nadia asked what she should do about a cough that wouldn't go away. Patti asked if Advil is the same as ibuprofen.

When the health educator put up a poster showing the female reproductive system, Homera gasped, then lay her head on her desk so that she could see nothing. Nadia averted her eyes, but Tharaya, Velida, and Patti carefully studied those drawings.

The health educator explained menstruation. As she discussed fallopian tubes and ovaries, Tharaya and Nadia giggled nervously. Homera turned beet red. Patti listened closely, then asked, "What does it mean if you don't have a period?"

The health educator said, "If you are sexually active, it might mean you are pregnant. Otherwise, it could be stress, or maybe too much exercise."

Patti yawned in an exaggeratedly indifferent way and asked, "How do you know if you are pregnant?"

The health educator told her about pregnancy kits then moved on to feminine hygiene. She asked if any girls in the room used tampons and all the girls said no. Even Patti, Velida, and Tharaya thought that if you used a tampon you would lose your virginity. The health educator said that wasn't true, but she didn't persuade anyone. Homera put her hands over her ears so that she could not even hear the lecture.

As the girls passed around the tampon, they handled it like it was hot or infectious. Patti seemed curious about the tampon as a cultural artifact. She asked when it was invented and what was its purpose. But she said, "I will never buy these."

Tharaya asked why she felt so tired when she had her period. The health educator suggested that she get a blood test for iron deficiency.

The health educator pulled out a rubber model of a breast and explained breast exams. She explained the mammogram procedures by saying it was just like making a hamburger patty out of the breast. Patti held the breast models to her chest and the girls laughed. Nadia and Homera wouldn't touch the breast model. Tharaya said it felt like Jell-O. Velida passed it on as if it were a plate of spaghetti and she was full.

When the health educator put up a model of male anatomy, Homera asked to leave. The health educator said, "Okay, go to the library," and Homera rushed gratefully out.

Nadia looked at the picture, but only her desire to understand a medical lecture kept her in the room. How could she be a doctor if she couldn't sit through this? But when the health educator used the word *ejaculation,* Nadia covered her ears.

On the other hand, Patti, Tharaya, and Velida were attentive. Patti asked about condoms. The health educator stressed that abstinence was the safest and best form of birth control and she urged the students to wait for sex until they were older. However, she answered Patti's question and stressed that condoms did not always work and could only be used once. She told of two couples who had sex in a car. The boy in the front seat passed his condom to the boy in the backseat who turned it inside out and reused it. The girl in the backseat got pregnant but with the front-seat boy's baby.

By now all of the girls looked a little stunned. This class had covered too much too fast. The bell rang. These girls needed more discussions. Could they teach their mothers to do breast exams? What was a Pap smear? A pelvic exam?

Many of the mothers had never had a physical exam or any health care because they wouldn't see a male doctor and there were no female doctors in their areas. Many women from Africa had medical problems as a result of female genital mutilation. I wished we could have a campaign that explained the health problems associated with this terrible practice.

One fifteen-year-old girl from Tajikistan had been taken from school for an arranged marriage. The girl's father was dead and her mother had been afraid her daughter would lose her virginity in America. So she lied about her daughter's age and signed papers giving permission for an arranged marriage to an older man. The girl went from learning grammar and fractions to being a pregnant wife in a matter of a few weeks.

An Albanian girl became pregnant while in a refugee camp. Her pregnancy was discovered here when she had her routine physical. She was six-months pregnant and swore she had never had sex. It was unclear if she even knew what sex was and that it had a connection to the pregnancy. Her mother was dead and no one had ever talked to her about the facts of life. Because of malnutrition and trauma, she'd never had regular periods. I asked her if she had been raped and she stared at me confused. It was a stupid question. The term "consensual sex" had no meaning to a young woman who had been scared, hungry, and hopeless in a refugee camp.

The class was over. Hurried and cursory as it was, this would be all the health information these girls received. There was so much more to teach—about nutrition, exercise, stress management, addictions, and regular checkups. Still, I was grateful to the health educator for what she did say. I walked to the library to check on Homera.

Day 170—May 19, 2000

Mrs. Kaye announced she would not be returning next year. She had accepted a job in another city. She didn't explain why, but I suspected that dealing with the gang kids had exhausted her. Nobody in this class liked her decision. Velida and Tharaya looked as if they were about to cry. Homera said, "You are my best friend in America." Anton and Faisal poked at each other to distract themselves from their feelings. Both Liem and Nadia looked suddenly depressed.

Alberto asked, "You're joking, aren't you?"

But Cahn and Khoi were the most upset. Khoi said, "I will move with you. I will help you at the new school." Cahn shouted out, "If you are not here at school, I am not here." Then he said, "I am a little kid. I want my teacher." He began to suck his thumb. He tried to make a joke of this, but the thumb-sucking looked pretty genuine. The other students stared at him in amazement. Patti asked softly, "What are you doing, Cahn?"

Nobody, except Alberto, really wanted to leave school. The world looked much colder and harder outside the school. Refugee students are understandably afraid of change. Some gang members purposefully fail twelfth grade so they can stay in school another year. One Laotian girl attempted suicide on graduation day.

As I watched the students react to Mrs. Kaye's news, I realized how much we all had changed over the year, how we had all grown together. Homera was more relaxed. She still dressed in her traditional way, but she spoke in class and sometimes even joked around. She looked everyone in the eye now, even boys. Only when her husband showed up did she become an obedient, demure wife.

Miraculously, Anton had not been beaten up by Cahn and Khoi. He hadn't calmed down much, but his English was better and he had made it through his hard first year. He still didn't have any real friends although it wasn't for lack of trying. He pestered Velida and Tharaya daily to be his girlfriends. His mother had forgiven me for suggesting therapy. Recently she had sent little cakes to class to celebrate Easter.

Patti was pregnant. Apparently the sex education class hadn't come in time. She hadn't publicly identified the father, but I suspected it was Khoi. He had been especially kind to Patti, and several times recently, he had actually turned in his assignments.

Cahn had started using heroin. Twice this month he'd fallen asleep on his desk. Mrs. Kaye had referred him to the drug counselor, but he wouldn't go. Regardless of where Mrs. Kaye worked, I didn't think Cahn would return to school next year.

Velida rarely came to school now. Her tumors were back and she had many severe headaches. But whenever she came, she was cheerful and kind to others. She was grateful for every small blessing.

Zlatko, Liem, and Nadia had all progressed academically. They were in regular classes pursuing their long-term goals of college educations. Zlatko and Nadia continued to think of helping people in their home countries. Liem wanted set a good example for his younger siblings and to make his parents happy.

Alberto wouldn't be back next year. He had a job at a body shop and didn't want to continue school. He had made some Mexican friends and had avoided the gangs. His English had improved and he seemed happier.

Faisal had been arrested twice. He had made very bad choices about friends and activities. He had learned all the wrong things about America. I felt sorry for him and for his parents. I worried about what would happen to him over the summer.

Tharaya had blossomed. She was a resilient girl with good coping skills. She had been awarded a summer school scholarship to the university. Her family and her community were very proud of her.

Mrs. Kaye announced that today she would read "I am from" poems, an identity exercise. Many teens love poetry, which allows them to express their feelings and to bracket the past with words that heal. She explained that the assignment was to write poems that included something about place, religion, and food. My "I am from" poem began this book.

Mrs. Kaye read poems from former students. Senada had written, "I am from parents that always had pain inside them and from the big beautiful oceans that I flew above." Sara had written, "I am from Shiraz, the city of flowers, the city of poems. I am from teachers that beat children with thick sticks." Boa had written, "I am from a house made of leaves, and when it rained, water dropped into my bed." Pablo had written, "I am from people who work really hard to get minimum wage. I am from a family who is always missing the ones in Mexico."

Vu had written, "I live in a world of peace, freedom, loneliness." Koa had written, "My heart is breaking / I'm going for a long walk / to forget the past." Manuel had written, "I dream I have a ton of gold / So I can help my family / And I help other people so no one would be homeless." Ivan had written, "The war begins when two / or more politicians decide / to get more land / power and money. / But they do not care / about the people / the people suffer and do not want war."

Khairi had written, "I am from the country of sadness and dying people / because of too many wars / I am the one who got lost in this world / and I do not know what my real nation is." Zohra had written, "I am from Afghanistan / in the heart of Asia / with high mountains that hold emeralds and rubies. / I am from a country that has rushing rivers / that wash the blood of people / who lost their bodies." Lana had written, "I am from a country / where the sun stopped shining, where the butterflies stopped flying and where mothers' hearts started crying." Tavan had written, "I am from where the waterfalls drop like a bird in the sky / From a place where the land is green and beautiful all summer long and in the fall the leaves fall like diamonds from the sky." Mrs. Kaye read these beautiful poems, then she said, "Now write your own poems for tomorrow."

CHAPTER 7

YOUNG ADULTS—"IS THERE *a* MARRIAGE BROKER *in* LINCOLN?"

JASMINKA
"I would like to remember nothing."

Jasminka's teacher wanted us to meet. She had great respect for Jasminka, who was in school and also worked to help her mother support her younger siblings. I interviewed Jasminka in the cafeteria at our community college where she was studying business administration.

Jasminka was twenty, a tall and strong-looking young woman with straight dark brown hair. She wore a striped sweater, tight jeans, and earrings shaped like camels. I mispronounced her name and Jasminka looked at me angrily. When I apologized and corrected myself, she smiled and opened up to me. Over grilled-cheese sandwiches and tomato soup, she told me her story.

Jasminka was a Muslim Albanian born in Kosovo in 1981. She was the second of seven children. At the time of her birth, demonstrators marched daily in Pristina and people were being shot and put into prison. Her grandfather was in his tenth year of prison for protesting on behalf of the Albanian population. The year of her birth, her father developed heart problems. However, shortly after she was born, things quieted down for a while. Jasminka's family had "sort of a normal of a life."

Then in 1989, Pristina was once again in crisis. Schools were gassed by the Serbs, and soon all Albanian children were being educated in basements by volunteers. Jasminka said that, under these conditions, it was hard to learn. The teachers were compassionate, but they had no books, desks, or even paper.

People were killed in the streets, arrested at their jobs, and taken away forever. Her oldest brother, who was in the Kosovar Liberation Army, slipped out of the country. In 1995 Jasminka's father died of his heart problems. When Jasminka told me this, she lost her matter-of-fact tone. She hadn't cried when she talked about the corpses in the streets, her grandfather in prison, or her brother fleeing for his life. But she sobbed at the mention of her father.

Clearly he had been a good man. Unlike some Muslim men, he'd wanted his daughters to attend college and to go out with their friends. He'd told his family, "I love education and I love freedom. Why would I not want these things for my daughters?" He'd also said, "My girls are good girls. I can trust them anywhere with the family honor."

I dug out some tissue and waited while Jasminka cried. Finally she wadded up the Kleenex and smiled bravely. Her soup was cold and she pushed it away. She said, "I am too fat." I said, "You have the American attitudes toward weight." She shrugged and sighed, "It is the universal attitude now."

Jasminka looked at me as if to say, "Listen carefully. You really need to understand what I will tell you next." Then she continued. After her father's death, the family was strapped for cash. The second oldest brother drove a delivery truck. He was quite successful, but every day he was in danger of being shot.

In 1998 this brother was arrested and imprisoned for his KLA activities. Jasminka's voice rose as she told me about this horrible time. Many men got sick or died in prison. Others went crazy from fear and torture. In April 1999, many Albanians in Kosovo were slaughtered by the Serbs. Jasminka trembled as she told me of the night the Serbs came to her house. She said, "The Serbs did terrible things to women."

Seeing her struggle to control her face, I extended my hand. She was quiet for a few minutes. Then she said, "I would like to remember nothing."

I said, "It's hard to forget and hard to remember."

She said, "My mother told me to pretend I was having a bad dream."

She swallowed and continued. Shortly after that night, Jasminka, her mother, and her four younger siblings escaped to Macedonia by train. Jasminka said, "I had to leave my kitten behind. I don't know if she is alive today." Of the journey, Jasminka said, "We were loaded like cattle into the cars." Her brother had escaped from prison, but he stayed behind to fight in the KLA.

At the Macedonian border they were stalled for several days, sleeping in muddy fields beside the train. They had no food, water, or blankets, not even newspapers to cover their heads. Then they were admitted into a crowded and unsanitary camp. During the five weeks her family was there, they were not able to take showers or have a hot meal.

Jasminka said her mother helped her survive this place. Her mother believed that even the worst life was better than death. Jasminka said, "I don't believe that, but our lives did get better."

After five weeks in the camp, the family was flown to the United States and assigned to Lincoln. They would have much preferred to live in Germany or Sweden; none of them spoke English and they hated to be so far from their own country. But they had no money, no papers, and no choices. Jasminka said, "My mother cried all the way across the ocean."

In Lincoln she and her mother found jobs sorting mail. She worked nights and finished her senior year in high school during the day. At first, she was terrified of Americans. Some students were racist, but the teachers were kind and she loved to learn. She said, "My father would be proud to see me in college."

After high school, Jasminka had enrolled in the community college. She said, "I made some friends at college. One American girl has helped me in every way she could. I invited her home to meet my family. But most of the students are too immature and wild."

She was deeply upset about pregnancies without marriage. She also disliked some of her classmates' sloppy dress and their obsession with getting high or drunk. She said, "Sometimes guys I hardly know put their hands on me." She made a grimace of disgust. "They should respect women more."

Jasminka showed me a picture of her mother, a pretty woman who looked like Jasminka, and she said, "I could never lie to my mother. She would look in my eyes and know I was lying."

Jasminka said she would not date until she was ready to marry, after she finished her business degree and found a good job. She would never marry an American, because he wouldn't understand her history or her religion and she would never marry anyone who didn't love her mother. Jasminka said, "I go out with my friends. My mother even trusts me with young men. She knows I will never betray the memory of my father."

Jasminka said she had bad dreams and flashbacks. She often woke in the night thinking she was in a basement being bombed. She worried she would go crazy if anyone in her family died. On the other hand, she was hopeful about her life now. She was working for her family and for her own future. Her little brothers would not need to serve in the KLA. In school it was hard to compete with students whose first language was English. She had trouble understanding her teachers and she couldn't afford to buy all the textbooks. Still, she was passing her courses and hoped to be an office manager someday.

Jasminka seemed less tormented by identity issues than many of the young adults I met. This was because she lived at home and had great respect for her family. She had the memory of her father to hold her life in place. She was reasonably adept at cultural switching.

We took our trays to the dish line. I thanked her for the interview and offered to help her in any way I could. She wrote down my phone number. As I watched Jasminka disappear in the swirl of students, she looked like an American college student, but she was not. She had a history and a belief system very different from the other students. She would have an arranged marriage when she was in her late twenties. She was a devout supporter of the KLA. Her dreams were Albanian dreams.

WORK, RELATIONSHIPS, EDUCATION, AND IDENTITY

In some ways, young adults are our most vulnerable newcomers. Many are on their own, American style, but with no money,

education, or connections. Often they are less adept than adolescents at cultural switching. They are behind educationally and
slower than teenagers to learn English. They are at an age when
they can get into all kinds of American trouble—with drugs, alcohol, gambling, and credit cards.

Young adults usually want to go to school, but there are
many hurdles. After age twenty-one, refugees are no longer allowed to attend high school. They may have serious gaps in
their educations and have no idea how our system of community colleges, universities, and trade schools functions. Without
a cultural broker interpreting the arcane language of academia,
refugees have trouble making it through the college system.
One Syrian student worried her brain wasn't good enough to
learn physics. With her limited discretionary money, she bought
ginkgo to improve her memory. A Turkish student noticed
there were no people who looked like her on campus.

Those young adults who remain with their families are
often the primary wage earners and the liaisons to the English-
speaking communities. In many cases, their parents are slow
to adapt or disabled, and the young adults must shoulder the
burden of supporting the family. They often are the drivers,
the schedulers, and the ones who fill out forms and translate.
And yet, in many cases, they are expected to remain deferen-
tial at home and they are not allowed the freedom of young
Americans.

When the parents are dead, young adults also become the
legal guardians of their younger siblings, which means they
must be present at doctors' and dentists' appointments and meetings with the schools. In the role of family workhorse and
leader, young adults can rapidly become overwhelmed and they
burn out.

Young adult refugees have many memories of home and there is a stronger sense of exile than with younger people. They must ask, "Who am I in this new land?" Young adults may also have come from cultures in which identity is derived from caste, family, or position in one's tribe. The whole concept of individual identity is new and yet, in America, many of the markers for the old identity are not present.

Finally, negotiating sexual relationships and finding a marriage partner is problematic. Dating, sexual relationships, and courtship are complex even for native-born Americans. These activities require judgment and the ability to send and receive subtle signals. They involve understanding the nuances of flirting and knowing how to set limits and negotiate consensual sex.

In our culture, dating begins as early as age twelve or thirteen. By the time most Americans are in their mid-twenties they have been learning to date for over a decade. As young adults, they have had trial-and-error learning and they've talked to dozens of friends about their experiences. They have read books, listened to songs, and seen movies that have taught them how to manage their dating.

Newcomers often have had none of these experiences. Many come from cultures in which young men and women have no contact with members of the opposite sex, except for their relatives. They have no scripts for actively seeking out a partner, winning that partner's affection, and negotiating a relationship. Our ways of dating are incomprehensible to many newcomers. Indeed, what we consider dating, they have been taught is deeply sinful.

Many young adults want to marry, but they have absolutely no idea how to go about finding a mate. If they proceed as Americans do, they will alienate members of their own culture.

They are not supposed to be dancing and talking to members of the opposite sex. However, if they wait for someone to arrange their marriage, they will remain single. They don't know where to go to meet a potential marriage partner, what to say to a member of the opposite sex, what behavior is appropriate for dating, or how to ask someone to marry them.

Refugees in Lincoln may want to marry someone from their culture, but there are no potential mates in Nebraska. As young adults from the Middle East, Africa, Eastern Europe, and Asia have grown to trust me, they often ask, "Do you know someone I can marry?"

When refugees try to approach someone from another culture, they are liable to make serious mistakes. A local woman tutored a Congolese man in English. At their second session he asked for her hand in marriage. He was very upset when she turned him down. He assumed that if she spent time with him she wanted to marry him.

There are many misunderstandings about the signals certain behaviors send. Many women from traditional cultures dress in fashionable and sexy American clothes but would be deeply offended by American-style sexual advances. Or they have been warned that all American men want sex and they are frightened by even the most innocent offers of friendship.

In some cultures a kiss is a prelude to sex. Women are very careful about whom they kiss because to them it signals a sexual commitment. Once they have kissed, they will have sex. American men find these women incredibly cold—until they talk them into a kiss. Then they are amazed at how rapidly the women hurl themselves at them. On the other hand, the women are deeply disappointed in American men. They think that a kiss is a marriage proposal and are heartbroken and angry when the man doesn't offer to marry them.

Dating and courtship are emotional minefields. The mis-understandings that inevitably occur are so often embarrassing, scary, or painful that newcomers withdraw from all attempts at courtship. Then they are lonely. A woman from Belarus spoke of "womb pain," which she attributed to the desire of her womb to carry a child. But she was thirty-three years old, spoke little English, and was unlikely to ever marry and have the children she so deeply wanted.

One women from Moldova kept falling in love with her married supervisors at work. She felt ashamed and guilty about this. She couldn't understand why this happened. I told her, "You are falling in love with the idea of a good husband, someone who is respectable and would care for you. Your yearning for this is understandable." She was grateful for my explanation, but I couldn't find her that caring man she so deserved.

Lonely adults from countries without any tradition of dating or courtship need help navigating the stormy seas of dating relationships. They are not going to find a partner in the bars, and they often don't have friends to introduce them to eligible partners. We could use a marriage broker in our town, or at least a class: Finding a Mate 101.

Of course, many young adults do find people from their own cultures to date and marry, and increasingly they date Americans or refugees from other cultures. We see interesting mixed couples in our cafés—Kurdish and Latino, Vietnamese and Afghani, Sudanese and Bosnian. Some young adults participate in arranged marriage in this country. And, of course, some do not want to marry.

The two stories that follow are of young adults in our community. The cultures and external circumstances are quite different in some ways, and yet all the young adults are struggling with work, identity, and relationship issues. No one is terribly happy. The late twenties is not a happy age for many people in America, especially if they are refugees.

THIEP

"I was born in the wrong time."

I met Thiep at the Student Union just after Thanksgiving. There was a fire in the fireplace and Christmas carols played in the background. Thiep was twenty-five, weighed maybe ninety pounds, and had an earnest face. She was pretty, but she wasn't about being pretty; her experiences had led her to a search for deeper meaning.

We bought cups of hot tea and settled in for a talk. I asked one question and then mostly listened. Thiep could have talked for hours.

"I was born in the wrong time—1975 in Vietnam," she began. "It was a time of distrust and disbelief, right after the war. Thirty-six hours after I was born, soldiers came to my house and arrested my father. It was six years before we saw him again. My grandfather and uncle were in prison, too. Many people starved to death."

While her father was in jail, she and her mother lived with her mother's family, simple country people. Their door was never shut and neighbors ambled in and out. She could go into any house in the village without knocking. No one cared about the war or politics, only food and shelter for their village.

After her father was released, they moved into his family home, which included seven uncles and two aunts who had moved to Saigon from the north so they could worship in a Catholic church. Before the war, this family had been wealthy and had associated with the French. Her father had been a captain in the army. He was a proud man who never learned to ask for favors. Now they were broke and the men were unemployed. Thiep's uncles were smart, but because of their history they were not allowed to study or work. These uncles and her father never recovered from the family's loss of status. Thiep's mother was a seamstress, the best wage earner in the family.

Prison changed her father, who had been optimistic and kind before the war but was now distrustful and bitter. When her family asked old friends for help, the friends would quietly disappear. Thiep interrupted herself to say that she didn't judge the people, but the times. It was dangerous to be helpful to a family like hers.

At school Thiep was teacher's pet and class president. But she knew her education would come to nothing. Because of the family's political past, Thiep would never be able to go to college.

Thiep paused briefly and looked around the cheery room. She said, "I want to tell you about my uncles. I think of them every day."

One of these uncles knew Latin and French and loved to write and conduct music. He lived an artist's life and didn't care for money at all. The other uncle dreamed of becoming a soccer player. They had no hope for a good life in Vietnam and they planned a daring escape. They slipped onto a boat with others who were escaping with the help of "snakeheads," or paid guides. They were at sea with sixty people when a storm blew in. The fishermen all rushed to shore, but the escapees couldn't go to shore or they would be arrested. So they chose to brave the storm, and at dusk the boat capsized. Everyone on board was killed.

Thiep's family went to recover the bodies. They found the body of her youngest uncle. It was a rainy day. Thiep thought, "God is crying with us." They never found the body of the educated uncle; they think he may have accidentally swum toward the sea. They made a cross for him by a tree and left an offering of chicken and wine. They brought the other uncle's body home. At his funeral, many women cried as the handsome soccer player was buried.

Thiep stopped talking and cried for a while. She said, "I have had more life than I wanted."

Thiep's family arrived in the United States jet-lagged and with pinkeye. That first night they stayed with a Khmer family, then they moved into a basement apartment. Thiep said they were like rats in a cellar. They didn't know how to cook on American appliances and no one came to visit. One day the baby had an ear infection. They called 911 but none of them could speak English. Later, the phone company traced the call and reported the emergency. A fire truck and policemen arrived but the family still couldn't explain why they called.

Slowly the family adapted. Her dad got a job as a floor polisher and learned to drive a car. Thiep had her first day of school. When she walked into high school, she couldn't even ask where to go. A Vietnamese student helped her get started and soon she was settled. She helped the other students and the teachers in any way she could. She rapidly learned English and passed through the ELL levels. She was what my aunt Margaret called "green on top," someone who loved to learn.

Thiep made many friends, but didn't feel close to anyone. "No one had my experiences." She felt that, compared to most Vietnamese young women, she was more serious and mature. She was unsure how to really be close to Americans or Vietnamese. She said, "I don't fit anywhere. I am not like the people in either country." She laughed. "I get along better with teachers than with anyone else."

Her teachers made her feel like somebody. She had never

felt like a real person in Vietnam. She wrote to a teacher, "ELL students are poor. But we have red hearts and we offer them to you."

At the university, she studied physics. She knew almost all the Asian students, but she was afraid of close relationships. She'd never had a boyfriend or even a date. She said, "I wouldn't know how to handle that."

Thiep was a strange mix of strong and vulnerable, confident and shy. She reminded me of a story my mother told of a man without a country, condemned to always keep moving, to never settle down and be at home. He sailed from place to place, always wanting what he could not have, terra firma, and an identity as a man from a particular place.

Thiep had job offers from big companies on both coasts. But she would never work for money. She wanted to help Vietnamese people keep their old culture, but with open hearts, ready to embrace what is good in America. She said that in many families the old spoke only Vietnamese and the grandchildren spoke only English so that the generations could not talk to each other.

Thiep wrote poetry and stories. She wanted to bring the generations together. But most of her themes were painful ones. She leaned toward me as she whispered, "I need to rearrange the landscape of my mind. I am not a very happy person."

THREE IRAQIS
"Is there a marriage broker in Lincoln?"

On a March morning, I interviewed three men from southern Iraq. We sat by a window as we talked and watched the harsh Nebraska wind blow crab apple blossoms from the trees. Soon the sidewalks were covered with what looked like pink snow.

Mamduh was a small man with sallow skin and bad teeth. He had a shy, engaging smile and he worried that his English wasn't good enough for our interview. Hamid was pudgy, but elegantly dressed in gray slacks, a gold vest, and white silk shirt. Saif wore a brown-and-gold ski sweater and tan slacks. He was tall and slim, with a Valentino elegance.

All three men were deeply religious, but they had very different personalities. Hamid was articulate and outspoken, the leader of the three. Saif was dignified and deeply sad. Mamduh was gentle and eager to do the right thing. They all had been in America for three years and in the camps of Saudi Arabia for seven years before that. Hamid worked at the same factory as Mamduh. Saif was visiting from Sacramento.

We talked first about Mamduh's life in Basra. His father had been a truck driver and he was the oldest of six boys. They lived in a big house with his grandparents and uncles. When Mamduh was thirteen, his father made a joke about the government; someone reported it and his father was taken to prison by Saddam Hussein's soldiers. Two years later he was released, but he was physically and mentally destroyed. He never worked again and soon died.

After his father's arrest, Mamduh supported the family by working construction. Often he got dizzy and passed out from heatstroke. Meanwhile, Iraq became more oppressive and Mamduh feared for his life. Almost all the men he knew were "drafted" by Saddam into an army that they hated.

During the Gulf War, there was a brief time when the Iraqi people believed the United States would help them overthrow Saddam's tyranny. While Saddam's armies were tied up in Kuwait, many people in Iraq hoped for a new government. But after the war, the Americans let Saddam alone. Mamduh felt

President Bush had changed policies and betrayed the Iraqi people. He believed that American soldiers even helped Saddam kill Iraqis.

After the war, Saddam ordered his soldiers to kill anyone who helped the Americans. He said, "Even their blood is filthy." People were made to drink oil, or they were shot and their stomachs were split open. The streets were filled with the bodies of the dead.

Mamduh knew that unless he left the country he would be killed. He couldn't tell his family he was leaving because they might accidentally betray him or be tortured later for information. So he slipped quietly away. He walked for two days until he met an American soldier and asked for refuge. He was treated as a prisoner of war and sent, like all the Iraqi soldiers, to a camp in Saudi Arabia.

The camp was supposed to be temporary, but it still exists today and is still filled with Iraqi men who turned themselves in during the Gulf War. It's located in the desert, far from the eyes of outsiders, and run by Saudis who these three men believe have contempt for Iraqis.

I asked Saif and Hamid how they had arrived at the camp. Hamid dismissed the question. "His story is my story. We all had the same story."

Mamduh said, "Over 54,000 young men were in the POW camps. There was no work and the water was salty. We went for years without seeing women or children. In the night, men were taken from their tents and shot."

Saif said, "I would wake up in the morning and the friend who slept beside me would be missing. I wouldn't even ask where he was."

Hamid said, "The soldiers called us dogs, camels, or donkeys."

This was upsetting to all three men. In fact, the worst damage seemed to be a loss of their dignity through this seven-year process of being herded from place to place without respect or choices. Many men in the camps committed suicide or escaped back into Iraq. Others just died because, as Saif put it, "They got tired of it."

I was struck by how different their version of the Gulf War was from the one I had seen on television and read about in the newspapers. I realized I knew very little about what our president had promised the Iraqi people or what consequences followed our policies after the war. I reflected while these three men watched their friends being killed, I was reading books and going to the movies. While they were being bombed by American planes, I was drinking coffee with my friends. Long after I had relegated that war to the dustbin of history, they were imprisoned in a camp, fighting for their physical and psychological survival.

Finally in the early 1990s, several prisoners slipped under the carriage of a supply truck and rode to a city. There they managed to speak about conditions in the camps to the BBC. After that, the UN sent observers and things improved slightly. By April of 1993 the men decided to go on a hunger strike and risk death rather than be treated like dogs. This strike forced the UN to allow some men out of the camps. But the process was slow and arbitrary. Many were refused permission, and this triggered suicides. Others went crazy from despair and stress. Many were still there. Saif said, "We hear from our friends that it is still terrible."

In 1997 these three men were released from the camps, arbitrarily assigned a country, and put on a plane. In New York they were met by immigration officials who gave them plane tickets to their assigned cities. Hamid and Saif, close friends since boyhood, were sent to different parts of the country. (Saif's forced separation from Hamid reminded me of the Ellis Island story of the man sent to Houston, Texas, instead of Houston Street. Now, as then, hurried officials, more concerned with paper than people, can wreck lives.)

At first, life was hard. They had nothing—no language, no money, no connections, no education or job skills. They didn't get much help finding work or places to live. No one explained about rental deposits or credit ratings, things they hadn't experienced in Iraq.

Saif worked first as a dishwasher, then in a fast-food place. I winced at the image of this proud, debonair man washing dishes. Mamduh and Hamid got jobs in a factory in Lincoln. Mamduh made a joke that he would always work with Hamid, who took care of him. Hamid put his arm around Mamduh and said, "I protect my little brother."

Now Hamid lived with an American woman that he met at the factory. Hamid said his "wife" had become Muslim because she liked how women were treated in Muslim culture. She even wore a head covering when she left their apartment.

Saif had a turbulent relationship with a California woman and he felt that their cultural differences were insurmountable. He said, "When I was growing up in a little village in Iraq, she was in San Francisco. When I was in the camps, she was in a rock and roll band. We do not think alike. Whatever I think is natural, she thinks is unnatural."

Mamduh desperately wanted to marry a woman from his own village. But he knew he would never have the money or the connections to find a bride and bring her to Nebraska. He asked me quietly if I could help him find a wife in Nebraska. I said I doubted I could be of help.

He asked, "Is there a marriage broker in Lincoln?"

Talking about women led the men into an animated discussion of the way American men treat women. They were outraged that, in America, women get pregnant without husbands and that many children don't live with their fathers. They compared our high divorce rates to the much lower ones of Middle Eastern countries. Hamid talked of the men at his factory who go to the bars on Saturday night and find women to "do dirty things with." He said, "An Iraqi man would not do that. He would respect women too much. We only want to marry and have families."

Saif told me a story to explain how different the rules were in Iraq. His uncle fell in love with a young woman he'd seen in a shop. He waited seven years for his family's permission to marry her. Meanwhile, he had no socially acceptable way to see her. So his uncle actually opened a store that sold women's products so that this woman would come to his shop and he could visit with her.

Mamduh said he encouraged the American men at his job to respect women and to marry. Hamid and Saif were so upset by the topic of how American women are treated that they were shouting. Mamduh had tears in his eyes.

I reflected how the two cultures have mirror-image beliefs about each other. Americans often see Muslim men as disrespectful of women, and Muslims see American men as disrespectful. These men clearly believed that Iraqi culture was better for women and children. They also felt that in Iraq, families were closer and happier.

In fact, to these men, life in Iraq was very good except for Saddam. People took care of each other and were trusting and generous. The men talked about how in America people were obsessed with "mine, mine, mine." There was such an emphasis on property and individual rights. They joked about how Americans worried over who paid what on a restaurant bill. Even though people were rich, they debated about pennies.

Saif marveled that Americans teach their children to guard their toys. Iraqi children were taught to be generous. He said that in Iraq, there was really no concept of private property, only the concept of need and distribution. Hamid told me, "If you need something, everyone, even strangers, will give it to you."

Saif told me a story to demonstrate Iraqi generosity. When he was first in Sacramento, he slept in the bed of a countryman who worked nights. He said, "When this guy had a night off, he would make me sleep in the bed. He slept on the floor beside my bed. He didn't even have a cover for himself."

The Iraqis laughed about how some Americans didn't want others in their driveways or on their property, or were afraid of each other. Once Hamid tried to help a man at an ATM. As he moved near him, the man looked scared and ran away. They had all been warned to lock doors and watch out for criminals. In Iraq, they all passionately assured me, except for the government, they could trust everyone.

These men seemed sad as we talked of Iraq. No doubt they had idealized some, but they also genuinely missed their homeland and their families. They all wanted to go back, but they felt it was unlikely they ever would. In America, Saif wanted to become a home health aid. He spoke earnestly of his desire to make the world a better place. Hamid and Mamduh wanted eventually to run a business together. Mamduh joked, "He will be the boss; I will be the employee."

Hamid said that working in a factory he felt like a person of no real value. Mamduh said that none of them could make enough money to buy a house or a car. They were trapped in poverty.

I feared this was true. In spite of their good manners and nice clothes, the fact that these men couldn't read or write in English condemned them to menial work. They had no family or community support and were working at difficult jobs for less than a livable wage. Yet, they were generous with what they had—time and stories. They had lost so much—their homeland, their youth, their language, and their hopes for a traditional life. What was striking was that they had held on to their humanity.

CHAPTER 8

FAMILY—"*A* BUNDLE *of* STICKS CANNOT BE BROKEN"

EVEN START

On a snowy night in late November, I arrived at my favorite conversational Even Start class. This class had three Vietnamese women, Yen, Ha, and Bao, and two Latinas, Rosa from Mexico and Maria from El Salvador. Even Start is a program offered by our public schools to teach English to the parents of ELL students. It is an expensive program, involving transportation, child care, special materials, and ELL teachers. Classes are held in different schools at different times of the day.

I attended an evening class of mothers from Latin America and Vietnam. They arrived on a bus with all their kids in tow and, while they studied and recited, their children played in the next room. Most of the mothers had been in factories all day, but they were happy to be in class and eager to learn.

Ha's husband was disabled and she supported him and five children by working at the water-bed factory. She was tired but good-natured, except when she talked about her teenage daughter. Bao was older than the others and she looked it. Bossy, funny, and filled with newcomer zest, she had most of the attributes of resilience, plus a close family and a community of friends. With her ponytail and makeup, Yen looked like a teenager, but she had six kids and worked full time with Bao and Ha. Rosa was fresh off the bus. She was shy and didn't work outside the home. She had two preschool-age children and was pregnant. Maria, from El Salvador, had six kids and cooked at a Mexican restaurant.

The teacher, Miss Wendy, a redhead from Montana, was all smiles and greetings. Tonight after she welcomed her students, she asked them to tell the class what they had done over the weekend.

Yen spoke first. She looked too pretty and peppy for someone with a full-time job and six children. Yen said she had taken her daughter to the emergency room because she had a sore throat and fever. Wendy expressed surprise because the emergency room is so expensive.

Yen said, "I called Ask a Nurse and she said I'd better go."

Wendy said, "Then you did the right thing. Is your daughter better?"

Yen nodded proudly. "I bought her medicine."

Wendy pointed to the thick bandage on Ha's hand. Last week she had injured herself when a sharp tool slipped as she worked on a bed frame. Wendy asked, "How is your hand tonight?"

Ha answered, "Not too bad. The doctor said I should rest, but I am the only worker in my family."

Wendy asked, "Could the doctor write you a note for work?"

Ha vigorously shook her head no. "I don't want any trouble. Good job." She changed the subject. "An American lady invited me to a candle party on Saturday."

The others looked impressed, but Wendy only said,

"Hmmm." She asked, "Do you know if your friend will be selling candles at the party?"

Ha looked confused. Wendy said, "Sometimes Americans sell things at parties. Remember you do not need to buy any candles. You can just enjoy the party."

Bao patted Ha's arm and volunteered herself as chaperone. "I will go with you if you want. Don't worry."

Bao pulled out her computer for translating and placed it in on the table in front of her. She flashed the group a big smile and said, "My family attended Thanksgiving dinner at the community center. I made seventy-five egg rolls for the party."

Wendy asked if it was fun. "Sure, sure. We had everything—turkey, pumpkin pie, pin-the-tail-on-the-donkey and bingo. I am very good at bingo." To demonstrate she yelled out, "Bingo!" a few times. We all laughed.

Watching Bao joke around, it was hard to believe she'd lost two children escaping Vietnam. She acted as if life were a grand adventure; she didn't complain and she hurled herself into learning. She was eager to make friends and to make money.

Maria proudly announced that she had found shirts at Kmart for 70 percent off. This elicited gasps of delight from the group. Maria said, "Go tomorrow. The sale ends Tuesday."

She elaborated, "They have Christmas decorations. Very cheap. I bought a Christmas card that sings all by itself."

Yen said, "I bought toys and coats at the Salvation Army for nineteen cent a pound."

Bao said, "I bought a Christmas tree, but the needles turned brown and it died."

"Did you water it?" Wendy asked.

Bao grimaced and said, "No, Miss." Everyone laughed.

Wendy turned to Rosa. "What did you do this weekend?"

"I had a flat tire," she answered shyly.

Ha said, "I had one of those last month."

Wendy asked, "How many of you know how to change a flat tire?" When no one raised her hand, Wendy said, "In the spring, I will teach you how to do this. It isn't hard."

Bao asked Rosa, "Do you have a driver's license?"

She looked embarrassed and shook her head no.

Bao clucked and shook her head. "This one should go to cultural orientation classes."

Wendy rescued Rosa from Bao.

"Rosa," she said, "stay after class and I will tell you what to do for your driver's license. Do not worry. You are not in trouble." Then she changed the subject. "How do you like the snowy weather?"

Yen said, "It is very hard, Miss. All my children fall down."

"My first snow in Nebraska, I put snow in a box to mail to Vietnam," Bao said. "I didn't know it would melt."

"What if the roads are closed when my baby is coming?" asked Rosa.

Maria said, "The hospital will send an ambulance for you, chica. You and the baby will be fine."

"My husband called in sick today because he is afraid to drive on snow," Yen announced. "He might wreck our car."

Wendy said gently, "Maybe your husband could ask an American to teach him to drive on winter roads."

"When we first came here, the snow made our lights go off. We were afraid the snow would cover our house." Ha shivered at the memory. "We sat in the cold and darkness for several days until our caseworker dug us out."

Wendy said, "Many newcomers do not understand cold. It can be dangerous. Please wear gloves, hats, and coats on cold days and make sure your children are dressed warmly. Be careful when you walk on ice."

I reflected on how much we take for granted. We Nebraskans know about hypothermia and wind chill; we have been walking on ice all our lives. Some of the lessons were verbal: "Walk on the grass, that sidewalk is too icy" or "Those shoes don't have enough grip. You'll fall down." But most of what we know has been learned through trial and error. Walking on ice involves knowing what kind of shoes to wear and how to step solidly and slowly, feeling our way, and it involves learning to evaluate surfaces for slickness and recognizing subtle gradations in texture and color that allow us to predict where we are most likely to fall. Newcomers, especially from the Global South, have none of that knowledge.

Wendy asked, "What kinds of food are good in winter?"

This led into a rousing discussion of food. Bao rubbed her stomach and said, "Fried catfish salad with eggplant."

Ha said, "Pizza is always good." Maria agreed.

Yen asked, "Miss Wendy, do Americans eat frogs stuffed with ants?"

"Not too often," said Wendy.

"Menudo is good in winter," Rosa said. "And pozole is delicious with Mountain Dew."

"My baby likes Mountain Dew in her bottle," Yen bragged.

Wendy asked, "Is this good for babies?" Three women said yes and two no. Wendy said, "Milk or juice is better."

Ha wanted to know why American grocery stores do not smell. "Vietnamese stores are very fragrant."

Maria said, "Shrimps in Mexico are much better."

Wendy said, "A shrimp must swim a long ways to get to Lincoln from the ocean." Everyone laughed.

Wendy joked, nurtured, and served as a cultural broker for

these women. She made class feel like a party. Her students arrived tired, but they grew less tired as the class progressed.

Wendy asked how everyone's kids were doing. Yen said, "My kids went to Chuck E. Cheese this week."

"I bought my daughter a new dress," Maria bragged. "She made straight A's."

"That is what I tell all my children," Bao said. "Make straight A's like Maria's daughter." Everyone laughed but Ha.

Ha shook her head sadly. "My daughter stay out late on Saturday night. She is a very bad girl."

"She is not a bad girl. She just has bad friends." Bao wagged her finger at Ha. "I told you, do not let her leave the house except for her job and school."

"My son is only three and already he has learned a naughty word from the boy next door," Rosa said sadly.

"Children are spoiled in America," Ha said. "Teachers here are too easy. In Vietnam if you made a mistake you had to kneel in the corner or teacher would hit you."

Wendy asked, "Do you want me to make you kneel in the corner if you make a mistake?"

Bao joked, "I am too fat to kneel in corner."

Ha remained serious and said, "In the United States, children lose their spiritual nature and become materialistic."

Maria said, "My oldest daughter comes home after school and takes care of the children. She cooks and cleans the house."

"If the oldest child is good, all the younger ones will be good," Yen said.

Ha said, "I worry my daughter is with gang kids."

"It is good you are learning English," Wendy said reassuringly. "You can help your children more when you understand our language."

Bao said, "I let my children study at an American school,

shop at the mall, and wear American clothes, but I make sure they think like Vietnamese."

"That is the best way to have a family," Wendy said. "Pick what is best from each culture."

She patted Ha's bandaged arm. "I am sorry your daughter is having trouble."

Bao volunteered, "Tell your daughter if she is a good girl, Auntie Bao will buy her a cell phone." Even Ha smiled.

Wendy offered, "Would you like to have an English lesson?" The women nodded happily.

Wendy distributed handouts and had them follow along while she read aloud a dopey story about a visit to a luxury beach hotel, an elegant place with tennis courts and a golf course. I thought it was cruel to make such poor women read about wealth. But, much to my surprise, they enjoyed it. They had no resentment of the rich. Instead, they all pretended to take a vacation to this hotel.

Yen said, "Someday I will go to a hotel like this. I will take my kids and we will build sand houses."

"Sand castles, you mean," said Wendy.

Ha giggled, "I would like to go there just with my husband for a honeymoon."

Rosa said, "What is a honeymoon?"

"Ahhh, chica. You don't know anything," Maria chided.

Wendy intervened. "It's good she is in our class. We can help her."

Bao pointed to the hotel scene on her handout and asked me, "Is it in Florida?" I nodded and she said, "I will make lots of money and buy my family plane tickets to Florida."

Maria said, "One time I went dancing at a hotel like this one."

Bao interrupted. "Dancing or kissing, chica?"

Maria blushed and Wendy cleared her throat and hid a smile. She said, "Let's look at the grammar in this story."

We worked on which prepositions to use when. The rules were complex and there were many exceptions—*on* the weekend, *in* the morning, and *at* night. We also worked on irregular plurals such as *foot* and *feet* and *child* and *children.* Wendy explained the difference between *flushed,* as in "a face is *flushed,*" versus *flush,* as in "flush the toilet."

After a while Wendy noticed many furrowed brows and tired faces. She said, "Let's put the books away for now."

She wanted to end things on a happy note. She said, "Each of you tell us what you think is beautiful."

The women all looked thoughtful.

Ha said, "The flowers in the mountains near my village; beautiful red flowers bloomed along the road and up into the trees."

Yen said, "The faces of my children as they sleep are very beautiful."

Everyone nodded in agreement. Bao made a joke that wasn't a joke. "My paycheck when I have worked overtime is very beautiful."

Rosa said, "The snow is pretty on the pine trees."

Maria said, "Our teacher is beautiful. She looks like Julia Roberts." We all chuckled, but Maria was serious.

Bao put her hands together in prayer and pleaded, "Please, Miss Wendy, don't go to Hollywood and leave us here."

Wendy said, "I'll take you with me. We'll all stay at a hotel on the beach and make sand houses." Outside it was snowing. Inside, the weather was tropical.

ACCULTURATION BLUES

From the moment of arrival, families face dilemmas: Do they let their children drink Coke and watch cartoons? Do they try to speak English or do they stick with their native language? What kind of clothes do they wear? Do they wear shoes in the house? Do they shake hands with strangers? Do they encourage family members to be individuals or to maintain a family-based identity?

Families arrive here intensely unified; they have survived great crises and stayed together. All have focused on the dream of reaching a safe good place. But once here, people develop individual dreams. These conflicting dreams create tension and sometimes break up families that have risked their lives to be together. It's sad to see a family that has survived bombs or crocodiles split up over a credit-card bill or a drinking problem.

Internal culture wars often ravage families. One sister may continue to wear her hijab while other sisters wear shorts and halter tops. A teenage daughter may want to dress like American girls and the father is horrified. Grandchildren watch *The Simpsons,* while, in the next room, their grandfather prays to his ancestors. A Laotian girl argues with her mother in a way the mother didn't even know was possible. A boy in high school wants to date and his father expects him to wait for his arranged bride.

There may be arguments about what language is spoken in the home. Wage earners pick up a new language more quickly than the stay-at-home parent. Old people have a harder time adjusting to a new country and a new language. Some don't even attempt to assimilate. They leave it up to their kids, but often the first thing the kids learn is to disrespect elders.

I once saw a vivid demonstration of power reversals in families. A psychologist asked members of the audience to stand in order of the power distribution of traditional families—old men first, then other adult men, then women by age, and lastly, children. He spoke about assimilation rates for the genders and different ages. Then he had the group stand in the order of who learned about America the most rapidly. The order was exactly reversed—first children, then younger women, then younger men, and last were the elderly.

Gender issues raise some of our thorniest problems. In traditional cultures the lines of power and authority are clearly drawn. Men and older people wield power over women and younger people. Men and women have separate spheres and distinct cultural roles, roles that are difficult to maintain in America. Because of economic pressures and laws regulating education, property, divorce, and domestic violence, traditional roles are compromised. For the first time, many women experience the freedom to work, to go to school, and to marry whomever they choose.

However, women may experience a lack of protection and support. They may be frightened by all their new freedoms and uneasy with the responsibility to choose that comes with them. Ironically, the freedom that women have in our country can lead to a tightening of male control. Men feel threatened by the changes and react by becoming more controlling. Gender role strains contribute to domestic violence or divorce.

Parents tend to be poor and overworked, often holding two jobs or working endless overtime and double shifts. Many parents rarely see their children. A man from Honduras drives a truck long distances and is home with his family at most one night a month. The rest of the time he sleeps in his truck. He cannot afford to call home. Once I talked about a book I was reading with a mother from Croatia. She said, "I wish that one day I would have time to read a book."

Families from certain parts of the world have not been exposed to advertising, sexually explicit materials, or graphic violence in the media. American sleaze is everywhere, and everyone in the family is vulnerable. Refugees have the same problems

we all have with MTV, Howard Stern, slasher movies, and sexist music. But they are less prepared. I met a three-year-old
Kurdish girl whose first word was *chalupa* from Taco Bell ads.
She only wanted to eat what she saw on television. A Syrian
mother told me with horror that her son had bought a *Penthouse*
magazine. I talked with a Russian man who was one thousand
dollars in debt two weeks after he received his first charge card.
These are new problems for traditional families.

Refugees' families can be marginalized by poverty and
racism. Newcomers learn to look at their cultures through
American lenses, and what they see isn't positive. Psychologist
Michael White describes people as being "recruited into prejudice," that is, they learn to see themselves as inferior by seeing
themselves through the eyes of prejudiced others. Prejudice,
what Latinos call *"mal trato,"* leads to depression and internalized feelings of worthlessness.

Among adults there are many psychological meltdowns.
Immigrants often feel like small children. For a while they lose
control of their lives and feel stupid, helpless, and lost. Lola's
husband was a soccer star in Yugoslavia, but here he can't find
work. He is depressed and helpless. Many fathers who are "re-
tired" or "too sick to work" are really incapacitated by stress.

CUSTOMS AND PRACTICES
ACROSS CULTURES

Children from traditional cultures depend on their parents for
emotional support and moral guidance for as long as they live.
Children owe parents lifelong respect, obedience, and love.
Daughters live at home until marriage, and sons often live with
their parents all their lives. In many countries, the old are revered
and cared for. Nursing homes are unthinkable.

From conception until death, things are done differently in different countries. For example, in Vietnam, pregnant women are believed capable of influencing the character of their children during pregnancy. A woman who reads poetry, thinks lofty thoughts, and looks at beauty will have a more aesthetically sensitive child. Expectant mothers don't eat chicken during pregnancy because they don't want their babies to have "chicken skin." Vietnamese babies are not named at birth but are given a "milk name" until they are a little older.

In traditional cultures, a birth changes dozens of relationships within the extended family. Children fall into a carefully arranged web of family members. Mothers are expected to care for babies, toddlers, and young children. Fathers, cousins, older siblings, aunts, and uncles all have prescribed roles. Grandparents often live in the same home and play an important role in the education of their grandchildren.

I know an Asian family that consists of the parents, both university professors, their teenaged daughter, and the mothers of both parents. They live together and while the couple works, the older women cook, care for the house, and supervise the daughter after school. The mother told me, "Our mothers have gentled our daughter. If they hadn't been with us, I think she would have found trouble in junior high. But they were waiting for her after school with snacks, attention, and affection. They held her life in place."

The American custom of putting infants in day care is shocking to many newcomers. No day care even exists in most of Central and South America and the Middle East. Immigrants wonder why we, in such a rich country, leave our babies with strangers.

Developmental milestones occur at different times across

cultures. In the Middle East and Southeast Asia, children are toilet trained very early by American standards. Latino mothers have more relaxed time lines for toilet training and weaning. In general, Latino mothers are more indulgent, talkative, and affectionate with babies than mothers from many other cultures. This is great for young children, but sometimes increases their separation anxiety when they begin school.

Traditional parents keep kids more involved with family and less involved with peers than do American parents. Our American ideas of overnights for children or birthday parties for friends of children strike many newcomers as odd. Children are expected to be with the family when they are not in school. In fact, often parents don't want their children to have friends because these friends could lead them into trouble.

Different cultures have different ideas about discipline and physical punishment. What many cultures consider appropriate, we define as abuse. Refugee parents have been told at cultural orientation that they will be arrested if they discipline their children with physical force. They are afraid to use what may have been their traditional ways of punishing their children, but they have no new ways. Children sometimes use their parents' fears of the law to bully them. One boy told his mother, "If you don't let me watch TV, I'll call the police."

Attitudes toward retirement vary across cultures. Middle Eastern people retire as early as fifty. Latino men generally do not retire while they are healthy. Often elders from traditional cultures watch children while parents work. Sometimes this works well, but sometimes it leaves elders lonely and vulnerable. Without English, elders may be dependent on grandchildren for the simplest things—answering the phone, helping them read their mail, or translating cooking instructions on a can of soup.

Sometimes their grandchildren cannot speak the language of the old country.

ADJUSTING TO THE NEW WORLD

Parents must learn English or they will lose authority and control of their children. As mentioned earlier, Portes and Rumbaut documented the benefits of bicultural families. They found that the best pattern was one in which the family carefully chose what to accept and reject in American culture. Second best was a pattern in which the whole family moved into mainstream America at roughly the same pace. Least healthy, but unfortunately quite common, was a pattern in which the children outstripped their parents. If the kids were in the lead, everyone was in trouble. Whatever their current stresses and past traumas, refugee parents must still be parents.

When I work with traditional families, I stress the importance of everyone learning about America. I encourage respect for parents and elders and reinforce the closeness of children and grandparents. I validate the family's past history of sticking together. I say things like, "I cannot help you if you don't help each other."

I have even been known to do a rather hokey demonstration. I set a number of small sticks out on a table. I have a volunteer from the family pick up one of the sticks and see if he or she can break it. Of course he or she breaks it easily. Then I gather all of the sticks together and tie them in a bundle. I hand this bundle to my volunteer and again ask him or her to break it. When the volunteer cannot break them, I say, "A bundle of sticks cannot be broken."

On the other hand, I encourage parents to reflect on the difficulty their kids have with our culture. I stress that this is a new place with very different expectations for children. Teenagers are not the same in the United States as they are in the traditional homeland. I encourage parents to listen to their children's point of view and to develop some empathy for the cultural switching kids must do.

I talk about the attributes of resilience. I encourage families to be flexible, focused, attentive, and hardworking. I stress that assimilation takes time. There is a lot of trial-and-error learning. Many of the problems families have are problems of transition. I reassure families that after a year they will have solved some of their current problems, although, of course, they will have new challenges.

I ask, What do you want to keep from the old culture? What do you want to accept from America? I reinforce the importance of connections to the ethnic community as well as to American cultural brokers. I teach families that time is their greatest wealth and they must spend it carefully. I recommend parents turn off their televisions and talk to and listen to their children. I urge parents to read to their children and practice English with them. I teach families to think carefully about choices and to be careful how they spend money.

I try to teach the best American parenting practices—how to set limits, to give feedback to family members, to hug, and to praise. We have the tools to resolve problems, negotiate conflicts, and respect everyone's point of view. My goal is to help people replace despair, stress, and denigration with pride, hope, and enjoyment. Pleasurable activities and laughter can bond families just as trauma can. Fun can be deeply healing.

Americans are good at having fun with children. Newcomers can learn from us how to have family vacations, picnics, and educational and recreational outings. In Nebraska, families enjoy the migrating sandhill cranes in spring and the wild geese in the fall. We celebrate birthdays and milestones of all kinds. We like family reunions and potlucks, events almost all people can enjoy.

ART THERAPY

I attended a group held at a community center for Afghani and Middle Eastern women who met for cultural orientation, English practice, and emotional support. I was invited by Leda, a Kurdish woman, who asked me to help her group heal from the past.

I had known Leda for six months. Her family had suffered in about every way a family could suffer. They had lost their home, their country, and their relatives. Her husband, Ahmad, had been forced to be a soldier and he told me, "In one battle that lasted forty days, I saw thirty thousand young Iraqis killed." He said, "Men who wouldn't fight had their ears cut off; but if they fought they would die, so losing ears was good."

After Ahmad escaped the army, he and Leda had no choice but to flee their country. Their youngest child was born in a meadow. The other children were educated on the run. At one point Leda tied the baby to her back and the family walked across the desert for weeks. They moved only at night and hid under bushes with snakes and scorpions by day. They were thirsty and had only dried bread. The children cried soundlessly for hours. One night they passed so close to soldiers they could see the embers of their cigarettes. As Leda put it, "We had months when everyone we encountered wanted us dead."

But they were doing well in America. Many times Leda prepared me meals in their home. That was the only place she was without her hijab, and she looked very different. Her beautiful long hair swirled as she moved, and her mobile face was filled with expression. Their small house was clean and calm, even with five children.

Our first meal together had been awkward. Leda served naan, shish kebabs and dolmas stuffed with rice, tomatoes, egg-plants, and peppers. I knew that she had worked all week in the factory and then spent her weekend cooking this meal. I was embarrassed that she wouldn't allow me to help serve and that she wouldn't sit down with Ahmad and me for the meal. As the two of us ate and Leda served, Ahmad stated, "We Iraqis treat our women like queens."

Leda and Ahmad had an arranged marriage. However, they clearly loved and respected each other. For his time and place, Ahmad was actually a feminist. He cared for the kids while Leda learned English. When she talked about her current job at the dog food factory, he looked sorrowful. He said, "I want Leda to get an American degree."

Leda said her job was very difficult and unpleasant. Some of her coworkers were kind, but many were unintelligent racists. She felt humiliated by this work, but she would do anything for the family.

Ahmad worked hard, too. In Iraq he'd been an architect. Here he worked as a clerk at a convenience store and as a baker. He believed girls and boys should be educated equally. He felt they could study together until junior high, but then they dis-tracted each other. He argued that adolescents were unable to work in the presence of the opposite sex, a point I found hard to dispute.

Leda disapproved of public displays of affection and the way American women show their bodies. She said, "Women are jewels, not toys. They should respect themselves."

Both Ahmad and Leda felt women should be able to divorce and keep legal rights to their children. Neither believed men should be allowed to beat their wives. Still, they disapproved of the high divorce rate in America. Ahmad said, "In Iraq, marriage is a shirt you wear the rest of your life. If you tear it, you mend it."

Both Ahmad and Leda were unfailingly kind to me. In spite of their economic situation, they often gave me gifts, not only of the meals but of flowers or books by Iraqi writers. When I left, Ahmad would say to me, "I am your brother. Leda is your sister."

It was Leda who encouraged the women in the support group to talk openly to an outsider. Thanks to her, I had been greeted as a friend. I'd been coming for a while now and I approached the meeting with eagerness but also anxiety that my skills were not adequate to the sorrow of this group.

Tonight it was early June. I walked under linden trees, with their sweet aroma, and entered the community center. The women were waiting for me at a table with hot tea, nuts, and dried fruit.

The Afghani women had been in Lincoln only a few months. They had come to escape the brutal civil war, the repression of women by the Taliban, and the famine. When the Taliban came to power in 1996, it prohibited women from going to school, working, driving, or leaving home without a male relative. All women were ordered to be covered in "black tents."

The Afghani women were coming from a place where seven-year-old girls were sold as wives for a few bags of wheat; where women who taught girls to read, even in their own homes, could be killed; and where villages were invaded and all the men between seventeen and seventy were lined up and shot. They arrived from a place where families froze to death and all women's health facilities were closed.

Leda knew the Afghani women from her work at a dog food company, rather grisly work for women who had seen so much blood and death. The four women in this group, Leda, Ritu, Zahra, and Nessima, were a complex combination of similar and different. All belonged to the community of the bereaved and downtrodden. Yet they brought very different characteristics and human capital into their new situations. Zahra was in her sixties and alone; Ritu, who was only in her late twenties, was widowed, pregnant, and supporting three children. Nessima was stoic and a hard worker, but she had been an arranged bride at fourteen and couldn't read or write in any language. Her husband was unhappy in America and sometimes took his frustrations out on his family.

Ritu was dressed in slacks and a shirt. Leda and Zahra wore traditional head coverings, and Nessima was totally covered in a long robe that even had black embroidery covering her eyes. The women spoke broken English, although Leda's English was amazingly good and she often translated for me with the others.

Zahra had lost almost everyone, including her husband, her three daughters, two of her sons, and her grandchildren. Her husband had been shot in front of her, her daughters raped and killed. Her daughters had tried to hide their attractiveness by smearing their faces with engine oil, but the soldiers had made them wash and then had raped them. Her only surviving son was in prison in Turkey with passport problems. He could buy his way to freedom, but neither he nor Zahra had any money.

Zahra was actually about my age, but she looked much older. I compared her life to mine. While she had worried that her children would be killed, my worries had been about my kids getting into graduate school or finding a nice apartment to rent. While she struggled to keep from starving and freezing to death, I had debated whether to become a vegetarian. Our lives showed in our faces and our bodies. Zahra had arthritis and decayed teeth. I had no serious health issues and had access to good doctors and dentists.

At first Zahra had worked cleaning office buildings, but she had been fired for moving slowly. She was unlikely to find a new job with her age, limited English, inability to read or write, health problems, and depression. Zahra was terribly lonely here, and she worried constantly about her son. I asked her once if she had any dreams and she had burst into tears and moaned, "I have no dreams."

She sat alone in her basement apartment watching the worst possible television shows and accumulating a great deal of misinformation. She had heard that Americans had half a million sex slaves hidden away in their basements. I said I doubted that. She had heard a computer could make all the airplanes in the world crash at once. I said I had never really thought about that. She asked me if all American men had mistresses. I offered a definitive no.

I advised her, "Please do not watch so much television. Sit outside under the trees or visit with your friends."

The one thing that gave me hope was that Zahra was interested in Ritu's pregnancy. She would feel Ritu's rounded belly and smile her toothless grin. "Baby," she would say. "Baby good."

Zahra had few visible attributes of resilience, no family, and a terrible history. She had no hope, energy, ambition, or trust. She felt cursed and wished she could visit a shrine and pray for forgiveness. She wondered what terrible crime Afghanis had committed that their nation was being punished so heavily. If anything could save Zahra, it would be this community of women who included her in their lives.

Nessima had a better situation. She was hardworking and healthy and her family was intact. But her lack of education would keep her in minimum-wage jobs. Her husband's family had checked her teeth like she was a horse the day they met and inspected her. She and her husband had always had a troubled relationship and in Nebraska it had deteriorated. However, at least they could both work and provide their four children with a home and adequate food.

Nessima often quoted sexist old sayings such as, "A woman in bed by night, by day a walking stick." She told me that when she and her husband fought, she taunted him, "If you're a real man, beat me." I responded carefully, "That isn't a good thing to say in America. It is against the law to hit women here. Your husband could go to jail. And, Nessima, you could be hurt."

Nessima's husband also worked at the dog food factory, first shift, so that he could watch the kids while she worked. He felt Americans were sinful and unfriendly. Nessima said of him, "*Hello* and *sorry* are the only English words my husband knows."

Nessima appeared to have mixed feelings about Nebraska. The world she believed in had grown murderous. In this new place, she was working and learning to drive. Her values remained conservative, but she enjoyed her freedom to shop, go to classes, and to drive her kids to Kmart and the parks.

She didn't enjoy her job—after eight hours on the killing floor, her bones ached and she stank from dried blood, but she liked making money for the first time in her life. Even though she handed her husband her check, they were both aware that she earned half their income. In Nebraska, power was more evenly divided between them; Nessima wasn't as humble as she used to be.

Ritu was a shy, pretty young woman. Looking at her in the support group, smiling and gentle, it was hard to believe she had witnessed the executions of all the men in her family. She'd escaped with her three children, traveling on foot to a refugee camp in Pakistan where they had survived a harsh winter with no tent. She had been raped in that camp, although no one spoke of this directly. Now she was pregnant with the baby of the rapist.

Generally in Afghanistan, rape is a great shame for the victim and her family. But this was America and the women were reacting in a new way. Ritu had no time for shame and the other women spoke of the upcoming birth with happy anticipation. They all did what they could to help. When Ritu worked double shifts, Zahra slept at her house. Nessima invited her home for meals, and Leda gave her used children's clothes.

Until the war came, Ritu had been a nurse, an educated woman with a husband she loved and healthy children. When the Taliban closed her clinic, she'd been forced to stay at home, knowing her patients desperately needed help. After her husband was killed, she and the children almost starved to death. Yet here in Nebraska, she never complained.

Ritu supported her family with a minimum-wage job. Her disposable income was probably about what I spent each month on café lattes. Still, she shared whatever she had with the rest of us. Today she kept passing me pistachios and encouraging me to eat. The only time I had seen her cry was when she told us about her baby's ultrasound and said the doctor believed the baby would be healthy. She'd asked me, "Why am I crying when I am happy? I never cried when I was sad."

In these women's stories, a lot of pain had gone under the bridge. But the women were clearly happy to be in America and in this group. They were delighted their children were well fed and learning to read. Ritu said, "We are grateful to Lincoln. It is a quiet, safe place."

Americans seemed lonely to them. Leda said in Iraq if a new family moved into a neighborhood, for a week they wouldn't lift a finger. Neighbors would bring them meals and do their chores. Fathers would help the men carry things and mothers would clean and cook for the wife to make her feel welcome. She sighed and said, "Everyone here is too busy." Ritu added, "In America everyone makes his own life, and that is a good thing and a bad thing."

As usual, the women discussed food and shopping. They all were amazed at the products in our stores. Nessima was surprised there were dolls that talked and that you could buy a mix to make a cake. The first time she went to Kmart she walked up and down the rows wondering what everything was for. Ritu told of seeing all the types of women's underwear at Kmart. At first she couldn't figure out what these objects were. She said, "They were so beautiful. All the colors of the rainbow."

The women all agreed that cooking was better in their homelands where food was sacred. Leda said Kurdish women won't cook when they are stressed. They believe negative emotions ruin the food. The Kurds eat together slowly, talking for hours.

Ritu said, "Middle Easterners eat slowly and calmly. We don't talk about bad things at meals. They are peaceful times."

Leda noted the casual attitude Americans take toward food. She said, "With Americans eating is just for physical need." She was shocked to see us eat on the run or while we were doing other things, such as driving or attending a lecture.

Nessima was amazed by vegetarians. Meat was very desirable in her country. She made a hand gesture near her brain to signal that she thought vegetarians were a little crazy. She told me, "They have never tasted my lamb curry."

All the women loved American buffets. Nessima oohed and aahed over the local Buffy's Buffet selection. Even Zahra had been taken there on her birthday. I remembered a *New Yorker* cartoon showing two pilgrims talking: "Actually the attraction wasn't freedom from religious persecution, but, rather, the all-you-can-eat buffet."

Ritu said, "Afghanis believe it is a sin to waste food." She was upset when her children made art with macaroni and uncooked pinto beans at school. She said, "I have many relatives who are hungry. It is disrespectful of the school to use food so foolishly."

At the mention of relatives, the room grew quiet. Leda looked at me. I asked gently if they remembered their assignment to bring pictures of their old homes. Leda brought out pictures of her house in Iraq. Then Nessima and Zahra showed pictures of their homes. All had nice houses with pretty gardens. As they passed these pictures around, all four women cried.

Nessima said, "Before the Taliban, Afghanistan was modern and happy. The streets were filled with neighbors talking. Now the streets are empty. Men are fearful they will be forced to fight for the Taliban. Women are prisoners in their own homes."

Zahra said, "Even young girls have to be completely covered to go outside."

"To escape, people walked or rode horses into Pakistan. Many died on the way," Nessima explained. "Children froze or fell off mountains."

Ritu spoke of her brother still in Afghanistan. "I don't even know if he is alive. It is impossible to exchange mail or call him. There are no airports. There is no consulate."

Leda said simply, "I, too, have seen a life of war. Every day I thought I might die. No matter how hard America is, I am grateful to be here. My children have a chance in this country."

I asked the women if they would like to do an art project. There is an old chestnut: Art turns agony into ecstasy. I didn't expect any ecstasy, but I did hope that drawing might help these women express feelings they couldn't express in their limited English.

They nodded in polite agreement. I pulled out paper and colored pencils. The women marveled at my supplies. I said, "Sometimes it is good to draw sad events, to take them out of your heart and place them on a piece of paper."

I said, "I know this may be painful for you. I wouldn't ask you to do this if I didn't think it would help you. I want you all to draw a picture of fear."

Zahra hesitated for a while, but the others drew eagerly and unselfconsciously, like schoolchildren. I realized most had never had an art lesson or even an opportunity to draw. They had no one's art to compare with their own.

Ritu drew women in black clothes scurrying around the corners of buildings looking for food. They looked like crows, all in black, skinny, trying to find crumbs. She drew herself in the robes she had been forced to wear by the Taliban. She told me, "The first time I wore that heavy cloth over my face I had an asthma attack."

She continued, her eyes blazing with emotion, "The cloth was hot in summer and cold in winter. I couldn't wear my glasses with the eye veil and I was blind without them. I fell down many times." She paused to collect herself and then said,

"Walking across mountains in the snow I threw it away. I couldn't wait any longer to get rid of what I hated."

Nessima drew herself and her children in black boxes that looked like coffins. She said, "We were prisoners in our small hut. It was a very dark time."

Leda drew her family on the run, a line of people with the father in the lead, then the mother, then the children in a row like ducks. Everyone was holding hands. Above the family was a crescent moon. In the distance, bombs were falling.

Zahra didn't draw anything for a long time. Then she drew slowly, her nose almost touching the paper. Watching her work, I had the feeling she had never drawn anything before. When she finally finished and lifted her head, I saw that she had drawn a meadow with sheep.

To me, it didn't look like an unhappy scene, just a crudely drawn meadow with stick sheep. But Zahra's face had been drained of color and she was trembling. I asked about this meadow. She shook her head many times and said only, "Something terrible happened here."

The women passed around their drawings. Nobody said very much. We could all guess at the feelings behind these sad pictures. I thought about the difference between the last five years of my life and the last five years of theirs. I wondered how I had ever had the nerve to complain about anything.

I collected the drawings and said, "I want to teach you an important word." On the board I wrote "hope" and I said it aloud several times. I defined it. They all smiled.

Ritu said, "Hope is good."

After the drawings of fear, we drew peace. The women drew their homes in America. The pictures, with big flowers and round suns in the corners, looked like the drawings of fourth graders. Leda put an American flag in front of her house. The other women admired that touch and they all drew flags in their front yards.

I talked about ways to relax. I suggested warm baths, lotions, and foot and back rubs from their families. I said that going outdoors and admiring the flowers and trees would be relaxing.

Zahra said her doctor said that swimming would help with her arthritis. Nessima said she would love to swim, but her husband wouldn't let her go to a public pool. Leda and Ritu both said they wouldn't feel comfortable swimming near men. I said, "I will check into a swim class for women only at the YWCA." I added, "Ritu, swimming is good for pregnant women."

The women gathered up their purses and books. Leda showed the others free tickets for the circus she had received from a local radio station. She said, "I will take my kids to look at lions and elephants. It will be a happy day for us."

Zahra looked sad and hunched over. She was heading home to her television with its tall tales and advertisements for things she would never be able to buy. I made a mental note to look into her son's situation. It would take time, but eventually we might be able to bring him to America.

Ritu touched Zahra's shoulder and said, "I am hoping you will help me with my baby. My time is soon."

Zahra straightened up as she agreed to help. As she left the room, she told Nessima, "Baby is good. Very good."

As I watched Ritu lift herself heavily from her chair, I thought about her coming baby. Ritu was already overworked, but she had never hinted that the baby would be a burden. In fact, she had told me she was very eager to see her baby take its first "breath of life."

I reflected on all of the stories from all over the world in which a child comes to end suffering. This may be our first and oldest human story. The Christmas story is one example of the many birth and salvation stories. A family wanders far from home, poor and scared, looking for a safe haven. A stranger is kind and allows them a place to rest. A baby arrives in a time of darkness and fear. The stars in the sky signal the glory of this event. The newborn brings its family great joy and the hope that he will save the world, at least the small world of the family. It's an archetypal story because it reflects our deep belief in the healing power of children. The face of hope is a newborn baby, not just for Zahra, but for all of us.

The ALCHEMY of HEALING—
HEALING—
TURNING PAIN
into MEANING

PART THREE

CHAPTER 9

AFRICAN STORIES

THE KAKUMA REFUGEES
"Education is our mother and father."

On Christmas Day 2000, Lincoln received its first refugees from the Kakuma Refugee Camp in Kenya. The family was part of a group called the Lost Boys of Kakuma, although I didn't like that name. First, who would want to be labeled a lost boy? It seemed condescending and it made the refugees seem hopeless. Second, in this case, there was a girl, Martha, the sister of Joseph, Abraham, and Paul.

By now the story of the Kakuma refugees is well known. They were children whose parents were killed in the Sudanese civil war, which began in 1983 when the government of the north attacked the southern tribal peoples. Eventually the south formed its own army, the Sudanese People's Liberation Army; both sides used a scorched-earth policy. Caught between armies, 2 million ordinary people lost their lives. Generally, girls were kidnapped by the soldiers, while boys fled into the wild.

The orphaned children banded together and walked first to a camp in Ethiopia, where they stayed for many months. But when new rulers came to power in Ethiopia, they wanted to get rid of the refugees. They bombed the camp and ordered soldiers to herd the refugees out of their country. The fleeing orphans had to cross the Gilo River. Many children drowned or were eaten by crocodiles crossing that river. The refugees walked to various places in Sudan, but in 1992 they ended up in Kenya in the Kakuma Refugee Camp. Of the roughly seventeen thousand kids who began the march, ten thousand made it to Kakuma. The others were killed by soldiers, starved to death, or were eaten by predators.

Kakuma was a large sprawling place with primitive huts and muddy roads. The temperature hovered around one hundred degrees. There was only dirty water that looked like tea and one meal a day, a porridge of lentils and grain. Disputes over food and territory broke out after dark. Of Kakuma, Abraham would later tell me, "I never knew if I would wake up in the morning."

Yet the camp officials deserve some credit. They took in thousands of children no one else wanted and organized schools for them. Many of the boys learned to read and write in English. Kakuma refugees were taught to say, "Education is my mother and father." Still, it was a place with too few resources and too many orphans. In explaining their situation, Joseph said, "We were worth even less than weeds."

The family, who came to our town, had lost their parents when Joseph, the oldest, was twelve and Paul, the youngest, was five. Their father had been killed when their village was first raided. They lost their mother as they all ran from the attack at the Ethiopian camp. She stopped for a moment, there were explosions, and they never saw her again. The children managed to stay together for ten years, crossing back and forth across three countries, eating weeds to stay alive, running from people who wanted to kill them, and finally living in the refugee camp in Kenya.

Our First Visit

The Kakuma family had arrived in Lincoln by plane, what the tribal Dinka and Nuer called "sky boats." The airplane meals had been strange to them. They hadn't seen vegetables or forks in the camps. At our small airport, they were greeted by a large contingent of Sudanese and they experienced their first escalator, cell phone, vending machine, and revolving door. Outside it was snowing and the wind chill was twenty-five degrees below zero. As soon as they arrived, the family began to shiver and really never warmed up until spring.

On a cold sleety day, my husband and I went to meet the family in their two-bedroom apartment near our downtown. Their apartment was furnished with donated furniture, but it was neat and clean. There was a television set in the corner, already turned on. The temperature in the apartment hovered around ninety degrees, but even so, the family all wore jackets and huddled together on the couch.

They had a visitor from Sudan: James, a Nuer man who had ridges of scars on his forehead from manhood ceremonies. In Africa the Nuer and the Dinka might have been enemies, but here in Lincoln the many different tribes mix. The Sudanese are a sociable, fun-loving people. When they are not working or sleeping, they visit each other. They share food, clothes, bicycles, cars, and money with their countrymen.

The Kakuma refugees didn't look like African Americans. They looked like handsome Dinka warriors in sweatpants.

Joseph was clearly the leader. He was tall and slender, with a broad smile and a handshake and greeting for everyone. I wondered where he had acquired such good manners.

Abraham was even taller and thinner than Joseph. He looked very much like his older brother, but more winsome and tentative. Martha was pretty and quiet. Unlike her brothers, she hadn't been allowed to go to school, and she spoke almost no English. Paul had an open trusting face and seemed heartbreakingly eager to please. He closely watched his older brothers and did exactly what they did.

Over time I got to know the family very well. Joseph was a wise leader, a workhorse, strong and proud, so proud it hurt him to make a mistake. He had sacrificed his own desires for so many years that he did that now automatically. Margaret Mead wrote that "Responsibility tends to ennoble and absolute responsibility ennobles absolutely." She could have been writing about Joseph. He had kept his family well-behaved and together through a holocaust. And he had done this as a twelve-year-old boy. In America, at age twenty-two, faced with a very different set of problems, Joseph would take the same heroic approach. He did what he had to do so his family could survive.

Abraham was spiritual, moody, and intense. Like most Dinka men, he spoke little, but he was tormented by all he had missed. Sometimes he was angry or heartbreakingly sad; other times his face broke into a sunshiny grin. He was charismatic and could light up or chill a room with a glance. Had he grown up in America, he would have been a poet or jazz musician, someone who made a living being sensitive. But because of his life, he would have a rough time finding a spot in Nebraska.

Paul was a fifteen-year-old hormone-filled adolescent who could really look like a sad sack when he didn't get his way. He was very tall with big hands and feet. He'd been well protected by his siblings, especially Martha, and he was clearly the petted baby of the family. But because of his age, he had to obey everyone in what turned out to be a very hierarchical family.

Martha was six feet tall and looked like a supermodel in her Goodwill clothes. She wore her hair in cornrows or other stylish African ways. She cooked and cleaned for the family. She was proud and slow to trust. At first, she had the mandatory silence of the non–English speaking, but as soon as she started school, her English improved rapidly.

On our first visit, the family was polite to us in the African way of being polite to elders, which meant they spoke softly and didn't look at us. They answered our questions and nodded as we talked, but they didn't initiate conversation. We Americans think it is polite to make eye contact, and it took us a while to get used to the downcast eyes and short answers to our questions.

That first day we all felt a little strange and awkward. The only whites this family had known were government workers or anthropologists. I pondered the irony that as a student at the University of California at Berkeley in the late 1960s, I had read about the Nuer and Dinka tribes and now I was meeting them in Lincoln, Nebraska.

Martha showed me their apartment. All the beds, the chairs, and the couches were covered with doilies she had sewn over the years so that when they finally had a home they would have beautiful things.

Jim and I showed them picture books of Africa and America that we'd checked out of the library. Later I would bring them a map and we would trace their travels through Sudan, Kenya, and Ethiopia. Joseph would speak of the days before the war when his family had grazed cattle along the southern Nile.

Their Nuer friend James had walked from Kenya to South
Africa to escape the war. He was angry that the United States
hadn't helped Sudan. He said, "Your country helped Zaire,
Rwanda, and Somalia, why didn't you help us?" Of course, I
couldn't answer. I really knew very little about Africa.

We had brought the family some Uno cards. We taught
them to play and we left them the cards. They were soon beating us at every game we taught them.

We gave them a calendar and showed them how to write
things down on it. I asked about their birthdays and wrote them
on the calendar. These birthdays had been arbitrarily assigned to
them when they left Africa. (An inordinate number of refugees
say they were born on January 1 or the Fourth of July.) Birthday
celebrations are a very American idea. They are about time and
individuality. Birthday parties are our way of teaching children
that the day they came into the world matters.

We took the family's picture—four handsome people sitting
on their couch, hands folded in their laps with big smiles.
Martha's doilies gave the couch a festive, homey touch. The
scene was one of excitement and hope. When we left that first
time, we asked if they wanted us to return. Joseph said, "You are
welcome anytime."

After our first visit, Jim and I talked about what role we
would play in the lives of this family. We had originally planned
to be their family therapists. But now it seemed like they needed
an American mom and dad. They needed practical help with
school, jobs, and managing time and money. They didn't need
family therapists as much as they needed cultural brokers.

America was going to be hard for them. We knew of a Sudanese man in Nebraska who had gotten overwhelmed and
killed himself. The best mental health plans for them seemed

preventative. Fred Rogers spoke of "loving people into existence." We decided to love them into a new life in America.
We would teach them to be Americans. We'd have field trips
and language and culture lessons. We'd make it up as we went
along.

When Jim and I stopped by a few days later, Martha was
cooking an omelet. Their canned goods were in the refrigerator
and the milk and produce were left on the counter. I explained
a few things about food storage. I also gently hinted that it was
good to turn off the television now and then.

The family seemed happy to see us. We had brought them a
few basic supplies—gloves and hats, scissors, a clock, and Scotch
tape. They had never seen Scotch tape before. They put their
hats and gloves on immediately. I could see I'd bought gloves
that were too small and I offered to exchange them. They said
the gloves were just fine and they kept their hats on.

There is a saying that if you want to know something about
the Dinka, ask a cow or a woman; the men will not talk. In re-
sponse to our questions, the family would answer, "Everything
is okay." Martha might have been more talkative if she'd known
our language. Joseph was unfailingly polite but volunteered little
information. Abraham seldom spoke but he communicated a
great deal nonverbally. Paul was a loving kid who occasionally
blurted out something, such as his request one day that I buy
him a Walkman.

One of the lessons I learned from the family was to be comfortable with silence. We Americans tend to talk all the time
when we are together. When I tried to do that with this family,
I felt silly and they were overwhelmed with the verbiage. I
learned to be silent and wait for a topic to emerge. It was restful
once I got used to it.

Sometimes they talked about the past in a matter-of-fact way. Joseph told of fleeing Ethiopia and of being stalked by lions. The children had been so hungry they'd eaten dogs, grass, roots, lizards, anything. Paul couldn't remember life before he lost his parents. All the years he should have been in elementary school, learning to play ball and swim, and just having a childhood, he was on the run. He reminded me of a line I'd once read: "I was born with a war in my eyes." He never complained, but when he was first in Lincoln, Paul woke in the night shouting, "Run, run." One morning, Abraham asked me how to get rid of nightmares and painful memories. He said, "I pray all the time for them to go away, but my prayers are not answered."

I said he would feel better with time. I reminded him that he was safe now. I showed him how to breathe deeply. I hugged him.

All of the Kakuma refugees had supercharged arousal systems. In a new place they had trouble knowing what was dangerous and what wasn't. Martha and Paul were especially afraid of animals. In the spring when the tornado watches and warnings came, the family were alarmed. They called tornadoes, "the big wind." We would call them and say, "Don't worry. What you see on television is just a watch for a county far from us."

On one visit we taught the family to play slapjack and solitaire. We showed them how to put a jigsaw puzzle together. These gifts seemed like a good idea because it was twenty below outside and they had no car. They needed ways to fill their time until they went to work or school. But I wasn't sure how much they enjoyed the gifts and how much they were just being polite to us. I worried that we were "inflicting help" on them, that when we left they were asking each other, "How do we get rid of these nutty Americans?"

One afternoon I asked the brothers to read to me. Joseph and

Abraham could read well. Joseph had actually taught English in the camp and had read many African and European novels. Abraham read softly, but with confidence. Paul refused to read alone, but when I read to him, he repeated exactly what I read. I learned later that the Kakuma kids hadn't been taught any phonics, only to repeat in rote fashion what the teacher had read.

That day Jim taught them how to change the burned-out lightbulbs in their living room. I showed Martha how to cook a frozen pizza and peel an orange, which she called a lemon. When we left, we gave them good-bye hugs.

Later at our three-story house filled with books and CDs, with our two cars in the driveway and our well-stocked refrigerator, I thought about the Kakuma refugees' humble situation. They had endured hardships I couldn't even imagine and, in our state, they were facing difficulties that they surely couldn't imagine—difficulties with education, work, money, culture shock, and prejudice. I truly hoped they would let us help them and that our help would be of some genuine use.

Before we met the family, we'd read Jon Holtzman's monograph, *Nuer Journeys, Nuer Lives.* Holtzman wrote that in Nuer culture, which is similar to Dinka culture, time is structured by seasons, births, and deaths. There are no calendars or clocks. In fact, there is no word for time or any sense of abstract time. The family didn't set up appointments to see friends. They did whatever came up next. When I asked Joseph if I could come by at eleven on Sunday, he said, "Come over anytime. You are always welcome." This meant I could drop by anytime, but it also meant he might not be there if I came at eleven on Sunday.

As we struggled to teach them the American view of time, I pondered what Joseph would teach me about time if I showed up on the southern Nile. No doubt he would tell me to throw away my watch, alarm clock, personal planner, and calendar. He would encourage me to watch the sun, the stars, the flow of rivers, and maybe the colors of grasses for information. He'd tell me to eat when there was food or when my stomach was empty. He would help me learn to be where I was for as long as I wanted. He would mentor me on not leaving a party because I had something else scheduled.

Over the next few weeks we checked on the family frequently. We took them clothes and articles about Sudan. We played cards and visited the natural history museum. We taught them how to put on a seat belt and count out money. We showed Joseph how to keep his bankbook and write a check.

America, with its ice and snow, its stores and machines, was clearly confusing to the family. How could it not be, after growing up in a world of grasslands, cattle, and forced marches? Mostly the family was glad to be here. They were stressed, sometimes too stressed to even speak, but relieved they were not at Kakuma. One day Joseph showed me a story about more kidnappings in Sudan. He said, "Here we are safe."

I often didn't quite know how to treat the family. They didn't know many things that Americans know and they seemed vulnerable in many ways. On the other hand, Joseph and Abraham were men who had lived through much more than most Americans do in an entire lifetime. They had survived years of dangerous situations. I would trust them with my life. I struggled to find the right tone with them. I wanted to be respectful but direct. They clearly needed guidance, but they didn't need to be patronized. Sometimes I wasn't sure exactly where the line was between the two. I said to Joseph, "If I were in Kenya or Sudan, I would ask your advice. Here, please ask my advice."

Especially the first few weeks, they were exhausted and spaced-out. They were fearful of making mistakes or getting in trouble. Once when I called to say that library books were over-due, I scared them and I had to say, "It will be okay. No one goes to jail for this problem." Another time when a clerk called Joseph to ask questions about social security numbers and vari-ous dates, he grew so frustrated that he hung up on her.

However, they remained a heroic family, deeply loyal and loving. Nobody ever complained about anything. The younger ones obeyed the older ones immediately. But Joseph and Abra-ham were not bullies and, in fact, made sure that Martha and Paul got the best of everything. I was amazed that a family with-out parents who had spent years hungry and running could be this well-adjusted. I had tremendous respect for their loyalty to one another and their ability to survive. Their saga was a reverse *Lord of the Flies* saga, and it spoke well for the human race.

Of course, they had up and down days. The day we visited the city library for a tour, they seemed overwhelmed. The li-brarian was kind, but the place was too strange for them—bright and filled with white people and machines they didn't understand. They had never seen computers or audiovisual equipment. They looked somber and scared.

We did have some good moments at the library. Martha and Paul liked the books about African animals. Joseph found the books of Chinua Achebe, the great Nigerian writer. Later, when he checked out an Achebe book, *Things Fall Apart,* the li-brarian told him she had read it. Joseph beamed.

Burger King saved that day. We went there afterward and bought everyone hamburgers and fries. The french fries were a hit. The family all knew how to eat them with ketchup, appar-ently a universal skill. I thought of Pico Iyer's line about "french fries, the universal language."

Sometimes I was anxious and frustrated when the family didn't bring up problems or ask for help. They didn't admit to

negative feelings or fears. They had a way of stuffing all their papers into a desk drawer and I had a feeling that is what they did
with issues and problems. I worried about what wasn't getting
discussed. I knew they should be asking more questions.

Keeping quiet and waiting had kept the family alive in
Kakuma, but here silence and passivity were not so adaptive.
We couldn't help them if we didn't know their problems. We
couldn't teach them if we didn't know what they needed to
learn. But I had to slow myself down or I would become one of
the people stressing them out. I had to remind myself that we
couldn't be responsible for everything, that their problems had
taken years and many wars in several countries to create and we
wouldn't solve them quickly.

Things got better. The Kakuma refugees were smart, resilient, and hardworking. The warm Sudanese community took
them in. They soon had the routines of church, school, and
work. Martha began to laugh and smile. Paul discovered basketball, and Abraham quickly became a leader of his peers. Joseph
got a job at a nearby hospital in housekeeping. Even though we
must have seemed like we were from another planet, they began
to trust us. When we showed up, they all rushed to hug us.

School

Joseph, Abraham, and Paul had been allowed to go to school
in Kakuma. Martha had been kept back, working in the home
of an elder in their clan. Her brothers had argued with this elder
when he refused to let Martha go to school. They had been
beaten for defending their sister's right to school. But they had
lost the arguments and Martha at eighteen had not learned how
to read.

At twenty-two, Joseph was too old for high school. He
had to find a job and support the family. But we would help

him study for his GED. The others were enrolled in our public schools.

Joseph and I planned to escort Paul and Martha to their first day of school. I went by the apartment early and they were dressed and ready. I gave them notebooks, pencils, book bags, and money for lunch tickets. They'd eaten only bread and milk for breakfast.

Martha wore a sweatshirt and stone-washed jeans with a red plastic coat. Paul wore a used marathon T-shirt and green plaid suit pants. The brothers wore stocking caps all the time, mainly to keep warm, but also because they liked them. Martha's clothing combinations were unique, but she always looked beautiful.

Joseph and I walked first to the middle school with Paul and Martha. I showed them how to cross busy streets. At first Paul and Martha chatted, but as we approached the three-story brick building, they grew quiet.

Inside, people were friendly, but it was bright, noisy, crowded, and very non-Kakuma. The American kids streaming past us seemed much shorter, whiter, louder, and more confident. As leader of his family, Joseph bravely trudged in, shaking hands and greeting school administrators. Martha was wide-eyed with fear but held herself with dignity. Paul followed behind, looking like he would bolt if we gave him a chance.

Our first task was to work the combination lockers. That had been a grueling experience in my school days, and it about did them in. Teaching Paul to work the lock was stressful for all of us. Joseph and I finally got the darned thing open, then Paul did. However, we struggled anxiously with Martha's lock for ten minutes before we finally gave up and went into orientation.

We sat at desks, not built for tall Africans, and listened as a teacher showed us a map of the school and went over procedures. Joseph was sweating in the cool room. Paul and Martha showed by their eyes that they had checked out completely. Then, the teacher handed Paul and Martha their schedules and read out Martha's classes, which included reading and piano lessons.

I looked at Joseph. He was smiling a small slow smile. He was thinking that the crossing, the cold of Nebraska, the difficulties of dealing with us beefy Midwesterners—all his efforts were for this. His sister was no longer a servant. She could go to school. She would learn to read books and play piano. She would be a respected person.

On the way home, Joseph said to me, "In five years I would like to take you to Africa."

I said, "I would like that very much, too. You could show us around."

"Sometimes we must walk for three days to see our friends," Joseph said.

I replied, "I am ready."

Outings

Over the next few months I had many field trips with the family. Once I took them to the supermarket, an amazing place to people who have lived for years on one meal a day of porridge. They got one cart and I got a cart for myself. Joseph ordered Paul to push my cart. Paul was so eager to be useful that he lifted items out of my hands to put them into my cart. I selected a few items and tried to explain to him why I bought spinach, brown rice, yogurt, and oranges. I taught him the names of some American products—peanut butter, cantaloupe, cornflakes, and dish soap.

Meanwhile, Joseph led the other shopping expedition. He selected several gallons of milk, lots of juice, and four cartons of eggs. Martha picked up three eggplants, which I suspected she liked for the bright purple color. I encouraged them to buy other fruits and vegetables. I explained how to cook zucchini and that they must spit out the seeds of citrus fruits. After they bought several packs of bologna, I reminded them to get bread.

Our shopping trip took a long time. They regarded the packages as we might regard objets d'art. They'd pick them up, examine them from all angles, and then discuss them intently in Dinka. Every row displayed a new set of exhibits. I explained what I could, but soon they were overloaded with food facts. The family passed the candy section and Joseph bought a bag of suckers. They had seen suckers before and were happy to find them in America. It was typical of Joseph's good leadership to buy a small treat for his family when they needed one.

By the end they were tired. They rolled our carts into line and with great curiosity watched the moving belt convey our products past the checker. As the clerk rang up our purchases, the family watched the computer screen above us as if it were a TV set. When the clerk asked Joseph for his food stamps, he handed him all of his coupons. The clerk counted out what he needed and handed the rest back. Joseph thanked him politely. He never got too tired to be polite.

Another time I picked up Joseph for a job interview. He wore a suit donated by a friend of mine, a good expensive suit. He had never had a real job before and was very eager to work. Before we left his place, I gave him a watch, that omnipresent American tool. I explained dry cleaning, so that he wouldn't ruin his suit the first time it got dirty.

There were many things to explain. I rationed lessons so that I wasn't lecturing all the time. But today I explained snow days. We were expecting a blizzard and I didn't want Paul, Martha, and Abraham struggling through a storm to schools that might be closed. Joseph was astonished that in America there was ever a time when schools shut down, when things didn't work.

On the way to the job interview, we prepared for potential questions. We talked about Joseph's work in Africa. I worried that he would be too quiet. He wasn't good at asking for or sharing information. I knew it was the Dinka way to be silent, but I encouraged him to speak up at the interview.

He looked scared and I said, "I know this is hard. Eventually, you will figure everything out."

The interview went fine. Joseph was quiet, but poised, and the interviewer liked him. Within a month of arriving in Nebraska, he had found a job. Now he would have to support his family of four on his wages.

Birthdays

The family had been assigned arbitrary birthdays when they came to America. Abraham's nineteenth birthday was the first one in Nebraska. We brought him a cake decorated with basketballs and bikes. We carried it to their apartment along with candles, matches, and presents.

Abraham greeted us. He was proud that he had a new job serving tables and washing dishes at a sorority. We kidded him about the Dinka custom of many wives and asked how many of the girls he would marry. Abraham said that if they were traditional Dinka, the brothers would have had their bottom teeth removed in a manhood ceremony. Jim asked how they felt about missing this ceremony and Abraham laughed and replied, "Very good."

Paul helped me light the candles. They had never seen candles before, much less a birthday cake. I carried the cake to their small coffee table and placed it in front of a rather embarrassed Abraham. Jim and I sang "Happy Birthday" and the others joined in when they could. We told Abraham to blow out the candles. He blew in short little bursts, taking forever to get all the candles blown out. Everyone laughed with him.

Soon after Abraham's birthday, Joseph had a birthday. Many friends were at the house that day, including their new neighbors, Mohamed and Bintu from Sierra Leone. They greeted us warmly and Mohamed spoke with great earnestness and intelligence about the problems of his country. Bintu struck me as kind-hearted and beautiful. It was hard to believe she had just arrived from a refugee camp in one of the most tragic places in the world.

We gave Joseph a cake decorated with cows and cars. We gave him a map of the United States, an umbrella, and two books, the Holtzman book on the Nuer and one by Achebe. He blew out the candles with more panache than Abraham, but he had no idea how to cut his cake. When I offered to help him, he said yes adamantly and gratefully.

After the party Jim and I assisted with homework. Today Abraham pulled out his math assignment and Jim helped him with it. A teacher had told us that Abraham was respected by all the other students. She felt he could go to college if he had a chance. Paul drew dinosaurs from a library book and I helped Martha read. I showed her vowel sounds and we worked on sequences like *bit, but, bat* or *hit, hut, hot*. All of a sudden, she realized that she could sound out words and make sense of those black marks on the page. She beamed with pleasure. I felt like Anne Sullivan the day she held Helen Keller's hand under a water pump and Helen spelled out *water.*

Another day we invited the family to tour our house, only a moderately successful experience. Abraham hit his head on a lintel. Martha was afraid of our cat. We served hot chocolate with marshmallows, which the family disliked heartily. I asked if the food in Africa was spicy and Abraham said angrily that Africa was many countries.

Joseph kept commenting on how big our place was. They were all interested in our automatic fireplace. I switched it on, and then they switched it on and off many times. They asked about the wood, the heat, the lack of smoke of this "fire," and they held out their hands to see if they warmed up. We also had a greeting card from the Audubon Society with a computer chip inside that made bird sounds. All of them regarded the card as magic. Paul kept lifting the card and holding it to his ear and smiling as he heard the birds.

During our first few months of friendship, I wish I could claim I was always confident and patient. But I had many self-doubts. I wondered if the family even liked us, if they thought we were pushy, weird, or crazy. Sometimes, I felt they took us for granted. Once I got angry when I heard that on the same day that Abraham had told me everything was fine, he had cried in class. I told him I wanted to know how he was feeling and when he had problems. He was upset by my reprimand and I felt guilty later that I had troubled someone who had so much to cope with.

One day Joseph reminisced about grazing cows with his father along the Nile. He said he could recognize his father's cows in a herd of five thousand cattle. There were twenty words to describe the color of a cow and many other words to describe the shape of its horns, etc. Cattle were the currency of life, used to establish status, for bride prices, and for barter. Milk was considered the best food. Cattle were not commodities, but rather the Dinka's perfect partners.

Just as Dinka social and economic life in Africa was organized around cows, in America it was organized around cars.
Holtzman quoted a Nuer man as saying, "A car is a bad cow."
Nuer and Dinka men in America wanted cars. Cars turned a
supplicant into a patron. Men helped each other get money for
down payments for old beaters.

Unfortunately, many Sudanese men drove their cars before
they obtained driver's licenses, insurance, or registration. They
were ripped off by used-car dealers all too eager to exploit their
lack of sophistication. And they didn't understand much about
car maintenance or mechanics. Holtzman reported that within
three years of buying a car, over 84 percent of the Nuer had an
accident, abandoned their car because it didn't work, or had it
repossessed.

The second day Joseph worked, he asked us to help him buy
a car. We told him it was better to wait until he had a license and
a little money. We made up our own slogan, "A bike is a good
cow."

We stressed that bikes are cheap, easy to maintain, and don't
require having a license, paying taxes, or buying gas. Also a person is unlikely to get in trouble with the law on a bike. We
found two bikes for the family and bought helmets.

But, by the next week, Joseph had bought a car with the
help of Sudanese friends. He now had the extra financial burden
of a monthly car payment. In spite of his poverty, Joseph was a
responsible car owner. Insurance cost him almost a thousand
dollars every six months, but he bought it. And he passed his
driver's test. He became one of the main drivers for people in
the Sudanese community. Jim taught him how to check the oil.

A couple of weeks later Joseph proudly showed us a pay
stub. Jim taught him basic bookkeeping and stressed he must

never write more checks than he had money to cover. We helped him formulate a budget. Joseph was making $1,100 a month. Abraham had lost his job when the spring semester ended and the sorority women went home. Joseph's salary supported four people and his car, and soon he would need to pay our government $200 a month to repay the cost of four plane tickets to America. The government no longer helped with food stamps and there was barely enough money for food. Joseph said, "We do not eat much."

I was angry when I looked at the numbers. Joseph had been deprived of a childhood and now he was locked into an adulthood working difficult jobs for less than a livable wage. I wished our country would make it a little easier for him and his family. At the very least, we shouldn't be charging them for their plane tickets. If they paid that bill, they would go hungry for many months. And they had to pay it, or their refugee status could be compromised.

Postscript

Eight months after their arrival, the family is adjusting to Nebraska. They are leaders in the Sudanese community and they help newcomers from Kakuma fit in. Their apartment is often filled with people who have stopped by for a visit or to ask for help. I am honored to be their friend.

Joseph works long hours, drives many Sudanese to their job interviews and dental appointments, and pursues his GED. I have yet to see him angry, rude, or upset with anyone. He has, however, taken up smoking.

Abraham has successfully completed a year of high school. He is popular at school and in the Sudanese community. He wants to go to college and become a policeman. Right now he is looking for a summer job.

Martha is learning to read. Her English has improved greatly and she is the star of her sewing class. She has developed a fondness for fried chicken, red soda pop, and orange "lemons." We have a close relationship. Martha said to me, "I am always happy with you. I pray to God all the time that He will make you happy."

Paul plays basketball and loves to swim. He had one bike stolen but was given another one by Mad Dads. He likes pizza, Pepsi, and Zesto ice-cream cones. He recently worked a day for a neighbor and was paid his first American money. He immediately spent the twenty dollars on a video game.

I worry the most about Paul, who is young and easily influenced. His older siblings are busy and he has too much unsupervised free time. The family lives next door to a halfway house for registered sex offenders and men recently released from prison. Paul spends his days wandering around the neighborhood. He might as well be wearing a T-shirt with VULNERABLE written on it. I am worried bad company will find him. This summer he is in summer school and day camp. I hope that is enough structure to protect him until he returns to school in the fall.

The Kakuma refugees are wonderful people with almost all the attributes of resilience. They are survivors on a level I can hardly imagine. However, even as I admire and cherish them, I worry about their future. They have been terribly traumatized and their history is one of physical and developmental deprivation. They are young and have missed many of the lessons that parents teach their children. They come from a culture as different from ours as is possible. Most of what they do know about the world isn't useful here.

Furthermore, their external environment in Nebraska is harsh. The bleak situation is that a twenty-two-year-old, utterly unprepared for modern life, with limited education and skills, is supporting four people and paying off travel debts on a minimum-wage job. Joseph recently told me, "In America we are protected from animals and people who want to kill us, but it is very hard to stay alive."

MOHAMED AND BINTU
"Sierra Leone is the worstest place on earth."

I picked Mohamed and Bintu up at their basement apartment, which was in the same building as the Kakuma family's apartment. Their place was sparkly clean and African-style in arrangement with several couches and a small television tuned to cartoons. They had been in America about two weeks and already colorful stuffed animals were on display and library books were piled up on their coffee table.

This was a gentle couple, clear-eyed and kindhearted. Mohamed had a wise, respectful demeanor. He was formal and unfailingly polite. Bintu was small, round, and effusive. She smiled and hugged easily. Bintu wore her hair in tight braids laced with colored beads. They spoke English, but Sierra Leone English is different from Nebraska English and there were times we had trouble understanding each other. Still, we muddled along on our mutual goodwill. I gave Bintu some jonquils and she laughed and put them in a juice glass.

We drove to a small coffee shop not far from the employment office. I bought us hot tea and we settled into a corner table. I asked where they were from and what brought them to Lincoln. Mohamed was born in a village in 1970, which made him one year older than my own son. Bintu was born in Freetown in 1973, which placed her age between that of my son and daughter.

Mohamed said he had a happy peaceful childhood. Many people remember their lives before a war or tragedy as a sort of Eden or Camelot, a time of innocence and happiness, and Mohamed was this way. He remembered that at dusk all the people in his village would gather and tell stories. He said softly, "They were very good stories."

He described his school without any irony as "built by our colonial masters for the sons of chiefs." He said it was an expensive school and his parents worked hard to pay his tuition there.

Bintu also had a happy family with four sisters and three brothers. Her mother stayed home to care for the family and her father ran a shop. She attended a private school, but what she remembered with a smile was how much her family liked soccer. She said, "I grew up watching soccer."

Then the war came to Sierra Leone, first to the rural areas, then to the cities. The war was started by outsiders who wanted to destabilize Liberia and Sierra Leone. At first, the people accepted the rebels. They'd had twenty years of a dictatorship and were ready for a change. The military overthrew the dictatorship and they invited the rebels to join them. But later there was a split between the military and the rebels. Civil war broke out. Sierra Leone became, to quote Bintu, "the worstest place on earth."

Mohamed explained that he had encouraged people in his little hamlet to vote and work for democracy. Thus, he was targeted early as someone to be killed. When the soldiers came to his house he was away at a meeting. Perhaps his family would have fled earlier but they were waiting for him. He had heard that if the family didn't stick together they could lose each other forever, so he had warned them to wait until he returned.

Mohamed wasn't there when two of his brothers were stabbed with machetes and his two sisters were "raped to death" in front of his father, who was forced to applaud while this happened. It took Mohamed three months to get back home. First he heard everyone was dead, then he discovered that one brother had survived. He said, "I tried to focus on my joy about that brother."

Mohamed escaped to Freetown where he met Bintu. She was lively and pretty and had her own fabric business. They decided to marry and later they had three children.

Bintu told me what happened next. As part of her business she traveled in the provinces to sell and buy cloth. She said, "One day my car was ambushed. I was abducted by the rebels and taken into the bush. I was kept for eight months and guarded all the time so that I couldn't escape."

She said softly, "I had to cook. I had to do whatever they told me to do."

Finally the rebels went into Freetown. When they entered the city they used children as human shields. This tactic worked for them, as the other soldiers had a hard time shooting innocent kids. There was a great battle between the rebels and the West African Intervention Force. During the chaos Bintu escaped. She said, "I was totally naked. I ran and ran until I came to the houses of my friends." These friends were afraid to open their doors, but eventually someone did help her. She was able to escape to the camp in Ghana.

Bintu lifted the shirt from her back and her arms and showed me the deep scars she had from being beaten by the rebels. She said her faith helped her survive. She had been Muslim but was now a born-again Christian. She was deeply grateful that "God kept me safe" and that Mohamed remained her husband after she had been kidnapped by rebels. She said, "Many men in my culture wouldn't have stayed."

Meanwhile Mohamed was in a terrible situation. In the

chaos of the war, he had been separated from their children. There was an attack on Freetown, one of the bloodiest attacks in the history of the world. Hundreds of houses were burned. Six thousand people, including children, had their limbs chopped off. Mohamed said, "We are a nation of amputees."

During the war, Mohamed heard that someone had seen his brother with the children. But almost immediately afterward the area where his brother and children were seen was bombed. He hasn't been able to find out what happened to them. Mohamed also heard that Bintu had been killed. Later he heard she was alive. He had no real idea, just rumors.

Eventually Mohamed escaped to a refugee camp in Ghana. As the war raged on, refugees with terrible stories flooded into Ghana. Sierra Leone was out of control. The rebels abducted five hundred United Nations peacekeepers. For almost a year there was no government at all. The illiterate rebels closed all the schools. If people went to work, they risked being shot by one group; but if they didn't go to work, another group would kill them. There was no way to be safe or stay out of trouble. If people were on certain lists they could be killed by some groups, but if they were not on those lists, others would kill them. No one knew how to stay alive.

Many of the survivors of the disasters in Sierra Leone arrived at the camp in Ghana. Mohamed escaped Freetown and made it to the camp where he was elected to the executive council. He showed me pictures of a communal cleanup to prevent cholera, of women cooking, and of a party at the camp with feasting and dancing. But it was a hard life; the huts were filled with snakes and scorpions; many girls became pregnant because they gave themselves to men for food.

Mohamed helped people who were traumatized. He said that people avoided anyone who had seen them tortured or raped in Sierra Leone. They felt humiliated around people who knew what had happened to them. When people first arrived they trusted no one, but gradually they would trust again. Mohamed talked people into eating, joining a work group, and registering to look for family members. He felt the cures for all the pain were love, work, and communal events. Food and laughter were important to healing.

After he and Bintu were reunited in the camp, they tried unsuccessfully to find their own children through the Red Cross. They helped the orphaned children in camp and informally adopted eight of the kids, some of whom were amputees. They weren't allowed to bring these kids to America with them, but they hoped to save money and bring them later. Bintu asked me for an international calling card so that she could call and check on the children.

We had to leave the café for their job interviews. I was struck by the contrast between their tragic stories and this restaurant with its scones and Italian sodas. I pondered the weirdness of time and place. While Bintu was being held captive, my daughter was a Fulbright scholar in Thailand. When Mohamed's family was killed, my son was in graduate school in California and learning to surf.

I could not believe that these terrible things had happened to these quiet, loving people. How could they go on? How could they keep from killing themselves?

But they weren't thinking of killing themselves. They were wondering how they could get bicycles. As we walked outside, Mohamed told me they were taking computer classes at Lincoln Action Program. They walked to these classes far from their apartment. They had heard that after ten classes they could get a free computer.

We looked at our capitol building, currently enshrouded in scaffolding for repairs. I told them about the beautiful murals inside. Bintu said, "We will walk there today. We love to see beautiful things."

Postscript

Many things have happened to Mohamed and Bintu since they arrived six months ago. Mohamed has found a mosque and Bintu has found a church. Mohamed has two jobs and sends money to the camp in Africa to help the children. He has his driver's license.

Bintu works as a cook in a local institution. She has made many friends there, including a "mother" who gives her rides to and from work. Bintu calls me mother as well. She is gifted at loving people and has quickly adopted an enormous family that includes Jim and me, the Kakuma refugees, and many other Africans and Americans.

They have had trouble with their apartment. Sewage from apartments upstairs leaks into their basement. They are neat and clean but cannot control the stench from the "black water" that fills their place. Mohamed has called the landlord many times and I have called the city health department, but as of now the problems remain. Until they have more money, they are stuck there.

Bintu remains tormented by her eight months as a captive of the rebels. As the one-year anniversary of her capture approached, she was very distressed and asked me about therapy. On the date of Bintu's kidnapping, I was away, but my husband took her and Mohamed out to dinner. At the dinner they made a solemn toast to those left behind in Africa.

Bintu can be haunted and overwhelmed by her tragic memories. I respect her great suffering but I am also aware that she is moving forward into the future. She has compassion and energy for others and she appreciates what she can. The evil inflicted upon her has not turned her into a hater. Bintu can be one of the most joyful people I have ever known. When she enters a room, her face lights up when she sees her friends. She hugs and kisses everyone. She jokes with us all, calls us nicknames, and teases us in ways that make us feel loved by her, a great gift. Whenever I take her flowers, she kisses the bouquet and says, "I love you, sweet flowers."

Mohamed and Bintu epitomize the human spirit at its best and strongest. No one has lost more than these two people. Even here in America they are without family and countrymen, in a very inclement environment. And yet, they do not complain. They are supporting themselves and sending money to the children in Ghana. When I see them, we laugh and hug. They speak of their hopes for college educations, good jobs, and a reunited family here in America. I am never with them without feeling inspired and grateful that they came into my life. I am honored to share this time and place with them. They are my teachers.

CHAPTER 10

HEALING *in all*
TIMES *and* PLACES

*The most interesting thing about the world is its fantastic and
unpsychoanalyzed character, its wretched and gallant personality,
its horrible idiocy and its magnificent intelligence, its unbelievable
cruelty and its equally unbelievable kindness, its gorilla stupor,
its canary cheerfulness, its thundering divinity,
and its whimpering commonness.*
—William Saroyan

On Lake Como in Northern Italy there is a beautiful villa
whose gardens stretch down to the lake. About one hundred
feet out from these gardens, in the lake, stands a brick tower
with a terra-cotta roof. This tower has a small window facing
the lake and inside the window is a statue.

About two hundred years ago, a wealthy young couple lived
in this beautiful villa. They had a five-year-old daughter who
played in the garden every afternoon. One day, when they
called her to dinner, she didn't answer. They looked everywhere
but never found her body. They presumed she fell into Lake
Como and drowned.

The little statue is of the mother with her hand on her brow, shielding her eyes as she looks over the water, searching for the body of her daughter. That is what the real mother did for the rest of her life, and what the statue mother has done for almost two centuries.

We all suffer. Pain and sorrow find a niche in every household. Most of us do not carry the burdens of Bintu or Joseph, but our lives are not easy. All of us have lost people we love. We have been betrayed or abandoned. We have made serious mistakes and have needed to forgive ourselves. As Wynton Marsalis's grandmother said, "Life has a board for every behind."

In all places and times, people have needed to know how to heal. Ten thousand years ago, a woman whose husband was killed in a hunt for wild game must have wondered, "How can I go on?" Parents who buried their children must have asked themselves, "Will we ever feel happy again?" Perhaps the oldest and most universal question is, How do I get over this?

Just as suffering is universal, so are systems of healing. All cultures have wisdom to offer their own members and the rest of us. This chapter will examine ideas about healing from all over the world and discuss what enables some people, but not others, to heal. It will ask, Why, with tragedy, do some people break like glass while others are tempered into steel? And, Why does suffering brutalize and coarsen some people and ennoble others?

THRIVE

I started the Thrive Project with a group of mental health professionals. We trained mentors from different cultures to be cultural brokers on mental health issues. The project began with ten classes that included everything from explaining the difference between a psychiatrist and a psychologist to discussing when Americans toilet train their children to describing how to deal with a suicidal person. Mentors educated professionals as well, teaching us how other cultures deal with emotional pain. The mentors then worked with people from their own countries, easing them into our system or helping them in more traditional ways. Therapists supervised and supported their work. The lessons of Thrive pervade this book.

The value of the project was not what we taught the Bosnian, Vietnamese, Kurdish, Russian, and Caribbean mentors, but what they taught us. They spoke honestly about how their cultures perceived our mental health system. They told us about the psychological problems that people from their countries experienced, and they listened to our advice. Often, they politely told us why our advice wouldn't apply.

The mentors defined their roles broadly. They were action-oriented and they didn't wear watches. If their clients were stressed by hungry children, rather than discussing stress management theory, the mentors drove them to the grocery store. A traditional supervisor might say that these mentors didn't have good boundaries. But I came to see it differently. The mentors were not compartmentalized the way we Americans are. They didn't make distinctions between clients and friends, between professional and nonprofessional relationships. By their behavior they said, all of us humans need each other's help.

Early on, I noticed that the Thrive mentors who were the least like mental health professionals were the most popular with their own people. The ones who acted the most like us were not in great demand. What the busiest mentors had in common was that they were holistic. For example, once when I chided a Sudanese caseworker for taking calls at night, he said to me, "You don't understand. All the Sudanese people are my family. I will help them all day and all night. It is not a job to me. It is my life."

When our Vietnamese mentor had a client who needed emergency shelter, he invited her home to sleep in his daughter's bedroom. His wife fixed her a big Vietnamese meal and his family temporarily adopted her.

When our Bosnian mentor met people from her country, she gave them her heart. She had a client who had lost twenty-two male family members in Srebrenica. The woman said to the mentor, "My pain has killed my soul." The mentor listened to the woman's stories, then she invited her to the circus, which she told me later "was a big hit."

This Bosnian mentor had another client who had suffered many previous losses. All she wanted was a child and she feared she couldn't get pregnant. The mentor took her to a women's clinic where the doctor reassured the woman she could have another child. Then the mentor invited the woman and her husband to her home. The two families stayed up all night drinking plum brandy and singing.

The Bosnian mentor was my most creative mentor. She was warmhearted, helpful, and good-natured. She had common sense and intelligence. When she heard I was writing a book on refugees, she said, "Tell families to get a kitten. We were very lonely and sad until we got our little kitty. Now we have reason to laugh. My daughter jumps out of the bed every morning to check on her kitty. It is the best thing."

At first, the goal of Thrive had been to train mentors to use our system and to encourage their people to use it. As the group proceeded, I found myself wondering why had I assumed that our system was better.

REFUGEES AND PSYCHOTHERAPY

Refugees don't seek therapy for a variety of reasons, some practical and some cultural. First, they often don't know that such a thing exists. They have no transportation to appointments, or they work all the time and cannot schedule sessions, or they have immediate concerns that take precedence over dealing with past pain. Usually therapy is lower on their priority lists than work, housing, or transportation.

Refugees resist therapy because of language and trust issues as well as a lack of understanding about our mental health system. Many refugees come from cultures with no cultural analogue for talking about problems outside the family. Certain things cannot be discussed even within the family. Domestic violence and rape are taboo subjects. In many cultures, the expression of certain emotions, such as anger, is not tolerated.

Often refugees label what we call mental health problems as spiritual problems, physical problems, or the result of a curse or the evil eye. Depending on the labeling process, different kinds of healers are required. A Vietnamese Catholic might talk to a priest. A Kurdish person might consult a tribal elder or visit a sacred shrine. Others might go to a shaman, a curandero, or a medicine man.

Even if refugees come from a culture that acknowledges mental health problems, these problems often are seen as shameful. Many people believe that only crazy people see therapists. Often times, mental health professionals are not trusted. The Vietnamese have a saying: You have to be crazy to understand crazy people.

Beyond these reasons there is another universal reason for

avoiding therapy. Talking about trauma is not easy. To remember pain is to reexperience it. Many people just try to blot it out and pretend things didn't happen.

When I first worked with refugees, I thought that, with access and understanding, many would want our services. They were traumatized people who could use therapy to work through their past tragedies and current stresses. Of course, there were refugees who wanted our mental health services. However, I now realize that many refugees choose not to be in therapy. Even when it's affordable, accessible, and user-friendly, and even when they truly understand what therapy entails, they turn down our offers of help.

Refugees are able to partake of the services they truly want in our communities. Because newcomers quickly see their value, they find our schools, job counselors, libraries, doctors' offices, and cultural centers. But in spite of our efforts to make therapy more available, we can't lure many people in. Most refugees don't want to sit in a room with a perfect stranger and talk over their traumas. Many listen to descriptions of what therapists do and then decide, "I'll help distribute clothes at the Asian Center," or "I want to watch movies," or "I'd rather go fishing."

And if refugees do show up in our offices, they are likely to come for practical advice, not help processing the past. They are likely to bring a form they need help filling out, or they'll come in with the classified ads and ask for advice on buying a washing machine. They bring up problems with a supervisor or a landlord, or they ask for help finding a used car.

PROBLEMS IN PSYCHOLOGY

Psychology was founded in the late Victorian era by middle-class white men. There was no concept of cultural relativity. For example, at Ellis Island, the IQ tests were given only in

English. In 1917 psychologists announced that 83 percent of Jews, 80 percent of Hungarians, 79 percent of Italians, and 80 percent of Russians were morons. About this time, Margaret Mead entered graduate school in psychology. She administered the Otis IQ test to foreigners and found that their scores were related to their English ability. However, her findings weren't accepted. She was out-maneuvered in a sea of powerful male psychologists and she left psychology because of its racism and sexism.

Fortunately, since then our field has worked to become less sexist, racist, and ethnocentric. While there is still resistance to dealing with culture in therapy and also a lack of sophistication about cross-cultural issues, many psychologists have devoted their careers to understanding diversity and increasing tolerance. However, in this time of transition to a multicultural society, psychologists often rely on models dusty with age. The field tries to fit people from all over the world into models developed for a very different time and place.

Psychologists ask, What does Gestalt theory or Jungian theory have to say about the Kurds or the Sudanese or the Vietnamese? These are the wrong questions. Better questions are, What models could we develop from our experience with refugees that would allow us to expand our knowledge of the human race? What are the universal components of healing? What are the aspects of resilience?

Sometimes psychologists have proselytized like missionaries. We have taught "Follow Sigmund Freud and Carl Rogers and you will be saved." We have said, "Our system is better than yours. Trust us to know you better than you know yourselves." But we have had an abysmal conversion rate. Our Western mental health system is dependent on verbal expressiveness, self-disclosure, and a belief in individualism. It splits the personal and the professional, the sacred and profane, and the mind and the body. Our system is also expensive, hard to schedule, and involves sitting in small rooms baring one's deepest secrets to perfect strangers.

Our ideas about how to deal with pain do not seem relevant to many newcomers. Catharsis and self-analysis are by no means universally respected as ways to heal. Not many refugees can be persuaded they will feel better if they talk about trauma. Psychologists have a metaphor for healing—a wound must be washed, cleaned to heal. It may be painful but it is necessary. The Vietnamese also employ the wound metaphor for healing. But they say, "A wound will only heal if it is left alone."

COMMON REACTIONS TO LOSS

In his introductory psychology text, David G. Myers writes, "Most political dissidents who survive dozens of episodes of torture do not later exhibit post-traumatic stress disorder (Mineka and Zinbarg, 1996). And, although suffering some lingering stress symptoms, most American Jews who survived the Holocaust trauma, experiencing starvation, beatings, lost freedom, and the murders of loved ones, went on to live productive lives. In fact, compared to other American Jews of the same age, these survivors have been less likely to have seen a psychotherapist (18 percent vs. 31 percent) and more likely to have had stable marriages (83 percent vs. 62 percent). Moreover, virtually none has committed a criminal act."

These statistics suggest we should be extremely cautious about assuming that traumatized people are necessarily suffering clinical syndromes. Yet extreme situations induce extreme reactions. People who suffer terrible things have a time when they are sadder, angrier, more agitated, more withdrawn, and more passive. They are temporarily disorganized by grief and permanently changed by the tragic events.

One of the most common changes is a shifting of priorities. With tragedy, what is most and least important changes. Often people value family and friends more and care less about property and money. Spiritual concerns become more salient. Many Americans experience this change of priorities after a cancer scare or heart attack. They stop worrying about unfinished housework or job promotions. They spend more time with their grandchildren, travel, and watch sunsets.

Depression is certainly one of the most common reactions to trauma. Almost all the Afghani women I met were severely depressed. However, depression is a confusing word in this context. Who wouldn't be depressed after suffering these experiences? Depression implies pathology whereas reacting to trauma is normal, even healthy. Perhaps a better phrase for what we have called depression would be bone-deep sadness.

Avoidance is also common. A Kurdish woman could hardly bear to think of her past. And, most likely, her ability to push aside her memories was adaptive during her years on the run. Now, however, she had a therapy appointment once a week that she always forgot. After many weeks of no-shows, her kind therapist sent a car for her. Every Tuesday the Kurdish woman was shocked when the car pulled up. Her memory was generally excellent, but she'd blocked out her appointment. She wanted to avoid reliving those terrible years. Slowly, in her sessions, she talked about events that had once been too painful to recall.

Guilt is a big problem. Some of this guilt is survivor guilt, or the irrational feeling that one is somehow to blame for having stayed alive while loved ones died. Some guilt comes from situations in which people were forced to make terrible choices.

Other people genuinely behaved badly. They took food from hungry people or killed others so that they might escape. Under abnormal conditions, normal people do very abnormal things. Human beings, afraid for their lives, don't always function at their best.

Anxiety and restlessness are common reactions to severe stress. People are startled at the smallest of events—a door slamming, a car backfiring, or a shadow on their floor. Many newcomers cannot fall asleep. Or, they wake easily, have nightmares and night sweats.

Paradoxically, torpor and lassitude are also common reactions. People just don't see any reason to get out of bed in the morning. They don't have the energy to cope with the complex new situations they are in. They don't have the energy to brush their teeth.

One common, and generally not very adaptive, way refugees deal with their pain and difficulties in America is to move. Moves are common among refugees as they find one town difficult and hear rumors that the grass is greener in other places. Generally these moves don't make things better; they are expensive, disruptive of the family's relationships with schools and community resources, and they don't solve the original problems. Still, it's understandable that geographical moves would appeal to refugees. After all, they have moved before to solve problems.

Refugees also are at risk to become hooked on drugs, alcohol, and nicotine as ways to cope with stress. They desperately want to forget reality and drugs help with that, at least in the short term. Many refugees come from places where they had limited access to alcohol and other mind-altering drugs. They also come from places where there were no traditions for helping people learn to drink responsibly and where there was no education about drugs and nicotine. It is tragic to see a person who has endured terrible things and escaped from a dangerous place become enslaved by gin or heroin, surely as cruel a jailer as any in the old country.

Reactions to trauma depend on many things. In general, one discrete traumatic incident is more easily handled than years of chronic stress. The Kakuma refugees and Bintu and Mohamed, who had long periods of great stress, had more trouble healing than refugees who had one terrible experience.

Whether a person is singled out for victimization is also important. It is easier to deal with abuse that is random or the result of membership in a group than with abuse that feels personal. Torture is a great injury to the human spirit. No matter how serious the physical wounds, the spiritual wounds are worse.

ATTRIBUTES OF RESILIENCE

Psychology has documented with great precision all human inadequacies. We have the *Diagnostic and Statistical Manual* to catalog our problems, but we have no equivalent inventory of human strengths. Writing this book, I discovered certain qualities in resilient people from all over the world, and I labeled them the attributes of resilience. Few refugees had all the attributes, but the ones who were successful at adapting to America had many of them. Those refugees with few or none of the attributes were in a great deal of trouble in America.

All of us can benefit from the attributes of resilience. As we cope with loss or adjust to new situations, we will do better if we have a sense of humor, if we are hardworking and honest, and if we know how to stay calm. On airplanes, we hear, "If needed, an oxygen mask will appear automatically." In times of crisis, these attributes are our oxygen masks. This list of attributes of resilience, while neither perfect nor exhaustive, summarizes what it takes to adjust to new and difficult environments.

Attributes of Resilience

1. Future Orientation

Future orientation is about letting go and moving on. It is about newcomer zest. All refugees must put their hearts into America if they are to succeed in our country. Bintu is a good example of someone who has experienced great sorrow, but who looks toward the future. She began computer classes right away and made plans for bringing her "kids" from Ghana over to America.

Having a future orientation doesn't mean repression of memory or silence about the past. On the contrary, dealing honestly with pain often allows refugees to leave the past behind. Nor does it mean leaving loved ones behind. Many of the most successful refugees are deeply tied to their homeland, and often much of their motivation to succeed is because they want to help people in their old country. However, having a future orientation does mean that refugees have plans and purpose. They do not live only in the past; they can envision a better future.

2. Energy and Good Health

Adjusting to America and recovering from loss requires an enormous amount of energy. Just facing each day, with difficult jobs and coworkers who are hard to understand, is exhausting. Life is hard enough for the healthiest refugees, but it is almost impossible for refugees who are in chronic pain from injuries, who cannot work because of disabilities, or who have previous histories of mental illness. The children at Sycamore School, filled with life and wriggly with energy, exemplify energy and good health. I think of Khoa and Ly, so lively they could barely sit in their chairs. Youth is a great advantage in a new culture.

3. The Ability to Pay Attention

Paying attention means being aware of subtle cues, knowing whom to trust, and accurately sensing danger. It means catching on to patterns and rules, picking up on how things work, and not repeating mistakes. Paying attention includes being empathic, remembering, and detecting small changes in tone and nuance.

The Kurdish sisters had survived by paying attention. All of them could expertly read other people and respond quickly and sensitively to the slightest needs in others. I was struck by how rapidly they responded to changes in my face or mood. The Kurdish sisters didn't miss anything and they learned things the first time. We joked that they remembered my life better than I did. I said, "Don't move away or I won't know who to ask what I did last year."

4. Ambition and Initiative

Being a hard worker requires motivation and stamina. It requires time-management skills, the ability to work with others, and the ability to do what one is told and more.

Mohamed exemplifies these attributes. Within a few weeks of his arrival, he'd signed up for GED classes and was going to a mosque, working two jobs, and sending money to Africa. His employers respected him because he always offered to do more than his share of work. He was on time and never called in sick. He was taking driving lessons and computer classes in his spare time.

5. Verbal Expressiveness

One of the most important attributes is simply being able to express one's needs clearly and appropriately. Being able to communicate thoughts and feelings, to ask good questions, and to articulate problems are all aspects of this attribute.

Walat at Sycamore School was able to communicate clearly. He knew what he knew and what he didn't know. He asked for help when he needed it. In contrast, Trinh and Abdul were silent about their needs and feelings and hence were much harder to help. Knowing one needs information and knowing how to ask for it are critical survival skills.

6. Positive Mental Health

Many people have "a talent for happiness." Long ago La Rochefoucauld seemed to know this when he wrote, "Happiness and misery depend as much on temperament as on fortune." Positive mental health requires an optimistic nature, a sense of humor, and the ability to appreciate and enjoy what one can in the midst of sorrow.

Bintu is a good example of this. In spite of all her misfortune she is a joker and a seeker of fun. The Even Start mothers also exemplify this attribute. They worked all day in factories, then cared for their families and came to class. Many had lost children, husbands, and homes. However, I have rarely been with a happier group of women, all jokes, smiles, and high hopes and kindness to the teacher and one another.

7. The Ability to Calm Down

These skills, which include deep breathing, putting things into perspective, and optimistic thinking, allow people to stay calm and positive, to forgive themselves and others, to sleep nights, to avoid addictions or impulsive behaviors, and to control feelings in the face of great sadness and trauma. These are the skills Martin Seligman teaches in his work on "learned optimism" and Daniel Goleman teaches as "emotional intelligence," a concept pioneered by Peter Salovey and John Mayer.

Many people get into trouble because they cannot tolerate pain. They run from it, try to drink it away, or inflict their pain on others. Stoicism, or being able to endure pain, is an important attribute of resilience. Wendy Kaminer defined stoicism as "the strength to tolerate sorrow."

Because refugees have experienced pain and chaos, many of them have had a chance to develop good coping skills. Tharaya and Velida could tolerate the pain of their pasts. Velida even coped with her brain tumor in a stoic and heroic way. Even as the Afghani women struggled with great sadness, they did what they needed to do to take good care of their children.

Nithal was a high school student from the Nuba Mountains in Sudan. She helped her mother with many younger siblings, made A's at high school in her fourth language, and gave talks about her people to raise money for supplies. Nithal was shy, but she spoke clearly as she told of the tragedy of war in her country. One quarter million of her people had died and the attacks on them continued. Nithal's father was Yousif Kowa, leader of the Nuba people. He stayed in the Nuba Mountains to fight for his people, but he sent his family to America to be safe. While I wrote this book, Yousif died. Nithal said of her father's death, "He has been gone so much. It's easy to think of him as on a journey. I like to think that this trip is a safe one. We will be together when it is over."

8. Flexibility

Flexibility means simply that one can behave differently in new situations. One can assess the situation and act accordingly. It's being adept at cultural switching. Flexibility also involves understanding the concept of point of view, that is, knowing

that different people have different perspectives and that all behavior is contextual.

The high school students come to mind as moving between
worlds, being traditional at home and American at school. Liem
is an example of someone adept at cultural switching. He adopted
Vietnamese ways at home and mostly American behaviors at
school. He managed to stay out of trouble and work toward his
goals in a very complicated environment.

Anton was having more trouble. He was in a safe place now,
but his behavior remained that of a person in a war zone. His
mother also had trouble being flexible. She and Anton would
have had an easier time if they had been able to change a little
and trust others in a new, more trustworthy place.

9. Intentionality, or Being Thoughtful about Choices

In the United States, where there are so many choices, it's
imperative to make careful decisions, to choose wisely what to
do and not do. It's also important to be able to pick wholesome
friends who will help with adjustment and to make good choices
about work, housing, schools, time, and money. It's necessary to
rapidly develop consumer skills and some sophistication about
media and advertising. One of the most useful skills is knowing
the difference between what one wants and what one needs.

Mohamed was an intentional person. He realized cars were
expensive and decided to bike as long as he could, at least until his
first Nebraska winter. He knew to stay away from credit cards,
nicotine, alcohol, and useless products. He was a good judge of
people and soon had solid, intelligent friends around him.

10. Lovability

Lovability is a complex attribute that includes many qualities
from other attributes. Certainly energy, verbal expressiveness,

empathy, and good character are all part of being lovable. It's an elusive quality, but we all know it when we see it. Lovable people make us feel good. We want to be with them and we want to make them happy.

There were no refugees more lovable then the Kurdish sisters. With their bright eyes and hearty laughter, their jokes and eager curiosity about the world, and their enthusiasm for parties, for dressing up, for camping trips and adventures, they were easy to love. I never was with them without enjoying myself, without feeling cared for and appreciated, and without learning something new about the world.

11. The Ability to Love New People

Originally I thought lovability might be the most important attribute of resilience. People who are loved are granted favors, given advice and privileges. They are invited to events and awarded scholarships. But I now realize that even more important than being loved is being able to love.

Caring for others is what motivates humans to get out of bed in the morning. It gives life purpose and meaning. Especially if one has had great losses, the best cure is to find new people to love. Zahra, the bereft Afghani grandmother, was saved when she became interested in Ritu's children. Bintu befriended needy refugee families here and worked for the children in her refugee camp in Ghana. With all that had happened to Bintu, if she did not have this skill, she could not have survived psychically. She cared for herself by caring for others. And there was Ly, the Vietnamese schoolgirl who thought I, a very ordinary fifty-four-year-old woman, was beautiful.

A man in our town lost his wife in the same time period that one of his daughters had triplets and the other had twins. He alternated nights at his daughters' homes, getting up to help feed and change the babies. Mercifully, he had five new people to love as he dealt with the loss of his wife.

A friend of mine lost her daughter to cancer. Shortly after this untimely death, her first grandchild was born. This new baby came into her life at a time of great need and gave my friend a reason to keep on living. My friend said, "I can see my daughter's smile in the baby's smile, my daughter's eyes in her eyes." When we lose people, as we all do, we must be able to find new people to love. They cannot replace those who were lost, but they can give us joy, hope, and a sense of purpose.

12. Good Moral Character

Good character is vital to success. Honesty, responsibility, and loyalty all help newcomers succeed. One of the joys of writing this book was that I met many heroes. Joseph worked to support his siblings and studied bleary-eyed for his GED. Often I could hear his stomach rumbling with hunger. Leda commuted hours to a job that made her cry, then on weekends she cooked meals of nourishing Iraqi food and cleaned the house. Deena from Sycamore School helped her overwhelmed family cope with their first year in America. She found time to pull Trinh, a withdrawn Vietnamese girl, into the life of the school.

CROSS-CULTURAL HEALING

Freya Stark wrote that "People who have gone through sorrow are more sympathetic, not so much because of what they know about sorrow but because they know more about happiness— they appreciate its value and fragility and welcome it wherever it may be."

Laughter, music, prayer, touch, truth telling, and forgiveness are universal methods of healing. Talking to friends, sharing food, enjoying children, and watching the stars have soothed us

humans for thousands of years. Many cultures have healing ceremonies, purification and forgiveness rituals, often with a spiritual component. Karl Marx called religion the opium of the
people. Described more kindly, religion is the healing balm for
all people. Faith is an important aspect of healing, faith that one's
suffering has not been in vain and that the future will be better.

Traditional healers and customs work because they are believed to work. Almost all mental health cures are about placebo
effects. Placebo effects aren't negligible. They are about hope
and faith. Langston Hughes wrote, "Hold on to dreams for
when dreams go / Life is a barren field frozen with snow."

In the Middle East, troubled people often visit "saint's
houses." Usually these are peaceful retreats with kind people
to assist the travelers. The guests visit with food to share. They
pray, cry, talk to others, and rest. Most return home feeling
much better.

Buddhism has an ancient and sophisticated set of practices
for calming and healing. Breathing properly, meditating, and fo-
cusing on the impermanence of all things are healing activities.
In fact, some of our most successful psychotherapy incorporates
aspects of Buddhism.

Praying works whether or not people believe in God. Prayer
is a more active, trusting process than worrying. It is more calming and hopeful. Talking to God is generally more satisfying to
people than talking to Freud. Also, with prayer, there is no need
for diagnosis, treatment, or authorization from managed-care
representatives.

Rituals are often part of healing. They vary in their depth
and intensity. Sometimes they reflect deep cultural values, sometimes they merely allow people to go on with their lives. They
mark transitions and allow the next step. They acknowledge
that something has happened and allow people to say what

needs to be said. The flower ceremony at Sycamore School was a simple ritual that helped the children heal from loss.

Art is also a great connector. Art and music don't require a common language, they are a language. They allow people to express pain they may not be able to communicate in any other way. Sometimes art allows people to transcend pain, to turn pain into meaning and beauty.

Refugees seem to understand the value of positive emotions and joyful events. There is an Iraqi saying, Three things are calming—the color of grass, water, and the face of a beautiful woman. Latinos have all-night fiestas. The Vietnamese are masters of potlucks. All cultures like food, dance, music, and parties. The Africans came from places where whole villages of people had been slaughtered and children had been stolen from their parents. We offered them therapy and doctors, but the first thing they wanted was to get all their people together and have a celebration. And they wanted a community center so that they could be together and plan more festivals. They knew that before housing, jobs, medical care, or money, community is what heals. It is good to share pain, but what is really healing is to share joy.

Social activism provides meaning and assuages survivor guilt. Documenting the abuses of an authoritarian regime or working for human rights is what saves many victims of a repressive government. Bringing family over from the old country is profoundly healing. Toni Morrison put it well when she said, "The purpose of freedom is to free someone else."

Refugees are great role models for resilience. They don't fit our theories. With all their stress and sadness they should be the most miserable of people. Still, for most, healing occurs with the tincture of time. Slowly most people learn to relax and trust again. And after trauma, instead of being bitter, many people become more loving and more appreciative of life. They often describe their characters as greatly improved by their experiences. They see the world in a more layered, complex, and empathic way.

After a few years, refugees find themselves humming as they walk to work or smiling as they hang clothes on a spring morning. They have babies, learn how to e-mail their friends, and form neighborhood support systems. In fact, refugee communities are often our most vibrant, bustling, and hopeful communities, filled with people who believe in the American dream.

HEALING PACKAGES

Sara Alexander, a psychologist from Boston, talked about her collaborative work with refugees to create "healing packages." She helped refugees design healing packages from a smorgasbord of activities that included reading to children, exercising, finding a mosque, taking a class in English, looking for a better job, or going out to eat. Healing packages were about joy, contentment, recreation, physical pleasure, rest, and social connection. Not all refugees included psychotherapy in their healing packages.

This lack of interest in therapy is quite consistent with the findings from Thrive. Refugees chose circuses and dances, GED classes and job fairs, over opportunities to talk to mental health professionals. Thrive mentors demonstrated that refugees could only be helped when they were seen as whole people with physical, spiritual, social, intellectual, and vocational needs. They also showed us the importance of love, work, fun, and community in healing.

However, therapists can be part of healing packages, especially if we take a problem-solving or psycho-educational approach. An educational approach involves sharing information or teaching skills such as stress management, assertiveness, or relaxation techniques. Many newcomers resist psychotherapy, but most people like to learn. Education carries no stigma, no shame, and no hierarchy.

Psycho-education can help people look at the circumstances at the time of their trauma and understand that they were powerless to stop certain events. Just because they felt vulnerable and frightened doesn't mean they were weak. A mother whose baby starved needs to hear, "You did all you could. There was nothing to eat." A father whose son washed away in a river needs to hear, "You could not help how swiftly the current flowed."

Therapists' best work emphasizes empowerment and control. Identifying strengths and celebrating victories build trust and pride. It is good to ask, "How did you survive all this? What helped you stay sane?" Or, "Are there things you did that you feel proud of?" It's good to find out what people do well and encourage them to do more.

Therapists will be more useful to refugees if we broaden our roles and become cultural brokers, college advisers, drivers, teachers, case managers, advocates, or cooks. We can help with life planning, mediation, money and time management, and strength building. We can ask people to elaborate on their strengths, although this can be overdone. I complimented one man on not going crazy and he asked me, "How do you know I am not crazy?" Our specialty areas can be dealing with emotions and resolving conflicts. We can empower with information. If what we offer is useful, newcomers will want to come see us. They won't need to be coaxed, they'll beat down our doors.

Therapy can happen anywhere—in homes, schools, community centers, churches, cars, parks, and cafés. I'm reminded of a story about Willie Sutton, the famous bank robber. He was asked, "Why do you rob banks?" Sutton answered, "That's where the money is." If the question is "Where should therapists do therapy?" The answer is, "Where refugees are."

Not too long ago, I listened to a roomful of professionals discuss how to help traumatized people. People suggested various forms of therapy, all of which involved facing pain. Fair enough. In many cases, pain needs to be faced, but no one in the room suggested anything pleasant such as music, art, parties, pets, or walks in the countryside. This serious discussion seemed a metaphor for our blind spots as a field. We have focused on narrow, and not necessarily the most palatable, of treatments. We have ignored some of the oldest, most useful, and most universal healing procedures.

After thirty years of being a therapist and several years of working with refugees, I have found certain constants in the healing experience, certain experiences that help people in all times and places. These constants include some things we've seen with the Thrive mentors—fun, useful work, the support of community and family, and religious beliefs. And the constants include some of the essential elements in psychotherapy—safe, calm places; caring relationships; finding hope and meaning in painful events. In the future, good therapists will use elements from healing from all over the world.

SAFE SPACE

Calmness is a language that the deaf can hear
and the blind can read.

—MARK TWAIN

A calm, safe environment begins the healing process. The best treatment facilities for refugees know this. The Center for Victims of Torture is housed in an old home near the University of Minnesota. There is a fountain in the lobby that makes splashy,

soothing water sounds. The house has lots of skylights and windows and no small rectangular rooms. Artifacts from many
cultures remind visitors of their homelands. The Universal Declaration of Human Rights is translated into many languages and
framed on the walls. Offices are homey and noninstitutional,
with easy chairs, couches, and soft light. Classical music plays,
flowers decorate desks and tables, and outside a garden flourishes.

The best treatment programs for refugees are user-friendly
systems. Paperwork is kept to a minimum. Greeters and gifts,
such as pizza and free TB tests, draw people in. The best treatment is holistic and incorporates school, family, and community
resources. Dr. Keller at the Bellevue/NYU Program for Survivors of Torture put it this way, "Whatever problem a person
has, we try to find the nicest person we can to solve it."

Therapy is very much about the construction of a space for
people to think, talk, and work out their problems. But the ideas
about a quiet space are much older than psychology. Almost all of
the great religious leaders found enlightenment when they were
alone in the wilderness. Many tribes encourage their members to
go away from the community and be alone to seek knowledge
and to heal. Healing rituals from all over the world involve isolat-
ing people from others and decreasing the amount of stimulation
they receive so that they can calm down and think.

Time alone outdoors is an ancient and a modern remedy.
Some of our most cutting-edge therapy recommends wilderness
experience. A local social worker, who was one of the wisest
people I knew, walked on our prairie for hours every day to heal
from the death of her husband.

HEALING RELATIONSHIPS

The first casualty of trauma is trust. After being tortured or witnessing murders, people lose their protective shields of invulner-

ability. They have no illusions that they are safe. They know what humans will do to each other. This puts them in a difficult bind. They cannot heal without relationships, but relationships seem dangerous.

Earlier we discussed the importance of family, friends, and community in the healing process. Just knowing that someone cares is therapeutic. Healing occurs when a real person connects to another real person, that is, when people are comfortable enough with each other to be who they truly are.

People who have been betrayed by the human race most need a person who asks, "What is your experience?" then listens closely to their answers. This person can be a family member, a friend, a cultural broker, or a religious leader. It can be a shaman, a curandero, or a therapist. The important thing isn't the label, but the relationship, which is nurturing, consistent, and respectful.

This healing relationship often relies on what psychologist Celia Jaes Falicov calls "the power of small gestures." When I visit Bintu, I take her flowers. In fact, whenever I visit people who have suffered, I try to take a small gift. When grief-stricken people visited my aunt Grace, she offered them pie. Sometimes what heals is as simple as a touch of the hand, a smile, or the expression of sympathy.

Relationships reintroduce people who have suffered to the community of love. If they have been dehumanized, caring can rehumanize them. Warmth and respect can rebuild a person who has been systematically humiliated and degraded by torturers. Many people have been pulled back from the precipice of despair by one person who let them know they mattered.

Linda Simon wrote of William James, one of our best psychologists, "He was a birthright member of the great society of encouragers." We can all be in that great society of encouragers.

We can ask people about their feelings and allow them to cry and rage. And we can be what Donald Meichenbaum called "purveyors of hope."

Love and hope are necessary to keep people's heads above water when they are in dire straits. A truly good listener manages to convey, "You have lost a lot, but you have not lost everything." In the end, healing relationships are about finding dignity adequate to the sorrow. I think of the three Iraqi men from the prison camp in Saudi Arabia. The most important thing for them was to find meaning in their experiences, to understand what happened to them in a way that allowed them to see themselves as men, worthy of respect.

HEALING STORIES
All sorrows can be borne if they can be put into a story.
—Isak Dinesen

People survive because they partake of the alchemy of healing. They turn their pain into a deeper understanding of themselves and of what it means to be human. As Pico Iyer wrote, "The final destination of any journey is not after all the last item on the agenda but rather some understanding, however simple and provisional, of what one has seen."

To say that people can grow and learn from any experience is not to justify their experience or even to say that they couldn't have learned from an easier life, but it is to say that healthy people learn and grow from everything, even trauma.

Almost all who become wiser and stronger after trauma do so because they develop a sense of purpose that transcends their immediate survival needs and allows them to focus on the future. They survive so that their children can become citizens and go to college, or so that they can become doctors or teachers and help others from their country, or so that they can bring their grandparents to America or write the truth about a bloody regime. This sense of purpose, as necessary to life as oxygen, propels refugees into the future

A woman from Colombia saw her husband shot by drug dealers. He was an honest judge who was unlucky enough to live in the wrong place and time. She was an educated woman who wrote books and worked all over the world. Afterward she spent her life writing and speaking about the problems of her country. She said, "I honor his memory by fighting for justice."

Healing stories might be about courage or generosity under fire, wresting victory from the jaws of defeat, or hard lessons learned. Stories should focus on what can be remembered with pride. Healing stories help people cast their lives in epic terms. Often just a slight spin can turn a story of misery into an epic of danger, heroism, sacrifice, and reward. Joseph's story can be told as one of victimization or as one in which he is a hero who saves his younger siblings. All of us need to see our lives as a quest for something more enticing then mere survival. All of us need to be a superhero to someone. The best question to elicit healing stories is, "What did you learn from your experience?"

Talking to the Sudanese and Kosovar refugees, I found that no matter what they had suffered they all said they had gained from their experiences. Many mentioned increased self-awareness, stronger love for family, closeness to other refugees, and witnessing acts of heroism or great generosity. One woman, who had been about to be shot, told of a stranger who placed his body between her body and the executioners. Another woman talked of people who gave away their only food.

Suffering is redemptive when it leads us to a deeper, more nuanced understanding of ourselves and other humans. For countless generations humans have used their pain to grow souls. Through tragedy many people realize they are capable of much better behavior than they thought possible. Or perhaps they realize how much they are loved. After she had broken her ankle, a woman from Azerbaijan was carried across a war zone by her husband. She said, "I never realized how much he cared for me." A Croatian boy said of his sister, "She was starving, but she handed me her last piece of bread."

Perhaps refugees have been heroes, much braver, more competent, or kinder than they ever suspected they could be. Through suffering, people learn the importance of kindness. They learn that love is all that matters. They develop a sense of perspective and scale. They learn tolerance and empathy. After much is lost, they learn appreciation for what remains.

I spoke to my aunt Grace the day she lost her only son. He had lived nearby all sixty years of his life and died of a heart attack mowing Grace's lawn. My aunt sounded old and tired on the phone. At the end of the call, she told me, "We'll just have to love and take care of the ones who are left."

My aunt was very wise. Her simple statement of purpose really sums up the nature of healing. After great loss, we must find who is left to love and resolve to care for them. That is all we can do. In most cases, the great miracle is that it is enough.

Samuel Beckett wrote, "Ever tried, Ever failed. No matter. Try again. Fail again. Fail better." We tend to underestimate our own resilience. Striving and overcoming obstacles can bring joy and focus to life. One of the great ironies is that stressful lives often provoke positive emotions, while easier lives can induce laziness and apathy. Who is happier, a mountain climber or a person who sits around and watches television all weekend?

The psychologist who has most understood healing and the relationship between pain and meaning is Viktor Frankl. In *Man's Search for Meaning,* he wrote that while he was in a con-

centration camp, he discovered that everything can be taken
from a person but one thing—the ability to choose one's attitude to any given set of circumstances.

Nelson Mandela discovered the same great truth. He was
locked up for twenty-seven years. At a certain point, he realized
that, "My enemies could take it all, everything but my mind and
heart. I decided not to give them away." This insight helped
him reestablish his dignity and personal integrity.

Human life is not freedom from conditions, but freedom to
take a stand on conditions. To live is to suffer. To survive is to find
meaning in suffering. Working for the welfare of others is the best
antidote to despair. Working to help extended family left in the
old country, testifying about human rights abuses, working for
democracy—all these activities give life meaning and help refugees heal. No one comes out of a holocaust to sell sausages. To
truly recover, one must find a deep sense of purpose and meaning.

Americans who have suffered find similar ways to cope.
They work for worthy causes, reconnect with friends, recommit
themselves to their religious faith. They decide to spend more
time with family, to read all of Shakespeare, or to visit the national parks they always wanted to see. They give their money
to the needy.

Resilient people tell themselves a story that gives their lives
meaning and purpose. The African American and Native American communities are especially good at using proverbs and stories to build meaning. Throughout their histories, these cultures
have created stories that allowed them to laugh, to learn, and to
find dignity in situations of oppression and despair.

In an ideal world we would learn about healing from one
another. We would draw on the wisdom from all times and
places. We would be intentional in our healing. That is, we
would select from all cultures that which might work for us. In

an ideal world we would all be able to pray, to dance and to feast, to watch sunsets and moonrises, and to talk to each other about our pain. We would use both laughter and tears and that great antidote to despair, being useful.

We would create healing ceremonies. We would find symbols that gave meaning to our grief. We would teach each other to endure, that greatest of human strengths. I remember an old saying my mother taught me: There are three cures for all human pain and all involve salt—the salt of tears, the salt of sweat from hard work, and the salt of the great open seas. Years ago when my mother told me this, I was a teenager and I believed the reference to open seas was about the escape one could make on the open seas, the escape from family or memory. Now I believe it is about the healing power of the natural world. After my time with refugees, I appreciate even more the truth of this saying about salt.

On the eve of January 1, 2000, National Public Radio commentator Daniel Schorr named Anne Frank Person of the Century. He praised her for keeping her humanity and faith in humankind in the face of all the horrors of the Nazi experience. I was touched and pleased by his choice. Ever since I read Anne's journal when I was thirteen years old, she has been a moral beacon for me.

She had all the attributes of resilience. However, she wasn't a disembodied saint, but a real person, capable of anger, self-doubt, tears, and joy. All through her last years, up until the end, she managed to remain awake, aware, and profoundly human. Even at the end of her life, in the concentration camp she was capable of grief when the gypsy girls were led to their deaths. Patricia Hampl wrote of our yearning for this girl who embodies resilience, "We seek her still, this sane person that we long for at the end of our terrible century that tried so desperately to erase her."

CHAPTER 11

HOME—*A* GLOBAL POSITIONING SYSTEM *for* IDENTITY

We find ourselves, I believe, in the midst of the
most massive shift in perspective that humankind has ever known.
We are living in a time—and I see this all over the world—
in which our very nature is in transition.

—JEAN HOUSTON

We need a psychology of place. As Einstein once said, "Everything has changed except our thinking." Right now we barely have the words to discuss what is happening to the human race. Our economy and our technology have changed much more rapidly than our conceptions about what it means to be human. In our rapidly changing world, we need research about the effects of global meld on people.

We are living in a world that is falling apart and coming together at the same time. It is both Babel and EuroDisney. All the world is becoming more like America at the same time that America is becoming more diverse. The sun never sets on MTV or Coca-Cola, and Nebraskans can shop for jicama and kimchi, listen to music from Eastern Europe, or pray in a Buddhist temple with people from Laos and Vietnam. Global citizens know Michael Jordon, Julia Roberts, and Tiger Woods.

New York City, Los Angeles, and San Francisco have always had global moments, incongruous scenes of cultures colliding, but now we are having those moments in Nebraska. Increasingly, our lives are filled with moments that reveal how mixed together our world is becoming. Nebraskans now travel to Machu Picchu and Nepal. At the Fourth of July parade, Latino and Vietnamese children fly the biggest flags. Everyone eats onion blossoms and corn dogs.

The changes have come upon us quickly. We are reeling from culture shock. Yet, we are only dimly aware of how different our world has become. We are now living in a universe of infinite choices. Every act requires an existential decision. Are we Buddhist, Christian, or Jewish? Do we serve bread, tortillas, or naan? Do we use chopsticks or a fork? Do we listen to Los Lobos, the Chieftains, or Didi Kembola? Do we shake hands or bow? Do we watch the Superbowl or World Cup soccer?

In this changing universe of home, we all need a global positioning system for identity. At one time, to be born a Cuban, Japanese, or Inuit was to live a certain kind of life. Identity was totally determined by gender, clan, birth order, and place. There was very little choice involved. Today, identity from sense of place is no longer a given. Demographic clusters have replaced national identity as the great definers. People in these clusters share the same habits, activities, opinions, and tastes, whether they live in London, Milan, Hong Kong, or Lincoln. "Soon the question where do you come from will be as antiquated as what regiment do you belong to?" wrote Pico Iyer. Or, as British sociologist Michael Featherstone put it, "We are all living in each others' backyards."

We need to take care with our words, as they shape our perceptions and experience. We are not living in a global village; rather we're quartered in a chain hotel in a global strip mall. In global shopping malls, the stories and metaphors are not our own, but rather are designed to sell us stuff. Everything is about money. Globalization means the world is for sale and that there is no place left where we can hide.

In our increasingly fragmented "hotel society," we have more freedom and more possibilities of making serious mistakes. All of us must construct our own identities and become experts at cultural switching. Sometimes that leaves us feeling like we are motherless children, or as one friend said, "We need a tribe."

Refugees have much to teach us about staying connected to a "tribe" while moving in many cultural contexts. One of the greatest challenges for refugees is to create a niche that allows them to maintain their ethnic identity and become American. This shouldn't be an either/or, but rather, a both/and situation. Pride in ethnic background shouldn't preclude acquiring a national identity. But as African Americans have long acknowledged, it's difficult to balance racial and ethnic identity with national identity. In 1903 in *The Souls of Black Folk,* W. E. B. Du Bois wrote, "The American Negro longs to merge his double self into a better and truer self. In this merging, he wishes neither of the older selves to be lost. He would not Africanize America.... He would not bleach his Negro soul in a flood of white Americanism.... He simply wishes to make it possible for a man to be both a Negro and an American."

Maintaining a both/and identity is complex. As a Mexican American teenager said, "I have to be more Mexican than the Mexicans and more American than the Americans. It's exhausting."

However, by now all of us struggle to maintain multiple identities. We exhibit multiple personalities, not the disorder, but the coping strategy. We do a lot of cultural switching, and we also do an awful lot of making things new. We all have "designer lives," creating our own ecological niches from our collective identities.

We have a great deal of psychological research that shows the adaptiveness of what social scientists call "bicultural or multicultural identity." Bicultural or multicultural people who identify with both their own groups and with America tend to feel the best. People who identity with neither their country of origin nor their new country have the hardest time.

The following story is of a refugee who falls in this last category. My work with Chia was to help her build attributes of resilience and to find a moral center. I helped her settle in our town and make connections with both her ethnic community and our American one. Over the course of our relationship, Chia developed a stronger identity and skills for coping with our complicated country.

THE LOST LADY

Chia, a sixteen-year-old Laotian girl, was sent to me by her high school nurse because she was not sleeping well and seemed depressed. She'd been coming into the nurse's office and talking for hours and the nurse felt Chia needed an adult who had time and attention just for her.

Chia was pretty in the way most Laotian girls are pretty— small and slim with shiny hair and delicate features. At first, she was shy with me, but once she relaxed, she was a nonstop talker. She had a thick accent and sometimes I had to slow her down and ask her to repeat.

Chia began our first session by complaining about lower back pain. I suggested swimming, but she said, "Laotian people don't swim." I suggested she ask a friend for a back rub, but she said, "I have no friends, Miss."

It became clear that while Chia complained about her problems, she didn't want to accept help. When I offered her suggestions, she was oppositional. So, I resolved to stop suggesting ideas and just try to understand her.

Chia's mother had died shortly after she was born. She'd been cared for by an aunt who had also died. Chia and her father had left his mother behind in Vietnam and come to America five years ago. She was learning English, but her father wasn't. He worked as a night watchman at a power plant and Chia cooked and cleaned for him. She said, "When my father comes home he is tired. He watches television and falls asleep."

Chia and her father had high utility and grocery bills and could barely live on his salary and Chia worried about her grandmother's high cholesterol and blood pressure and about her father's chronic cough. She had nightmares that both her grandmother and her father had died. She said, "Then, Miss, I would be all alone."

I asked gently if she was lonely now.

"Yes, Miss." Chia looked at her hands and for a moment was silent. I asked her about school clubs. She said, "I must go right home and cook for my father."

"Do you and your father have Laotian friends?"

"No. My father is very tired. He doesn't want to spend money. It's better if we are just alone."

I gently noted, "Everybody needs friends."

She pondered this as if it were a truly novel idea. She said quietly, "I am afraid if anyone likes me they might die."

I said, "Let's talk more about that."

Chia lived in a world without relationships. Except for her

father, her distant grandmother, and a few kind teachers, she was deeply alone. She had little understanding or empathy for others and few ways to attract others' interest. She was fearful of closeness because closeness meant loss. She'd lost touch with most of her Laotian world, but she hadn't connected to much in our town.

She was struggling to decide when to be Laotian and when to be American. She seemed very traditional in her behavior and beliefs, and yet she dressed like an American girl. Because of her English, she had responsibilities in her family very unlike those of a traditional daughter. She helped her father with everything, including his taxes, his bills, and his INS paperwork.

Chia's life was an odd combination of sad, stressful, and uneventful. I remembered the Jay Haley technique of turning tragedy into musical comedy. I couldn't go that far, but I decided a nickname might give Chia some identity and some hope. I said, "For now, I am going to call you The Lost Lady. That is the name of a beautiful young woman from a book by a famous Nebraska woman named Willa Cather."

She looked at me with interest and asked "Why do you call me that?"

I wrote out the words and handed them to her. I said, "The lost lady had many people telling her who to be. She didn't really know who she was. She was trying to figure out what her life meant to her and to other people."

This small naming ceremony was the beginning of my identity work. I wanted to have an enticing label that described Chia to herself. Chia had few external or internal resources, and small problems became big problems because she had no one to help her with them and no ways to calm herself down.

She needed nurturing, identity building, and help developing some of the attributes of resilience. She needed someone to tell her stories and to encourage her to explore her new environment. The first few months, I told her about our town, about its parks and other beautiful places, about it history and cultural events, and about where to find good Asian restaurants. I told her many stories, of life in America, of families experiencing culture shock, of parents and children working things out, and of teenagers who were stressed finding a path to happiness. Whenever I could, I told her stories of hope.

I asked Chia about college and she said, "It is too hard and it costs too much money." I asked her about her dreams and she said, "I have no dreams." I touched her arm. "Everybody needs dreams."

At the end of the session I praised her for cooking for her father. I said, "That is an important job." I asked her if she wanted to come back. She asked, "How is your health, Miss?"

Session 2

Chia again started with a physical complaint—her shoulder hurt. But I was prepared for this by now and I said simply, "I am very sorry."

Chia said, "My dad still has his cough."

I asked if he'd been to a doctor and she looked worried. She said, "No, Miss. The doctor costs money."

I said, "I'll call for a free appointment at the health department. Let's get this checked out."

Today, Chia brought pictures of her grandmother and her aunt who had died. They were old-fashioned pictures, from another world. Her grandmother looked like she weighed about eighty pounds and her aunt had stooped shoulders and several missing teeth. Both the grandmother and the aunt were barefoot and dressed in traditional silk dresses.

Chia also had pictures of herself and her father. He was a

skinny, wrinkled man in a dark suit, the same suit in every picture. But whenever he was with Chia in the pictures, his arm was on her shoulder. And Chia always wore pretty clothes that he had bought with his meager wages.

I pointed to his arm on her shoulder and said, "I can tell your dad loves you."

She said, "He is always crabby with me."

I told Chia I had read that Laotian parents didn't praise their children for fear that spirits would hear the praise and steal the children. Especially if parents had a wonderful child, it was good to insult that child. I said, "Your father loves you, but he is old-fashioned."

Chia nodded happily at this interpretation. I suspected that Chia's father wasn't a terribly well-adjusted person, but to criticize him was to criticize the only person who kept her tethered to the world. She needed ways to keep loving her father and yet become more confident and American. Somehow she needed to be able to feel loyal to him and to Laos and yet adopt some new behaviors.

I temporarily forgot my resolve to stop making suggestions and asked Chia if she and her father would consider visiting the Asian Center, a Buddhist temple, or the Catholic church that many southeast Asians attended. She shook her head no. I asked about a pet for her, or even a visit to the zoo. She said, "My father doesn't like animals."

I asked about a school dance that was coming up. Chia looked at me like I was crazy. "My father thinks that is too dangerous."

I paused and reminded myself of my earlier insight. At the very least, I needed to come up with less-ambitious assignments. I showed Chia how to breathe deeply and relax her muscles, and I gave her a relaxation tape to play when she had trouble sleeping. I also gave her a journal and said, "Every day I want you to write down two things you are proud of." She thanked me for the journal. "This is my first present. You have made me very happy, Miss." On the cover, she wrote her name and "The Lost Lady."

I said, "Next time, we'll take your picture for the journal." She smiled in agreement.

"I want you to surprise me by writing that you talked to some students here at school."

Session 8

Over the next few months Chia did begin to make friends, with Miki, a Bosnian boy in her homeroom, and Thao, a Laotian girl from her computer class. She still led a quiet life of school, housework, and sleep, but she smiled more.

We talked about the problems that came up with her new friends. She responded to problems by ignoring them, pretending everything was okay, or by disappearing entirely. In general, she wasn't very flexible, and I worked to broaden her repertoire of responses. When she asked questions about how to handle things, or when she discussed issues openly, I really praised her.

Our sessions were very ritualized. Chia began with a physical complaint. By now I realized this was her way of asking for nurturance and I responded with interest and caring. Then she asked about my health and I assured her it was excellent. I asked if she was doing her breathing and relaxation exercises. Sometimes she was and sometimes she wasn't.

Next I inquired if she had written two things a day she was proud of. Generally Chia pulled out her journal and read what she had written. I praised her for speaking to new people, for exploring our town, for being flexible, or for having fun.

We used the diary to help her define a self. I asked her, "What do you enjoy? How do you make decisions about what to do? What are you good at? What are your favorite books, foods, and flowers? What qualities would you want in a friend?"

At first, Chia struggled with these questions, but as we worked over the months, she began to have short tentative answers. She liked to sing. She liked carnations and roses. Maybe she would go to junior college if her dad had enough money. She liked kind, honest, and healthy people.

Today she was moody. Her father had attended a performance of her school chorus. But afterward he had told Chia, "You can't sing. Forget this chorus."

She was mad at her father and discouraged by his remarks. I reminded her of the old-fashioned Laotian belief that the gods might steal gifted children. I said, "Your dad must be very proud."

She said, "I wish he would act like an American father and give me a hug."

That led into a discussion we often had about America and Laos. Chia was beginning to sort out what she wanted to keep from both cultures. She felt that in most ways her home culture was superior. She respected her elders and she felt American teenagers were too wild. She planned to care for her father forever. She said, "I would never put him in a rest home like Americans do." However, she liked the American ways of joking around and having fun. She envied American kids' conversations with their parents.

We talked about her friends. Miki wanted to come to her house after school and study. Her father didn't want anyone to come over, but especially not a boy. He didn't believe in dating until age twenty. Then he thought Chia should only date the man she would marry. After struggling with the issue, Chia decided to tell Miki that she could only be his friend at school and that she couldn't be his girlfriend. She said, "I will marry a man from my country."

Her Laotian girlfriend Thao had invited her to a birthday party. Chia was afraid to go and she didn't have any money for a gift. After much discussion we decided she could afford a two-dollar carnation and a handmade card. I gave her copies of pictures I'd taken of her. I said, "Give one to Thao with her card and send one to your grandmother."

As we parted, I said, "Take a chance. Go to the party." It was a sign of real progress that she agreed to think about it.

Session 9

For the first time since we met, Chia came in without any physical complaints. I greeted her and asked if she had brought her journal. She proudly handed it to me. She had written, "I am proud that I told Miki I couldn't be his girlfriend. I am proud that I went to Thao's party. I am proud that I cooked noodles for my father and that I wrote my grandmother a letter."

I hugged her and praised her for her kindness and for taking some risks. She smiled happily. Chia liked American-style affection. She brought me pictures from Thao's party. It had been a small party, with just Thao, her brother, and her brother's best friend. They'd had birthday cake, the first Chia had ever tasted, and they'd walked over to the Sunken Gardens. In the pictures Chia looked almost playful.

Chia confessed she had been very nervous and had hardly spoken. I said, "That's all right. It was your first party. Next time you will talk more."

I said, "Don't worry if you aren't perfect in everything you try. Celebrate your victories."

She said proudly, "My father and I went to a free concert in the park."

I looked surprised and she said, "I told my father what you told me, Miss. I said we need to have fun."

I reflected how much Chia had changed in the three months I had known her. She was no longer so oppositional with me. She talked more to her classmates and she no longer seemed afraid that if she liked someone they would disappear. She asked more questions and admitted she needed help with her problems. She had developed a few ways to calm herself down—writing in her journal, talking to her Laotian friend, even going out with her dad. She had developed a few interpersonal skills. She slept better and was more energetic. She had a sense that she had some strengths. We were just beginning to sort out what she did well and what she enjoyed. I wanted to help her plan a future.

Working with Chia reminded me of something Fred Rogers once said: "There is a space between the needy and the person who is asked to help. That space is holy." I was grateful I had been allowed to listen to the problems of this quiet, decent person who was lost in our complex city. As we put away the party pictures, I said, "When I met you, you were The Lost Lady, but you have changed. You talk more in class. You enjoy your friends. You are more courageous. You are The Strong Lady."

She said, "Thank you, Miss. I am glad you have good health."

CHOICE AND IDENTITY

Psychologist Barry Schwartz has researched the problems of choice. He grew interested while shopping for a stroller for his grandchild. Instead of the two or three choices he'd had when his own children were young, he encountered several dozen models. Far from the additional choices being liberating and exhilarating, he felt confused, uncertain, and anxious. Schwartz realized that he had too many choices and he decided to explore this idea scientifically.

His stroller dilemma occurs in all areas of life. All domains— work, school, religion, entertainment, and clothes—have choices where once choice didn't exist. Parenthetically, while there are more things to choose from, our options are more alike. Travel agents offer ten tropical island vacations, but they are all at Club Meds. There are fifty pizza joints in town, but the pizza is all made from the same prefabricated ingredients.

Choice is a good thing, but only up to a point. Beyond an ideal number of options, people are paralyzed. The situation is too confusing. They don't choose carefully but rather give up and pick impulsively. Also, with many choices, people are more likely to experience regret. People are more likely to feel badly about a lackluster meal if they selected it from a menu with sixty items. They are more likely to second-guess their vacation choice if they chose from a hundred places instead of deciding between the Black Hills and the Ozarks.

Schwartz argues that freedom can be experienced as tyranny. "If you are free to do anything you want, you find there isn't anything you want to do." What seems best is freedom within constraints. Traffic laws are an example of how constraints give us more freedom. Language is another. With language you can say everything, but not anything.

For the first time in history, large numbers of people can lead the kinds of lives they want, unlimited by economics or culture. However, emotional depression is ten times more likely now than at the turn of the twentieth century. It seems counterintuitive that more choice leads to more depression. However, when we increase people's opportunities for control, we increase their expectations of control and their sense of responsibility for failure. When we have more choices in every domain, we must spend more time researching choices and negotiating these decisions with family members. Never in the history of the world have so many people spent so much time making decisions.

At one time cultures restricted options and circumscribed choices. Traditional morality served as preventive medicine protecting people from themselves. But, in a global shopping mall, many of the constraints from culture disappear. For our own positive mental health, we need to reconstruct some constraints. It is no accident that retreat centers are an increasingly popular vacation spot. Retreats restrict choice and thus, paradoxically, allow certain kinds of freedom. Another example of constraints is the Universal Declaration of Human Rights crafted by Eleanor Roosevelt at the United Nations after World War II. These rights exist for all people wherever they are. They set bottom-line limits about the choices governments have.

Cicero asked a question that's relevant today: "What is the set of rules that makes freedom possible?" The ideal culture would have exactly the right number of choices to maximize freedom and control in every domain. While citizens should have more choices than they are allowed under repressive regimes, prosperous American teens should have fewer. The perfect culture would be neither an authoritarian nightmare nor an existential Disney World.

WHAT REFUGEES CAN TEACH US ABOUT IDENTITY

E. M. Cioran wrote, "A civilization evolves from agriculture to paradox." As the world changes rapidly and becomes more riddled with paradoxes, we must deal with all that complexity. The challenge is to change in ways that allow us to experience our lives as continuous wholes. To be healthy, we must make choices to restrict choices.

We must prepare ourselves for a future that has arrived. We must educate our children to be global citizens who can live with all the paradoxes of identity, who can change while retaining a core of self. We want to give them the minimum daily requirements for identity. Otherwise, they will have a hard time holding on to their humanity in a world that increasingly defines them as consumers.

Identity is formed by art, writing, dance, music, and other forms of self-expression. It develops by answering questions about the self, whether via philosophy class, self-analysis, or psychotherapy. The questions are universal questions—Who am I? What do I want? How am I like other people? How am I different from other people? Am I a good person? Am I a talented person? Do I have something to offer? Am I loved?

To survive in this new century we all need what refugees need. We must adapt to a world that shifts constantly under our feet. We must be resilient or we will be lost. We need families who love us and will help us, rituals and traditions, and contact with the natural world and with our history. We need communities of friends to hold our lives in place and reasonable conditions in the external world—livable wages, decent schools and health care, safe streets, and opportunities to advance.

In a global village, identity is built by having the attributes of resilience and good moral character. In a world of infinite options, humans need a simple core identity and a solid set of values to sort through all the choices. To quote Beethoven, "Character is fate." Without a moral compass to guide behavior, one is adrift. One risks being swept along in the current of impulsive hedonism or running aground entirely, paralyzed by having the responsibility to choose without the wisdom.

Our moral sense becomes our global positioning system. A man told me that when he was a boy his Ozark grandmother told him that when we are born each of us has a soul like a clear blue pool of water. We are responsible for the care of our pool. Every day we make choices that will keep the water clear or make it muddy. The grandmother said, "When I get to heaven, I'll wait for you. The first thing I'm going to do when you get there is take a look at the color of the water in your pool." The man said, "Knowing my grandmother is waiting has kept me on track all my life." He had a strong GPS.

Aristotle wrote, "We are what we repeatedly do. Excellence is not an act but a habit." The Dalai Lama said, "My religion is kindness." Or, as Thomas Paine wrote, "My country is the world and my religion is to do good." Moral people tend to have good moral habits and a few simple rules, such as do unto others as you would have them do unto you. They are the North Stars for the rest of us. They give us hope as we try to orient on our spinning planet.

HOME

The love of your own country hasn't to do with foreign politics,
burning flags, or the Maginot Line against immigrants at the border.
It has to do with light on a hillside, the fat belly of a
local trout, and the smell of new-mown hay.
—BILL HOLM

The refugee experience of dislocation, cultural bereavement, confusion, and constant change will soon be all of our experience. As the world becomes globalized, we'll all be searching for home. There are two intertwined components to home: people and place. In fact, we can't really know people if we don't share a place with them over time. *Community, communication,* and *communion* all come from the same word, meaning "together" and "next to." Embedded in the word *community* is the concept of a shared place. An Internet chat room is not a place. The virtual university that "liberates students from time and space" may perform a service, but it is not a community. An electronic village is no village. Everywhere is nowhere.

William Riley said, "In a world without places there is no responsibility for yesterday and tomorrow." With place comes responsibility—to those who were here before us, to those who are here now, and to those who will come later. At a most basic level we behave better with people and places we will see again and again. We take care of the land, the water, the air, and the animals.

Gary Snyder advised, "Find your place on the planet, dig in, and take responsibility from there." It is a simple thing, to be in a place where good behavior is rewarded and bad is punished. In that sense, all morality, like all politics, is local. The farther we are from home, from our people, the less likely we are to see a strong connection between our own behavior and its consequences. In an avalanche, no snowflake holds itself responsible.

Some of the worst behaviors in America occur in airports and on interstates, places where we move among strangers. These are places where the people who will be hurt by our behavior have no names. In places where we are anonymous, we can do whatever we want. No one will be a witness.

Home is where you know the names of the people you meet. You know who is kind and honest and who lies, betrays, or fools around. Home is where people care if you have a speeding ticket or a fever. It's where people ask about your grandbaby and your daylilies and know your favorite kind of pie. For newcomers, one of the hardest things is simply walking down streets filled with strangers. All of us, wherever we are, search for "an old familiar face."

If you live in one place a long time, you have a history. When you talk with your friends, you don't have to discuss Tom Hanks or Benicio Del Toro; you have real people in common. If you get sick, people will bring you soup and flowers, shovel the snow off your driveway, or go to the pharmacy for you. To move away from home is to move away from life.

In Spanish the concept of home has almost sacred status. *Querencia* refers to an instinct that people and animals have to find a place where they feel safe and at home, a primal need, premammalian even. *Querencia* comes from the verb, *querer,* "to desire." It's the spot in the bullring where the wounded bull goes to collect himself. *Querencia* is a place where one can center and regroup. We all need *querencia* to find ourselves.

When former Speaker of the House Sam Rayburn was diagnosed with a terminal illness, he left Washington, D.C., to return to his small Texas town. He said, "There people know when you're sick and care when you die." That was *querencia* at its most basic.

The big questions for this decade are, Will we live in real places and have homes, or will we allow ourselves to be defined as consumers in a soulless global landscape? Of course, these aren't either/or questions. We will all be part of both a world culture and a local one, but the amount we participate in each will vary enormously. We have choices.

When Jim and I flew home from Alaska, we could see the northern lights exploding halfway across the bowl of sky over mountains of ice and snow, glacial rivers, and pale tundra. But as we watched out of our small thick window, we were watching alone. All the other passengers had their eyes on a video. It seemed a metaphor for our time, a crowd of people focused on a tired rerun of the news while missing news of the universe.

Refugees often come from places where, at least until the war or tragedy that drove them away, there was a true community, and they fare better in America if they find a new true community. What they need is a hometown. There is a great deal of difference between true and false communities.

In Nebraska, Oakland is a true community and White Clay is a false one. White Clay is a town built near the Pine Ridge Reservation. It has four liquor stores, a post office, a secondhand store, a grocery, a pawnshop, and an auto parts store. Each building is made of cinder blocks and has steel mesh over the windows. Nobody lives in White Clay because they enjoy it; they are there to make money.

Its civic events are shootings, fistfights, stabbings, and beatings. The shopowners keep loaded shotguns behind the counters. White Clay has only carry-out liquor sales, so the Native Americans drink in the town's abandoned houses. There are no festivals in White Clay, no churches, schools, parties, or farmers' markets. White Clay is what will happen to the whole world if we don't stop it.

In contrast, Oakland, Nebraska, is a sleepy little town that is a true community. Many of its children have left, but they come back for holidays and the Swedish festival. My generation of "Oakies" has created many new holidays. There is the Oakland Christmas party in Lincoln, the Ya Shoor bike tour, and summer parties on the Platte. Oakland is filled with characters with character. It is far from any action or centers of power and there is not enough money in town for anyone to bother to come steal. So it remains a simple good place.

Scott Russell Sanders writes, "I cannot have a spiritual center without a geographic one." He contrasts inhabitants to drifters. He speaks of the "malnutrition of the soul," of the "dissatisfaction and hunger that result from placelessness." The words *provincial* and *parochial* have traditionally had negative connotations, but they can also mean the sacredness of one's town.

Place is identity. There is a marvelous Francis Picabia painting at the Art Institute of Chicago called *Four Faces*. The faces are barely outlined. The painting is of the landscape of the islands, mountains, and the trees. His point is that we are landscape internalized. Our souls are etched with the geography of a particular place.

As we become global citizens, we need a home to hold our lives in place. We need to turn off our televisions, go outside, look at the stars, and visit with our neighbors. I think of myself on book tours, month-long marathons of speaking, signing books, giving interviews, and passing through airports and hotel rooms. By the end, I yearn for home. I weep at the smell of my father-in-law's pipe tobacco. I long for the sight of a jonquil or a sycamore. I search for a duck or a goose, even a starling—anything that connects me to home. Or, I think of a Kansan I know, a strong, smart man, who now lives in an East Coast city and works at a high-powered job. He falls asleep at night reading Laura Ingalls Wilder's *Little House on the Prairie*.

Paul Gruchow wrote, "The Plains Indians said that everywhere is the center of the world and so it is." American restlessness is overstated. We all come from immigrants, but if we look far enough back in our family trees, we will find a farmer. In *Grass Roots,* Gruchow makes the point that the average settler wasn't in search of a new world to conquer, but of a refuge, "a place with a few cows, a garden, a house of one's own, as far away from trouble as possible."

CHAPTER 12

BUILDING *a* VILLAGE *of* KINDNESS

TWILIGHT IN THE SUNKEN GARDENS

After a hundred-degree day, the earth is cooling as the sun sinks below the trees west of the city. Women in hijabs and burkas gather in a circle on the grass, their long skirts tucked skillfully beneath them, their faces in shadow. Between mauve and white hibiscus bushes, the grasses are yellow, but the splash of a nearby fountain provides the illusion of water in abundance, of water to squander on beauty. Shouting in Farsi, boys in shorts and T-shirts splash in the pool below the fountain. Their mothers are absorbed in talking to their friends and only occasionally glance their way.

Near the women, a dignified man in traditional clothes and sandals walks alone. I suspect he is the husband of one of the women, perhaps appointed by the other husbands to make sure the wives are not disturbed. Near the fountain, an older man with sad eyes walks with his young wife. They are speaking Arabic, but they don't mesh with the other families. She wears makeup, capri pants, and high heels. They look lonely in this setting, their eyes searching for the face of a friend.

Two girls in long flowered dresses and head scarves argue as they ride their bikes. The taller one pushes the shorter one down and she begins to wail. The taller girl is rather plain and I wonder what happens to plain girls from the Middle East. Do they have trouble finding husbands? For that matter, what happens to plain girls here? It may be easier for this girl to find a life partner than it is for American girls. Her parents may help arrange a marriage. Families will be connected and decisions will be made by cool heads, uninfluenced by beauty.

The women pass a gallon jug of water and a package of dates around the circle. Two laughing women take photos of each other and their babies in strollers. No doubt their husbands are working second shifts or are at home watching news in their own language on satellite TV.

This scene could happen almost anywhere in the world. It's a very old scene, women and children outside under trees, sharing food and water at the end of the day, enjoying the cool and the company, speaking softly in their ancient languages. Crickets serenade a tableau of flowers, trees, and an orange sun sinking. The people gathered here for these old rituals are from Eastern Europe and the Middle East. But this is Nebraska, what William Gass calls, "the heart of the heart of the country."

Our Sunken Gardens, built years ago by our European city fathers, is now an oasis for women in burkas who spend their days assembling computer boards or cutting up chickens.

Nearby, the Rotary Club benches built in memory of departed loved ones sit empty. We Americans are too busy to lounge around in parks, and besides we have air-conditioning. So, the cicadas and crickets sing for our new citizens. The cars pass nearby on Twenty-seventh Street. Tonight the women talk of what they have always talked about—of their men, their chil-

dren, and the price of rice. Starlings fly across the face of the setting sun.

WHAT REFUGEES TEACH US

I was a speck of light in the great river of light that
undulates through time. I was floating with the whole human family.
We were all colors—those who are living now, those who have died,
and those who are not yet born."

—JANE KENYON, *Once There Was Light*

For the most part, newcomers are filled with energy, gratitude,
and hope. They enjoy a walk, a cup of coffee, or a bouquet of
tulips. They are not jaded consumers. Everything is new and interesting to them. A trip to the ice-cream store or a concert are
great events. Many laugh easily, work hard, and do not complain. They are, to quote Jesse Jackson, "the kind of people who
get up every day and do what needs to be done."

Newcomers keep their pain to themselves. They don't tell
us about the child killed while walking barefoot across the
mountains into Turkey or their starving relatives in Haiti. They
don't tell us they don't have money for dinner for their kids or
a bus ride to the doctor. Newcomers do not reprimand us for
our wealth.

Many newcomers have excellent manners. From the first
day, the Kakuma refugees were among the most polite people I
had ever encountered. The Kurdish sisters never failed to offer
me tea and snacks, even when they had little food for themselves. Many Middle Eastern and Vietnamese women have
cooked me beautiful meals when I visited, and served them to
me as if I were a beloved family member.

A caseworker told of missing a day of work with the flu.
While she was gone, a Sudanese client called for her and was

told she was ill. When he next spoke to her, he said, "I told all the Sudanese people about your health and we prayed you would get well. Now we will thank God that he heard our prayers."

The newcomers can teach us about family loyalty. Many adults work two jobs so that they can send one paycheck to the old country to support family there. Or they eat nothing but rice and save every penny to sponsor family members coming to Lincoln. Many Vietnamese save for years to return to Vietnam. This is not for travel expenses, but rather, so they can give thousands of dollars away to needy family members.

Loyalty extends to the ethnic community where everyone is struggling with the same issues. For the most part, people help each other. They share food, clothes, and housing. They give each other rides to work, to medical appointments, and to church, temple, or the mosque. We humans have long valued communal experiences. At Neolithic sites, anthropologists have noticed that all the bones of game animals are often found around one cooking fire. They postulate that since the earliest times we have liked to share our food with other families. However, we Americans have been educated to value privacy and we tend to live in our own "isolation tanks." Working with refugees I began to appreciate what we are missing.

There is nothing more insulting to the poor than romanticizing poverty. However, lack of resources can lead to good things. Once I had a conversation with a refugee from Ethiopia in which he told me he had caught many big fish. Thinking to be helpful, I offered to let him store these fish in my freezer since he had far too many to eat at one time. He looked at me quizzically and replied, "I have no need to store fish. I will give them away to my friends."

Over and over, I have witnessed heroic altruism in newcomers. Poverty and crises allow people to help each other.

Likewise, prosperity can keep us from knowing how much people love us and will help us.

Descartes advised, "When living in the midst of others, do not stand out too much." For the most part, newcomers try to fit in and to do things the way Americans do. They are extremely reluctant to complain about anything, even serious problems at work or school. For the most part, refugees see Americans as kind, albeit fairly ignorant of the world. When they do voice any criticism it is about two main things— our children's lack of respect for authority and our lack of communal life.

Refugees value freedom. Refugees from war-torn areas often mention how much they value safety. They value educational opportunities for their children and work opportunities for themselves. Many mention how grateful they feel to have food and good housing. No one is more patriotic than newly arrived refugees.

Refugees are the biggest believers in the American dream. They live in an irony-free zone. They want a house, a car, a stereo system, and a dishwasher. In our strange and difficult times, one reason the American dream stays alive is that new people keep showing up who believe in it. And, because they believe that America is the land of freedom and opportunity and because they act on that belief, they sometimes make it true. As Willa Cather once wrote, "The history of every country begins in the heart of a man or a woman."

RACISM

Eleanor Roosevelt wrote in a letter to a refugee, "There are a lot of things that make me wonder whether we ever look ourselves straight in the face and really mean what we say when we are patting ourselves on the back."

We all have values about our own and other cultures. There

is no such thing as cultural neutrality. Unfortunately, some people do not understand that they are cultural beings. They see their culture as The Culture and all other cultures as inferior, or at least peripheral. Or, they may remain blissfully unaware that other cultures even exist. They have not yet learned the concept of cultural relativity and that we all lead contextualized lives.

Albert Memmi defines racism as "all that produces an advantage or privilege through devaluation of the other." He writes that fear of the other is basic to human nature. He points out that the word *allergy* derives from the Greek word for "other." Difference is disquieting and can seem dangerous. However, to deny that differences exist is to deny reality.

To acknowledge difference is not to be a racist. It is only racism when all positive qualities are attributed to the oppressor group and all the negative ones to the subjugated group. Memmi believes racism has four elements—an insistence on difference, a negative valuation of that difference, the generalization of that difference to an entire group, and finally the use of that difference to justify hostility and aggression.

Ironically, even idealizing other cultures can be a form of racism. Placing people or a culture on a pedestal doesn't allow us to acknowledge people in all their complexity. Even compassion can be contemptuous if it causes us to ignore the great range of people within an ethnic group.

Racism becomes a self-fulfilling prophecy. Discrimination leads to barriers and bad treatment of newcomers. This bad treatment in turn leads to poverty, bitterness, and social problems. On the other hand, respect and opportunities allow refugees to move quickly into mainstream culture. People will assimilate if they are welcomed; they'll cling to ethnic enclaves if they are not.

Soon we will all be together and more of us will be brown. The changes in our state are happening before our eyes. Our understanding of these changes must keep pace or there will be problems. Our social health requires us to fight the racism in ourselves, our communities, and our institutions. We will all benefit from a kinder, gentler world.

The first step in fighting racism is becoming conscious of racism in ourselves. It's admitting our deepest fears and anxieties about people we see as "other." Step two involves developing empathy for others, "becoming intimate with what is foreign," as Alice Walker put it. One of the best ways to do this is to make friends with whoever seems "foreign." Then that person stops being a stereotype and becomes a complex human being like oneself. I know a university professor of Latin American studies who has his students each befriend a Latino immigrant for the semester. A high school teacher requires his students to mentor junior high refugees. Both teachers report that their students are transformed by the experience. Step three is to condemn racism. This means correcting people who use racist language, teaching our children that racism is wrong, and writing letters to the editor about racism in local issues and events. Step four requires us to fight the conditions that create racism. Decreasing anxiety and fear always helps. Just as we support diversity and difference, we should also respect our common humanity. We can celebrate sameness as well as difference.

JUST PLAIN IGNORANCE (JPI)
Rumors race all around the world while the truth
is just putting on his shoes.
—MARK TWAIN

Historically, Nebraska has been a white Christian state. We have African Americans, Mexican Americans, Jews, and Native

Americans, but the power and influence have been in the hands of whites. Generally, Nebraskans are a well-behaved and well-meaning people, known for our quietness. We are not show-stealers. Most of us have rural backgrounds and come from places where neighbors help neighbors. It's just that our neighbors used to look a lot more like us. Now we are moving into a new world.

In Nebraska overt racism exists, but it isn't pervasive. Refugees are doing jobs no one else wants and bringing new life to many communities. Currently we have a steady acceptance and accommodation to newcomers. Our libraries are filled with gray-haired Nebraskans helping dark-skinned newcomers learn algebra or American history.

Reactions of locals range from altruism and interest, to lack of awareness and indifference, to fear and active resistance. Immigrants and refugees are a living Rorshach test. This test requires people to look at ambiguous inkblots and tell what they see. Because of the ambiguity of the cards, the story ends up being about the storyteller and the way his or her mind works.

Refugees generate protective and nurturing feelings in some, anger and contempt in others. Each person reacts according to the shape of her soul or the color of his heart. We do not see things as they are; we see things as we are.

We have had a few ugly incidents. Mexicans fight stereotypes that they are stupid and lazy. They are still, alas, called "wet-backs." Vietnamese report being called "gooks" and told to "go back home." Middle Easterners are accused of being unfair to women or of being terrorists. Laotians are asked if they eat cats and dogs. Many newcomers are suspected of odd customs regarding selecting and butchering animals. This is because every culture has a slightly different definition of meat and different procedures for killing animals. It would be hard to argue that our

American ways of treating animals, especially the ones we eat, are more humane.

On the other hand, one man I know works full time helping refugees in our community. Norm said, "I have found out just how similar we all are. Our differences are so minuscule. I am working to build a village of kindness."

One of my friends said of the newcomers, "Every different color, every different bone structure, gives me energy." A school administrator in a small town told me, "Immigrants bring us optimism and energy. They are transforming our dying town and saving our school."

Newcomers are helping us reexamine our attitudes toward the other. Sometimes there is less prejudice against the Africans than against African Americans. Working with Africans has sensitized many of us to long-standing racial issues in our state. Meanwhile, African Americans, Mexican Americans, and Native Americans are involved in efforts to help the new arrivals. They are already bicultural and can help the rest of us learn to be. They can teach us what they know about feeling like outsiders.

It's natural to feel shy and anxious around newcomers. We are all a little fearful of strangers. That first reaction is nothing to be ashamed of as long as our second reaction is to learn more about the other's humanity. One local said to me, "At first I noticed skin color and accent. Now I no longer see us and them. Nebraska is all just us."

Our mistakes are mostly due not to prejudice, but to just plain ignorance (JPI). Our attitudes about refugees have almost nothing to do with facts. We don't know much about the wars in Sierra Leone and Bosnia, the civil unrest in Sudan and Ethiopia, or the flight of Afghanis into Pakistan—all of which ultimately bring many people to our city. We are not terribly aware of what is happening all over the world. Like most Americans, many of us see three thousand advertisements a day, but very few public service announcements that encourage us to understand the plight of others.

Ten Common Beliefs of the JPI

1. Refugees are ignorant and have no formal education.

This is not true. Many were doctors, professors, engineers, and journalists in their native lands. Mohamed, for example, was a foreign exchange student to Austria when he was in high school.

2. The United States takes in most of the world's refugees.

We actually take less than 1 percent of the world's refugees. Many countries take a much larger share than we do. And many host countries are much poorer than the United States.

3. Most refugees are here illegally.

This also is not true. Most have the proper papers and are desperately seeking to comply with the INS. My INS story about Sadia and her daughter going to Hastings illustrated how difficult that can be.

4. Newcomers are taking American jobs.

In fact, they are filling jobs that Americans won't take and thus enabling businesses to prosper in a time when minimum-wage workers are hard to find. They are a tremendous boon to our economy, especially our rural economy. Furthermore, relations between newcomers and old-timers are not a zero-sum game. Refugees buy groceries and other products in our stores and introduce innovations that ultimately help all of us.

5. Newcomers do not pay taxes.

In fact, refugees pay taxes, including property taxes. Even

though they pay taxes, newcomers cannot vote or receive many government benefits and they were not eligible for the Bush tax rebate of 2001. They are taxed without representation.

6. Tax dollars go to teach refugees in their own languages.

Actually, the concept of ELL is that our publicly funded schools teach newcomers English.

7. Newcomers don't want to learn English.

Not being able to understand the languages of newcomers makes some locals uncomfortable. Some people think refugees are talking about them. Some locals have the mistaken belief that newcomers don't want to learn English. It seems ironic that we expect people to learn our language rapidly when so few of us speak any language but English. However, people who haven't struggled to learn another language have less empathy for how difficult it is to succeed with a new language. The fact is, most refugees, many of whom speak four or five languages already, are desperately trying to learn English.

8. Most refugees end up on welfare.

In fact, all of the refugees I know do 3-D work—difficult, dirty, and dangerous. And most were working within a month of their arrival.

9. Anyone who wants to can come to America.

This is not true. We have strict rules and quotas on new refugee arrivals. Most people are shocked to hear that asylum seekers are often put in detention centers, even though they have committed no crimes and are often here because they fought for democracy at home.

When asylum seekers arrive in this country, desperate for sanctuary from totalitarian regimes, they are often treated like criminals while they wait out a long process of adjudication to determine if they truly deserve asylum status. Many are sent back to their countries of origin, even though this may mean death or prison for them.

10. "Why don't they go back where they belong?"

Refugees are here because they had no choices but to be here. They couldn't stay where they were. I want to respond to this question by asking, "Would you stay where your children saw people being killed if they looked out the windows? Or where you were made to participate in your parents' torture and execution? Or, where you might be beaten until you could never work again for the crime of speaking to an American? Would you stay where your daughter could be raped and shot by soldiers?"

HUMAN RIGHTS VERSUS RESPECT FOR DIFFERENT CULTURES

Refugees bring in evil as well as good. Refugees, like other Americans, range from saints to psychopaths. All cultures have values that are loving and strength-producing and values that are punitive and deleterious. No culture has a monopoly on goodness or common sense.

Desperate people arrive having learned desperate ways to survive. Some countries export their criminals and fanatics. Our towns must sometimes cope with imported drug cartels and gangs. More routinely, some newcomers are unpleasant and difficult just as some old-timers are. Some are lazy, alcoholic, and misanthropic, just as some locals are.

Probably the greatest tensions are around finding the balance between respect for ethnic traditions and respect for human rights. For example, some men from traditional cultures will not allow their wives to leave home or to study English. Women are kept at home and denied opportunities to make friends, learn our language, and enjoy our city.

I witnessed the birth of a baby whose mother had experienced female genital mutilation as a girl. The mother had a terrible time with pain and bleeding. Her body required much repair work after the delivery. The baby had a hard time being born and barely survived. After seeing the effects of this traditional practice, I will never again be silent about female circumcision.

One of the best documents in the history of the world is the Universal Declaration of Human Rights, a bill of rights for the world (see appendix 3). It was formulated by the United Nations in 1948, right after World War II, and prohibits torture and slavery and argues for the right to equal pay for equal work and freedom of religion and speech. I would like to see this document hanging on the walls of our public buildings and cultural centers.

In fact, all over the world, support for the Universal Declaration of Human Rights is being challenged by those who argue in favor of cultural relativity. Some argue that it is "Eurocentric" to enforce human rights. Well-meaning people are often confused about how to proceed. Should they respect a local cultural act, even if it involves treating certain people badly?

An example of this changing perspective on respect for human rights comes from an English class. For years a colleague I know has taught college students Shirley Jackson's short story "The Lottery." In this story, a villager is selected by the others to be stoned in a traditional ceremony. This story once horrified students, but in the last few years, students have had a different reaction. Instead of reacting with sympathy for the victim of the stoning, they condone the villagers' behavior under the guise of cultural relativity. Apparently, to many people, even murder is all right if it's a cultural tradition.

Human rights should be universal. Cultural traditions are not set in stone. Cultures are not monolithic. Rather, they are processes, or sets of negotiations between members. Cultures are practical, active, and creative responses to specific conditions. They are constantly changing, and within any given culture there are many points of view and many different groups and members.

Culture isn't the property of just the leaders or the powerful. The right to interpret the cultural values doesn't belong to any one group. It is important to ask whose interests are served and whose are violated by a tradition. Who profits from maintaining the status quo in a culture? Who stands to gain with change?

For me, human rights trumps respect for ethnic traditions. Slavery may exist in certain cultures, but it is wrong. Dowry deaths may be a cultural tradition, but they are unjust. A rigid caste, gender, and class system has no place in a free world. Many countries value men over women, but that is wrong. Cultural relativity should be a liberating, not a constraining, concept. It should allow us to select from all cultures what is best for us humans, not hold us to that which is harmful in the name of respect for tradition.

Margaret Mead defined the ideal culture as one in which there was a place for every human gift. I have found no better definition of an ideal culture. Mead's definition includes both respect for the individual and a belief in community. It's a transcendent definition that encompasses all cultures in all times and places.

My own deepest belief is that the purpose of human life is to grow and become all we can be in order to use those gifts for the betterment of other people. The Universal Declaration of

Human Rights merely tries to set up minimal standards that allow people to develop into who they can be. Without it, our world is a very dark and dangerous place.

WHAT I'VE LEARNED

Such delicate goods as justice, love, honor and courtesy, and
indeed all the things we care for, are valid everywhere but they are
variously molded and often differently handled and sometimes nearly
unrecognizable if you meet them in a foreign land, and the art of
learning fundamental common values is perhaps the greatest gain
of travel to those who wish to live at ease with their fellows.

—FREYA STARK

My experiences writing this book have been satisfying on intellectual and emotional levels. I have always loved Culture and Personality studies and now I can be an anthropologist in my own town. Every day I hear incredible stories. All of a sudden, I am reading every word in the foreign news section of our paper. Because of my human connections, I am curious about the situations in El Salvador, Sierra Leone, and Macedonia.

Before I did my homework, I knew little about the Kurds or the Bosnians. I was woefully ignorant of Africa and the Middle East, and my knowledge of Southeast Asia was limited to the Vietnam War, which the Vietnamese call the American War. Now I am interested in the Sudanese government, the economic troubles of Tajikistan, and the geography of Africa.

Writing this book has changed me profoundly and forever. I have a much broader sense for what being human can entail. In *Fugitive Pieces,* Anne Michaels wrote, "There's nothing a man will not do to another and there is nothing a man will not do for another." I've been a witness to the truth of her statement.

When I first began working with refugees, I was anxious around them. I worried that I wouldn't be able to communicate or that I would accidentally offend them. The more time I have spent with Laotian, Kurdish, Croatian, and Romanian people, the more comfortable I have become.

I have worked to decolonialize my mind and examine my ethnocentric assumptions about everything from cleanliness to psychology to what is edible. It was easy to confuse local culture with universal human nature. It was easy to assume that the way we do things was the most sensible way. Refugees would often ask me, "Why do you do it that way?" and I had to ask myself, "Yes, why do I do it that way?"

Everything is more complex than it seems. Religion and politics are danger zones. I asked an Iranian, a liberal well-educated woman, about the Ayatollah and she glared at me and said, "We do not discuss Imam with Americans." When I first worked with ELL high school students, I was ill-informed about the war in Bosnia and Croatia. I barely knew the names of their countries and leaders. Especially given my ignorance of the politics of other countries, it was easy to say the wrong thing about foreign policy or the causes of the war back home. And what seemed like a small mistake to me felt like a giant insult to someone who had lost family members in a war I did not understand. I am trying to become better informed, and as I grow more interested, the world becomes much more interesting.

In my interactions with newcomers, I learned the importance of keeping things simple. Instead of grand gestures or big, overwhelming events, small quiet lessons worked best. Elaborate events tended to overwhelm newcomers and involved complicated scheduling, which could set things up for failure.

Expensive outings, dinners in restaurants, or concert tickets could make newcomers feel beholden to me in ways that made them uncomfortable. They couldn't repay the gifts and thus felt like lesser people. Generosity could be perceived as a burden and a statement about status. I learned to let refugees give me gifts and to make sure my gifts were small enough that we could have a reciprocal relationship.

Of course, sometimes giving money was absolutely necessary. But more often knowledge and love were what pulled people through a rough patch. As Greg Brown sings, "Stuff without knowledge is never enough."

What newcomers most valued was good information and acceptance. When these were present, most people could figure out a way to help themselves. People, not material possessions, were the most valuable resources. Over and over, I saw people help each other. Community relationships, not bank accounts, kept people's spirits high.

My interpersonal skills were given a workout with traditional people. I'm an informal person, very egalitarian, and not terribly respectful of gender and age differences. I had to learn to behave more formally. I wore dresses and nylons. I addressed people as Mr. and Mrs.

My experiences have given me a sense for the complexity and richness of life, for what, to quote Greg Brown again, he describes as, "a world filled with terror and grace." I have learned that truth is not the property of any one culture. Every culture has its strengths and weaknesses, its beauty and ugliness. It's especially important to listen to the quiet voices in a culture and to acknowledge that cultures change and that right now they are changing very rapidly. There is no one right way to think about anything. Carol Bly writes that civilization is "partly about noticing and appreciating what other people are doing." It's about appreciating the richness of a world with multiple points of view.

I learned the importance of simple good manners. For

instance, I learned to remove my shoes before entering the homes of people from many parts of the world. I have worked to learn who, where, and when I can touch. I learned that to touch a Vietnamese child on the head is an insult. I learned not to blow my nose in front of Asians. I stopped being so time conscious. Sometimes I slowed down to the speed of wisdom.

I went to the home of a Muslim family after the grandfather died. Thank goodness I had a guide who told me not to take flowers to the family. Flowers would have signified I was happy about the death. I was also told to wear black and not to smile. Smiling would also imply I was happy. I was told to take money or food—tea, rice, or oil. With all this coaching, I may have made it through my fifteen-minute visit without deeply offending people I liked and wanted to help.

Communication difficulties can be overcome. Most immigrants are eager to have American friends. They have been kind and generous with me. A kind heart and an eagerness to learn allow much to be forgiven.

When I meet newcomers, I have learned to ask, "How do you like to be greeted in your country? How do you like to be addressed?" If the content is right, the form can be awkward. The message must be, "I respect you, I want to understand your situation and be of use." Wherever I went, I learned to say, "Welcome. I am glad you are here."

Some lessons were funny. I learned that gender trumps body mass. Once my husband and I delivered a couch to a refugee relief center. A Laotian man weighing about seventy-five pounds insisted on helping Jim carry in this couch while we hefty Nebraska women stood by. I felt ridiculous, but I understood it was a matter of pride.

Other lessons made me ashamed. Watching *The African*

Queen with African friends, I was acutely aware that the heroes were all white. The non-whites were props—nameless, servile, and mostly stupid beasts of burden. Their culture was primitive and their personalities were childlike. I was embarrassed for us and for them.

Writing this book, I have learned more about my own city. Before my work with refugees, I didn't know what people experienced in our human service system, our community action program, and Catholic Social Services. I didn't know what it was like to be on food stamps or Medicaid. For years I had driven by factories and never noticed them. I knew nothing about our many large food-processing plants. I'd never called OSHA or the INS, or sat in the health department waiting to apply for the WIC program.

I'd never tried to rent an apartment for a large family with no wage earner. I hadn't noticed my city's pawnshops or check-cashing joints. I had no idea how much was bought and sold through our newspapers. Before my work for this book, I'd never been in certain parts of Lincoln. Studying refugees was studying my town from a very different angle.

In Lincoln I found two worlds. We have a prosperous middle-class culture and a culture of the poor. I had been in one and I began to move in the other. Neither culture has a monopoly on happiness or truth. I enjoyed the second culture a great deal. Sometimes it seemed more honest, more authentic and caring. Poor people can't afford not to share.

I felt schizoid. I'd spend time with my friends and we'd talk about new movies and CDs, and book signings we might attend. My friends talked about the stock market or whether they should remodel their kitchens. Then I'd visit refugees and talk about slavery in Sudan or how to smuggle insulin into Iraq.

Once I left a potluck party with tables filled with fruit, salads, and sliced meats and fish. I stopped by Bintu's to hear that two of her friends from the camp in Ghana had starved to death. They were allowed only four cups of rice a month. She said, "They will all die eventually if we don't get them out of there."

A friend told me about meeting a man from Togo. He had been the bodyguard to the king, but he had joined a small group trying to bring in democracy. He was arrested and sentenced to die. He swam with his family across a river to a refugee camp where they lived for seven years. Now he was in Nebraska. He asked my friend for a desk that had been carried to the street for trash pickup. My friend said he could have the desk and later saw him carrying the desk down the street on his shoulders.

Too often we Americans, myself included, indulge ourselves in the great white whine and complain about the .001 percent of our lives that is not perfect. There was a *New Yorker* cartoon labeled "Yuppie angst" in which a character driving a car says to his rider, "Oh no, I spilled cappuccino on my down vest." I realize that much of my misery is "Yuppie angst." I worry about a postponed hair appointment or a dying rosebush. Meanwhile, my refugee friends worry about whether their relatives will starve to death or their friends are being tortured.

Even though I always have played some variant of the globe game, that is to say, I have always been interested in others, I started this project as a white protected Nebraskan. I am Irish-English married to a Heinz 57 German. Most of my friends were of European background. As I've made friends with people of Mideastern, Latino, African, and Southeast Asian backgrounds, I've changed a great deal. I've stopped seeing myself as a member of a majority culture. Instead, I see myself as a member of a world culture that flourishes in my hometown.

I have grown both more and less aware of differences. I have more appreciation for the endless variations of the human experience, and yet I'm aware we are all more alike than we are different. Leonard Peltier described my feelings exactly when he wrote, "You reach across the world of otherness to one, and you touch your own soul." I have become part of that new American race that includes all colors and is characterized by Alice Walker as "people who love." Lincoln has become for me the middle of everywhere.

I'VE BECOME A COMPLEX PATRIOT

We hope the world won't narrow into a neighborhood
until it has broadened into a brotherhood.
—LYNDON BAINES JOHNSON

Researching this book has made me both more critical and more appreciative of America. I have seen through the eyes of newcomers how we treat our most vulnerable residents. During a time when we gave ourselves a tax cut, our government refused to allocate funds to support the Kakuma refugees while they attended high school. These refugees had spent their childhoods without parents, eating grass, and watching their friends being killed. Now, in this country, they desperately needed to learn to read. Instead, our government told them they must support themselves and even repay their plane ticket expenses. Meanwhile, we gave tax rebates to billionaires.

I don't like our isolationism and "America first" tendencies. We Americans are taking more than our fair share of the world's resources. To use Carol Bly's term, we are "lucky predators." We do not deserve more than other people. I would like to see a fairer distribution system and more aid going whenever and wherever there is great suffering. To quote David Brower,

"The world is burning up and sometimes all I hear is the sound of violins."

The INS is a mess, underfunded and burdened with red tape. And we criminalize the victims of our inefficient system. We have factories and businesses that use up people and toss them away. We have too many laws that favor the rich and the propertied and not enough laws to protect the poor. We make it very difficult to call OSHA and report health hazards at a factory. Our town has its share of sleazy landlords and salespeople.

But many of us are better than our institutions. I have seen the kindness of ordinary Nebraskans to the newcomers. Attorneys and doctors work for free. Churches sponsor families. My friends have delivered piles of supplies and clothes to my doorstep to help the families I know. One friend, not very wealthy herself, told me, "Call me if you ever need money for a refugee family." Another said, "I have too much stuff and will give it to anyone you suggest." A local businesswoman risked her life to take in a Laotian woman being stalked by an ex-boyfriend. When Joseph first went to work, his supervisor greeted him warmly, saying, "Welcome. We are happy you are here."

Even though I am critical of our government in many ways, I also realize how lucky we are to live in the United States. I bristle when I hear people criticize all government as bad. I have met many people who lived in places where there was virtually no government. We don't want to live in those places.

I have great respect for our constitution, our schools, and many of our institutions. But love means wanting to make things better. People can be greedy and imperfect; institutions have important roles to play in keeping us civilized. Having heard stories of governments crumbling and of lives changing overnight, I am more aware of the fragility of governments, even ours.

WHAT IF WE COULD?
The cry of the poor is not always just,
but if you don't listen to it, you won't know what justice is.
—HOWARD ZINN

Refugees are vulnerable people and like all vulnerable people they are exploited. They will work the worst jobs for the lowest wages, live in the lousiest houses and drive the crummiest cars, for which they are overcharged. Just because we can exploit newcomers doesn't mean we should. As Albert Camus wrote, "It is the job of thinking people not to be on the side of the executioners."

The Portes and Rumbaut research makes it clear that for newcomers the first few years in America are a critical period. They have an initial optimism and energy that enables them to work hard and in some cases achieve enormous gains. They will either move into the middle class in a generation or two or they will languish at the bottom of our socioeconomic hierarchy.

We are making it difficult for our newcomers to climb out of entry-level jobs in America. Today there is no longer really a ladder into the middle class. Of course, a few amazing people will always be able to make it, but there are too many barriers for the average refugee. We are leaving too many people behind.

Unless we once again develop that ladder, we will have a permanent underclass of disaffected, resentful people. We need a livable wage, housing subsidies, and more access to education and job training. We need stronger unions and better regulations to protect our most vulnerable workers. The INS needs to be reformed. Its procedures need to be faster, kinder, and more comprehensible.

Helping our newcomers with living wages, decent housing, education, and health care will be expensive and require commitment and compassion. These tasks will be hard, but we Americans have done hard things before. We underestimate each other's basic goodness. We could do this.

The worst thing about America is its exclusivity, and the best thing about America is its lack of exclusivity. We are not bigger or richer in natural resources than Russia or China. It is our open arms and hearts that have made us a great power. The central fact of our American identity is that we take people in. We make room for refugees. We are the city on the hill.

Community does not mean "free of conflict." It's inevitable and even healthy to have great differences. Diversity in community is as healthy as diversity in any ecosystem. Without diversity in age, ethnicity, and ideas, we don't have communities; we have lifestyle enclaves. Even conflict can lead to closeness. As Dennis Schmitz wrote, "Humans wrestle with each other, and sometimes that wrestling turns into embracing."

Long ago, Carl Rogers noted the paradox that the most personal is the most universal. The deeper we go into our souls, the more they look like everyone else's soul. Carlos Fuentes wrote, *"Reconozcamonos en el y ella que no son come tu y yo."* Or, "Recognize yourself in he and she who are not like you and me." At heart, we all want the same things—happy families, good health, close friends, and useful work. We want freedom and respect.

One time I sat at the health department with a pregnant Sudanese teenager. She was tall and wore her hair in dreadlocks. She had on a red polka-dot dress and purple slippers and was a marvelous, but unusual, sight. As she and I sat waiting for her appointment, a Vietnamese toddler approached us. The little girl stared at my friend for a very long time.

At first it was cute, then it grew a bit uncomfortable. The

toddler was examining my friend as if she were trying to decide if she was human. All of a sudden, the little girl smiled broadly and blew my friend a kiss. We laughed in relief, but the laughter was about something deeper than relief. It was about the ability of us humans to recognize ourselves in another. It was about our ability to see our common humanity and blow each other a kiss of welcome.

"Civilization can in a certain sense be reduced to one word—welcome," Stanley Crouch said on the Ken Burns PBS series on jazz. For all our flaws, we Americans have been, for hundreds of years, the people in the world who said welcome.

When Europeans arrived on this continent, they blew it with the Native Americans. They plowed over them, taking as much as they could of their land and valuables, and respecting almost nothing about the native cultures. They lost the wisdom of the indigenous peoples—wisdom about the land and connectedness to the great web of life. What a different America we would have today if the first Europeans had paid more attention to native traditions.

We have another chance with all these refugees. People come here penniless but not cultureless. They bring us gifts. We can synthesize the best of our traditions with the best of theirs. We can teach and learn from each other to produce a better America. This time around, we can get things right.

WE'RE ALL HERE NOW

On a sunny Saturday in July, my husband and I walked into our farmers' market which is down by the train station in the oldest part of town. We walked by Jim's friend of thirty years who was selling sweet corn. Gary looked hot and harried, so Jim stopped and gave him a quick shoulder rub. Gary smiled gratefully and began to joke again with his customers.

We walked past various brightly colored displays of Supersoynuts, kolaches, gourmet mushrooms, sausage, and prairie flowers. A Latino family sold gladiolas, iris bulbs, and catnip. Beside them a man in overalls grilled green onion sausage. Its spicy pork flavor filled the air. An Italian man and his son stood behind quart jars of homemade pasta sauce. An aged Vietnamese couple sold bean paste dumplings and egg rolls. Many Vietnamese families shopped at the market for fresh produce and flowers. I looked in vain for Ly, the student who thought I was beautiful. I would have given a great deal to see her smiling face this morning.

Women in hijabs examined tomatoes alongside women in shorts and tank tops. Children speaking many languages splashed in the fountain by the old train station. One boy I didn't recognize wore a faded shirt that looked like one I had given to Goodwill years ago. It was from a distant KISS concert.

I noticed Fatima and Deena sitting on the edge of the fountain giggling together, just as they did at Sycamore School. They greeted me happily and Fatima asked, "Miss Mary, please take our picture." I hugged them and asked them to smile for the camera.

American teens with tattoos and rings in their noses lolled around the Chilean musicians and African drummers. A woman in traditional Middle Eastern clothes strolled past with her husband. The couple looked happy, talking to each other, and carrying a bag of peppers and tomatoes. Patti, the student at the high school who had been interested in information about birth control, listened to the music with Khoi and her baby, a little boy who looked a lot like his father. Khoi clapped his son's hands to the music. Patti showed me their wedding rings and I snapped their picture.

Country people displayed hostas, pottery, quilts, and rag rugs. Mennonite ladies sold angel food cakes and dilly bread. A big guy dressed in high heels and a cotton dress sold cut flowers and bedding plants to somewhat puzzled locals. Our local community college had a chef-in-training booth. Fresh-faced chefs from many countries handed out samples of quesadillas and crepes. Long lines of people of all nationalities—Bosnian, Sudanese, Vietnamese, Afghani, and Mexican—waited behind pickup trucks for fresh sweet corn.

We stopped at our favorite booth to buy lettuce and greens. The air always smelled of basil and mint around this booth. Today Maren, the baby daughter of a friend, and my friend Twyla were celebrating their birthdays. Maren, wearing a hat made of balloons, nibbled on a pita from the Greek booth. Every time I saw her she was eating a new kind of bread. I photographed the birthday girls together.

Our friends Terry and Chris played music in the sunshine by the train mural. They played Irish songs, Civil War ballads, waltzes, and Czech polkas. All ages and kinds of people enjoyed the music played outdoors, where music sounds best.

The train mural was made of locally produced bricks. Already it had acquired a legend about a hidden image in the bricks—supposedly a picture of a naked woman. People of all ages have searched for this woman in the train smoke, clouds, and landscape.

As the musicians played a waltz, children and a few older people danced, and Leda tapped her toes and swayed. Maria and Rosa from Even Start showed up with all their kids and with Rosa's new baby in a stroller. I marveled at so many new babies on this sunny morning.

Chunky Nebraskans and smaller, darker newcomers shared ice-cream cones and sunlight as they absorbed the music, the color, and the aromas of this busy place and time. The beautiful Kurdish sisters were buying cucumbers and tomatoes. I waved to them and asked when Tanya would make me some biryani. Jim took my picture with the laughing sisters.

Patti and Khoi bought Asian eggplants, fresh lemongrass, and bitter melons. The longest lines were for the Norfolk melons. As I waited in line, I could almost inhale the hope of this Saturday morning. I bought a three-dollar watermelon and thought of a Greg Brown line about life, "It's like a thump ripe melon. So sweet and such a mess."

As I looked at our truck beds of sweet corn and nectarines, our booths of tomatoes and bread, our neighbors and musician friends, the refugees and old-timers, the blue sky above and the gladiolas and coneflowers below, I thought to myself that my healing package is my hometown. On a morning like this, it's the best healing package for us all.

APPENDICES

APPENDIX 1

WORKING WITH PEOPLE FOR WHOM ENGLISH IS A NEW LANGUAGE

There are two main rules: Don't assume anything and Ask questions. For example, How do you greet people in your culture?

Interviews are stressful and the setting is important. Try to have the setting be informal, friendly, and calm.

Even knowing a few words of a foreign language makes newcomers feel more relaxed.

Remember that without English, people can show you only the tip of the iceberg. Most of their personalities, intelligence, problem-solving abilities, and humor are hidden.

Communicating with Language

Use short simple sentences and speak slowly.

Pause frequently to check that you have been understood.

If you are not understood, do not repeat exactly what you said before; rather, paraphrase what you said with even simpler language. Do not move on until you understand and are understood.

Many times newcomers pretend to understand when they don't. Have newcomers repeat any essential information or instructions to make sure they understand.

Do not use jargon or professional language.

Avoid colloquialisms and slang.

Many newcomers have odd knowledge gaps. Don't assume people understand the whole because they understand part of a concept.

When possible use pictures and gestures to go with your words.

Write instructions down, even if the newcomer cannot read or write. Many newcomers have someone who can read the instructions to them.

A little information carefully selected and clearly communicated is better than lots of information that's misunderstood and overwhelming.

Good manners are always in order. You can't overdo please, thank you, and statements of respect, empathy, and appreciation.

Humor is appreciated and defuses tension. Laughter is calming for everyone. Try to have a little fun and make sure your last interaction is positive.

Clock-watching or rushing people is often interpreted as rude and uncaring. Take plenty of time.

Remember that different cultures have different ideas about the way to express emotions and about the value of emotional control.

Silence means different things in different cultures. In many cultures silence is a sign of respect and it is considered impolite to interrupt or to speak right after another person finishes.

Suggestions Concerning Nonverbal Behavior

Because language skills are limited, newcomers pay careful attention to nonverbal cues. Be aware of the message your posture, voice, facial expression, and eyes are sending. Use your body language to signal respect, attention, and optimism.

Be sensitive to cultural differences about touching. For example, many Muslim women are not comfortable shaking hands with men. Many Asians regard being touched on the head as an insult.

Be aware that different cultures have different ideas about personal space. Americans tend to be farther apart when speaking than most other peoples. This distance can be interpreted as coldness.

When Working with Interpreters

Seek interpreters who are both linguistically and culturally competent.

Be aware of problems with interpreters. They may be personally involved with the newcomer and not objective. They may be perpetrators of violence toward the newcomer's ethnic group. They may be gossipy, opinionated, or judgmental. They may be traumatized by what the newcomer says.

Try not to use children or family members as translators.

Make sure the newcomer is comfortable with the interpreter and also that the interpreter understands confidentiality.

Remember to keep your eyes on the newcomer.

Try to keep your sentences short and ask the newcomer to communicate in short simple sentences. (Most interpreters struggle with languages themselves and do not have strong memories.)

If the interpreter is abbreviating too much, ask politely, "What else
    did the newcomer say?" or say, "Please translate everything."
Before and after the session, talk with your interpreter. Make
    sure that he/she understands the task at hand and gets the
    help necessary to do a good job.

A P P E N D I X   2

BECOMING A CULTURAL BROKER

Why You Should Help

To learn languages
To learn about other cultures
To have greater involvement in international affairs
To put our own culture in perspective and see America in a new
    way
To feel useful and helpful

How to Get Involved

1. Visit with refugees whenever you can, on the streets, in
the stores, especially when you see someone looking lost or
confused.

2. Help when you can identify that help is needed. For example,
a woman in Lincoln knew a boy with an Afghani mother who
didn't have anyone to help him with homework. She volunteered to go to the school one hour a day and tutor him. Now
she wants to organize all our parent/teacher organizations to re-
cruit volunteers to help kids in their study halls.

3. Encourage your church or civic group to adopt a family.

4. Join a group that is helping new Americans learn English or work toward a GED. Teach classes to newcomers.

5. Volunteer at an agency that serves immigrants and refugees.

6. Make a contribution of cash or goods. Find a program that serves refugees and ask what they need. Cars, bicycles, clothing, furniture, appliances, and tools can be put to good use.

APPENDIX 3

UNIVERSAL DECLARATION OF HUMAN RIGHTS

Adopted and proclaimed by General Assembly resolution 217 A (III) of 10 December 1948

On December 10, 1948, the General Assembly of the United Nations adopted and proclaimed the Universal Declaration of Human Rights, the full text of which appears in the following pages. Following this historic act the assembly called upon all member countries to publicize the text of the Declaration and "to cause it to be disseminated, displayed, read, and expounded principally in schools and other educational institutions, without distinction based on the political status of countries or territories."

Preamble

Whereas recognition of the inherent dignity and of the equal and inalienable rights of all members of the human family is the foundation of freedom, justice, and peace in the world,

Whereas disregard and contempt for human rights have resulted in barbarous acts which have outraged the conscience of mankind, and the advent of a world in which human beings shall enjoy freedom of speech and belief and freedom from fear and want has been proclaimed as the highest aspiration of the common people,

Whereas it is essential, if man is not to be compelled to have recourse, as a last resort, to rebellion against tyranny and oppression, that human rights should be protected by the rule of law,

Whereas it is essential to promote the development of friendly relations between nations,

Whereas the peoples of the United Nations have in the Charter reaffirmed their faith in fundamental human rights, in the dignity and worth of the human person, and in the equal rights of men and women and have determined to promote social progress and better standards of life in larger freedom,

Whereas Member States have pledged themselves to achieve, in cooperation with the United Nations, the promotion of universal respect for and observance of human rights and fundamental freedoms,

Whereas a common understanding of these rights and freedoms is of the greatest importance for the full realization of this pledge,

Now, Therefore THE GENERAL ASSEMBLY proclaims THIS UNIVERSAL DECLARATION OF HUMAN RIGHTS as a common standard of achievement for all peoples and all nations, to the end that every individual and every organ of society, keeping this Declaration constantly in mind, shall strive by teaching and education to promote respect for these rights and freedoms and by progressive measures, national and international, to secure their universal and effective recognition and observance, both among the peoples of Member States themselves and among the peoples of territories under their jurisdiction.

Article 1.

All human beings are born free and equal in dignity and rights. They are endowed with reason and conscience and should act toward one another in a spirit of brotherhood.

Article 2.

Everyone is entitled to all the rights and freedoms set forth in this Declaration, without distinction of any kind, such as race, color, sex, language, religion, political or other opinion, national or social origin, property, birth, or other status.

Furthermore, no distinction shall be made on the basis of the political, jurisdictional, or international status of the country or territory to which a person belongs, whether it be independent, trust, non-self-governing, or under any other limitation of sovereignty.

Article 3.

Everyone has the right to life, liberty, and security of person.

Article 4.

No one shall be held in slavery or servitude; slavery and the slave trade shall be prohibited in all their forms.

Article 5.

No one shall be subjected to torture or to cruel, inhuman, or degrading treatment or punishment.

Article 6.

Everyone has the right to recognition everywhere as a person before the law.

Article 7.

All are equal before the law and are entitled without any discrimination to equal protection of the law. All are entitled to equal protection against any discrimination in violation of this Declaration and against any incitement to such discrimination.

Article 8.

Everyone has the right to an effective remedy by the competent national tribunals for acts violating the fundamental rights granted him by the constitution or by law.

Article 9.

No one shall be subjected to arbitrary arrest, detention, or exile.

Article 10.

Everyone is entitled in full equality to a fair and public hearing by an independent and impartial tribunal, in the determination of his rights and obligations and of any criminal charge against him.

Article 11.

(1) Everyone charged with a penal offense has the right to be presumed innocent until proved guilty according to law in a public trial at which he has had all the guarantees necessary for his defense.

(2) No one shall be held guilty of any penal offense on account of any act or omission which did not constitute a penal offense, under national or international law, at the time when it was committed. Nor shall a heavier penalty be imposed than the one that was applicable at the time the penal offense was committed.

Article 12.

No one shall be subjected to arbitrary interference with his privacy, family, home, or correspondence, nor to attacks upon his honor and reputation. Everyone has the right to the protection of the law against such interference or attacks.

Article 13.

(1) Everyone has the right to freedom of movement and residence within the borders of each state.

(2) Everyone has the right to leave any country, including his own, and to return to his country.

Article 14.

(1) Everyone has the right to seek and to enjoy in other countries asylum from persecution.

(2) This right may not be invoked in the case of prosecutions genuinely arising from nonpolitical crimes or from acts contrary to the purposes and principles of the United Nations.

Article 15.

(1) Everyone has the right to a nationality.

(2) No one shall be arbitrarily deprived of his nationality nor denied the right to change his nationality.

Article 16.

(1) Men and women of full age, without any limitation due to race, nationality, or religion, have the right to marry and to found a family. They are entitled to equal rights as to marriage, during marriage, and at its dissolution.

(2) Marriage shall be entered into only with the free and full consent of the intending spouses.

(3) The family is the natural and fundamental group unit of society and is entitled to protection by society and the State.

Article 17.

(1) Everyone has the right to own property alone as well as in association with others.

(2) No one shall be arbitrarily deprived of his property.

Article 18.

Everyone has the right to freedom of thought, conscience, and religion; this right includes freedom to change his religion or belief, and freedom, either alone or in community with others and in public or private, to manifest his religion or belief in teaching, practice, worship, and observance.

Article 19.

Everyone has the right to freedom of opinion and expression; this right includes freedom to hold opinions without interference and to seek, receive, and impart information and ideas through any media and regardless of frontiers.

Article 20.

(1) Everyone has the right to freedom of peaceful assembly and association.

(2) No one may be compelled to belong to an association.

Article 21.

(1) Everyone has the right to take part in the government of his country, directly or through freely chosen representatives.

(2) Everyone has the right of equal access to public service in his country.

(3) The will of the people shall be the basis of the authority of

government; this will shall be expressed in periodic and genuine elections which shall be by universal and equal suffrage and shall be held by secret vote or by equivalent free voting procedures.

Article 22.

Everyone, as a member of society, has the right to social security and is entitled to realization, through national effort and international cooperation and in accordance with the organization and resources of each State, of the economic, social, and cultural rights indispensable for his dignity and the free development of his personality.

Article 23.

(1) Everyone has the right to work, to free choice of employment, to just and favorable conditions of work, and to protection against unemployment.

(2) Everyone, without any discrimination, has the right to equal pay for equal work.

(3) Everyone who works has the right to just and favorable remuneration ensuring for himself and his family an existence worthy of human dignity, and supplemented, if necessary, by other means of social protection.

(4) Everyone has the right to form and to join trade unions for the protection of his interests.

Article 24.

Everyone has the right to rest and leisure, including reasonable limitation of working hours and periodic holidays with pay.

Article 25.

(1) Everyone has the right to a standard of living adequate for the health and well-being of himself and of his family, including

food, clothing, housing, and medical care and necessary social services, and the right to security in the event of unemployment, sickness, disability, widowhood, old age, or other lack of livelihood in circumstances beyond his control.

(2) Motherhood and childhood are entitled to special care and assistance. All children, whether born in or out of wedlock, shall enjoy the same social protection.

Article 26.

(1) Everyone has the right to education. Education shall be free, at least in the elementary and fundamental stages.

Elementary education shall be compulsory. Technical and professional education shall be made generally available and higher education shall be equally accessible to all on the basis on merit.

(2) Education shall be directed to the full development of the human personality and to the strengthening of respect for human rights and fundamental freedoms. It shall promote understanding, tolerance, and friendship among all nations, racial or religious groups, and shall further the activities of the United Nations for the maintenance of peace.

(3) Parents have a prior right to choose the kind of education that shall be given to their children.

Article 27.

(1) Everyone has the right freely to participate in the cultural life of the community, to enjoy the arts, and to share in scientific advancement and its benefits.

(2) Everyone has the right to the protection of the moral and material interests resulting from any scientific, literary, or artistic production of which he is the author.

Article 28.

Everyone is entitled to a social and international order in which the rights and freedoms set forth in this Declaration can be fully realized.

Article 29.

(1) Everyone has duties to the community in which alone the free and full development of his personality is possible.

(2) In the exercise of his rights and freedoms, everyone shall be subject only to such limitations as are determined by law solely for the purpose of securing due recognition and respect for the rights and freedoms of others and of meeting the just requirements of morality, public order, and the general welfare in a democratic society.

(3) These rights and freedoms may in no case be exercised contrary to the purposes and principles of the United Nations.

Article 30.

Nothing in this Declaration may be interpreted as implying for any State, group, or person any right to engage in any activity or to perform any act aimed at the destruction of any of the rights and freedoms set forth herein.

BIBLIOGRAPHY

Barber, Benjamin. *Jihad vs. McWorld*. New York: Ballantine, 1995.

Cather, Willa. *My Antonia*. Boston: Houghton Mifflin, original in 1918.

Daniels, Roger. *Coming to America*. New York: Harper, 1991.

Danquah, Meri Nana-Ama, ed., *Becoming American*. New York: Hyperion, 2000.

Eng, Phoebe. *Warrior Lessons*. New York: Pocket Books, 1999.

Fadiman, Anne. *The Spirit Catches You and You Fall Down*. New York: Farrar Straus and Giroux, 1997.

Falicoy, Celia Jaes. *Latino Families in Therapy*. New York: Guilford Press, 1998.

Frankl, Viktor. *Man's Search for Meaning*. New York: Pocket Books, 1963.

Friedman, Thomas. *The Lexus and the Olive Tree*. New York: Farrar Straus Giroux, 1999.

Galeano, Eduardo. *Open Veins of Latin America*. New York: Monthly Review Press, 1978.

Holm, Bill. *Coming Home Crazy*. Milkweed Editions: Minneapolis, 1990.

Holtzman, Jon D. *Nuer Journeys, Nuer Lives.* Needham Heights, Massachusetts: Allyn and Bacon, 2000.

Iyer, Pico. *The Global Soul.* New York: Alfred Knopf, 2000.

Jaranson, James M. and Michael K. Popkin, eds., *Caring for Victims of Torture.* Washington, D.C.: American Psychiatric Press Inc., 1998.

Kaplan, Robert D. *An Empire Wilderness.* New York: Vintage, 1999.

Lee, Evelyn, ed., *Working with Asian Americans.* New York: Guilford Press, 1997.

Marsella, Anthony, ed., et al. *Amidst Peril and Pain.* Washington, D.C.: American Psychological Association, 1994.

Memmi, Albert. *Racism.* Minneapolis: University of Minnesota Press, 2000.

Millman, Joel. *The Other Americans.* New York: Penguin Books, 1997.

Ohmae, Kenichi. *The Borderless World.* New York: Harper, 1999.

Portes, Alejandro, and Ruben Rumbaut. *Legacies.* Berkeley: University of California Press, 2001.

Raban, Jonathan. *Hunting Mister Heartbreak.* New York: Vintage Books, 1998.

Roy, Arundhati. *Power Politics.* Cambridge Massachusetts: South End Press, 2001.

Said, Edward W. *Out of Place.* New York: Vintage Books, 1999.

Serraillier, Ian. *Escape from Warsaw.* New York: Point, 1990.

Smith, James P., and Barry Edmonston, eds., *The New Americans.* Washington, D.C.: National Academy Press, 1997.

Sowell, Thomas. *Ethnic America.* New York: Basic Books, 1981.

———. *Migrations and Cultures.* New York: Basic Books, 1996.

Teitelbaum, Michael, and Myron Weiner, eds., *Threatened Peoples, Threatened Borders*. New York: Norton, 1995.

Weiner, Myron. *The Global Migration Crisis*. New York: HarperCollins, 1995.

Zinn, Howard. *A People's History of the United States*. New York: Harper, 1995.

ACKNOWLEDGMENTS

I want to thank my refugee friends—the Kurdish, the Kakuma, and the Sierra Leone families who moved from far-away places into my heart. My deepest gratitude goes to the many refugees who shared their stories, but whose names I cannot acknowledge for a variety of reasons including their safety.

Also, I thank Jim Pipher, Jane Isay, and Susan Lee Cohen, loving supporters of this project from the beginning. I want to thank Pam Barger, my heroic first reader, and my other readers—Marge Saiser, Karen Shoemaker, Dave Myers, Leon Caldwell, Sara Pipher, Jamie Pipher, Rachida Faid-Douglas, Sharon Stanton Russell, and Jan Zegers. I appreciate the help from Dr. Aladjem and Dr. Keller at the Bellevue/NYU Program for Survivors of Torture, from all the staff at the Center for Victims of Torture in Minneapolis, and from Peter Frazier-Koontz, Dean Settles, Maria Diaz, Kit Boesch, Deb Demuth, Benjamin Zinc, Amy Struthers, Suzy Prenger, the New Americans Task Force, Susan Garwood, Uma Gupta, Linda Roos, Sheila Jacobs, Suzan Connell, Dr. Christine Keim, Pat Leach, Hilde Dale, Barbara Colvin, Pat Boharty, Karen Christensen, Constance Kingston, Cindy West, Kay Marks, Sharon Kreimer, Betty Carpenter, Sue

Galvin, Judy Beste, Maria and Anton Vu, Hoa Tran, Vanja Ilic, Clover Sterling, Olga Podany, Zainab Al-Baaj, Melody Kenney, Christy and Dick Hargesheimer, Marty Seligman, Pauline Redmond, Beatty Brasch and the Lincoln Action Program, Dick Roy and the Northwest Earth Institute, the Center for a New American Dream, Tammy Weihe, Mike Schell, Pat Fraikes, Mary Christensen, Susan Kash-Brown, Julie Skonard, Chris Orr, Rita Chen, Dave Masilko from Work USA, Norm Leach, Laureen Van Norman, the Samaritan Center, Rose Esseks, Margo Foreman, and Pam Laws, and thanks to Jennifer Aziz, Susan Amster, Jennifer Holiday, Arlene Kriv, David Nelson, David Hough, Dan Farley, and all the other wonderful people at Harcourt, Inc. Special thanks to the Bellagio Study and Conference Center and the Rockefeller Foundation for giving me a wonderful place to work. Thanks to Gianna Celli, Alberta and Ed Arthurs, and Susan Garfield for making Bellagio a paradise for its scholars.

The stories in this book are all about real people in my town. Some people wanted their names used and others did not. I have respected their requests. With the students, with clients, and with others who were concerned about their privacy, I have changed identifying details. I also changed the name of the schools, again to preserve the privacy of the students.

For the most part when I have quoted refugees I have corrected their English. I was just not up to the job of transcribing the thirty-two varieties of broken English in our city. Occasionally I have kept a phrase or two, because it seemed important for capturing the flavor of an interaction.

INDEX